A Student's Guide to

British Literature

A Student's Guide to

British Literature

A Selective Bibliography
of 4,128 Titles and Reference Sources
from the Anglo-Saxon Period to the Present

ALIKI LAFKIDOU DICK

1972

Libraries Unlimited Inc.
Littleton, Colo.

Library of Congress Card Number 77-189255
International Standard Book Number 0-87287-044-8

LIBRARIES UNLIMITED, INC.
P.O. Box 263
Littleton, Colorado 80120

To Alexandra Lafkidou, my mother,
and Mary Papamoshou, my sister,
who guided my steps to literature,
this book is affectionately and
gratefully dedicated.

PREFACE

The main purpose of this work is to provide students of English literature with a conveniently structured, selective guide to the most important authors and writings from the Anglo-Saxon period to the present. Recognizing the problems faced by a contemporary student in his search for pertinent titles amidst a rapidly growing number of resources, the author has made every effort to restrict the materials included to those considered indispensable.

A working selection of basic reference materials which pertain to English literature in general is offered in the first chapter. Each entry includes complete bibliographic information—author, title, place of publication, publisher, and year of publication. Supplementing this general approach, a chronological arrangement is adapted in Chapters II through VII, with each chapter devoted to a specific literary period: Old English, Medieval, Renaissance, Restoration, Nineteenth Century and Twentieth Century. Immediate access to the 4,128 entries is facilitated by an author-subject index concluding the work.

With uniform internal structuring, the last six chapters first list bibliographies and criticism pertaining to a particular period as a whole. Following these general works, each genre (drama, poetry, prose) is listed alphabetically and is divided into 1) works pertaining to the genre as a whole (bibliographies, texts, criticism); and 2) individual authors or works of unknown authorship arranged alphabetically. Entries of individual authors are divided into four parts: 1) a chronological listing of an author's most important works including the date when a given work was written or, if this is not known, the date when the work was first published or performed; 2) bibliographies; 3) texts; and 4) selective criticism.

Each author is listed under the period and the genre to which the majority or the most important part of his work belongs. For instance, Shakespeare is listed under Drama and not under Poetry, and Ben Jonson is listed under Jacobean and Stuart Drama and not under Tudor and Elizabethan Drama, although part of his work belongs to the latter period.

Selection criteria have been based on the significance of individual authors as reflected in the standard histories of English literature. Consequently, all classics are included as well as some minor authors when they are typical representatives of a given genre or period. For example, Samuel Daniel is not a classic, but his contribution to Elizabethan lyric is important to the poetry of the period as a whole. Similarly, the romances involving Richard Coeur de Lyon are not classics, but their presence adds importance to the understanding of the genre in general.

In the process of selecting texts it was decided to include editions of complete or collected works; only when these are not available are editions of individual works listed. The majority of the works included in this guide are edited or written by American or British scholars and can be found easily in most American libraries.

Works of literary criticism listed in this guide have been selected according to their importance in contributing something new, significant, instructive, or interesting to the already existing voluminous body of criticism. On major works of literature, where the quantity of criticism often makes it repetitious (Chaucer, Shakespeare, Milton), the author has been more selective, but at the same time has been more inclusive on minor works where occasionally even one book is valuable in one way or another (the poetry of Caedmon, the Old English prose, etc.).

It is hoped that the 4,128 numbered entries represent a well-balanced selection of major works. It should be noted that in comparison to similar guides, this compilation is somewhat more comprehensive and differently structured. For example, the well-known A. G. Kennedy and G.B.A. Sands' *A Concise Bibliography for Students of English*, 4th ed. (Stanford University Press, 1960) covers English and American literature. The first five chapters of the Kennedy guide provide 2,150 entries arranged by literary form. Other bibliographies are much more selective, e.g., Richard D. Altick and Andrew Wright's *Selective Bibliography for the Study of English and American Literature*, 4th ed. (Macmillan, 1971) contains only 996 entries. Included in this total are many general reference books that only indirectly relate to English and American literatures. Similar emphasis is also found in Donald F. Bond's *A Reference Guide to English Studies*, 2nd ed. (University of Chicago Press, 1971).

The author cannot possibly acknowledge individually all those who have contributed to the preparation of this work through so many generous suggestions and recommendations. The author should like to take this opportunity, however, to express deep gratitude to colleagues as well as the editorial staff of Libraries Unlimited, Inc., for enabling her to look more closely and with a new perspective at the British literary scene.

TABLE OF CONTENTS

GENERAL WORKS

GUIDES TO ENGLISH LITERATURE

1 Bateson, F. W. A Guide to English Literature. Garden City, N. Y., Doubleday, 1965.

2 Bond, D. F., ed. A Reference Guide to English Studies. Chicago, University of Chicago Press, 1971.

3 Courtney, W. F., ed. The Reader's Adviser: A Guide to the Best in Literature. v. 1. New York, R. R. Bowker Co., 1968.

4 Rosenheim, E. W., Jr. What Happens in Literature: A Guide to Poetry, Drama, and Fiction. Chicago, University of Chicago Press, 1960.

5 Wright, A. H. A Reader's Guide to English and American Literature. Glenview, Ill., Scott, Foresman, 1970.

BIBLIOGRAPHIES OF ENGLISH LITERATURE

6 Abstract of English Studies. Boulder, Colo., National Council of Teachers of English, 1958– . Ten issues yearly.

7 Altick, R. D., and A. H. Wright, eds. Selected Bibliography for the Study of English and American Literature. 3d ed. New York, Macmillan, 1967.

8 Annual Bibliography of English Language and Literature. 1920– . Edited for the Modern Humanities Research Association. Cambridge, University of Cambridge Press, 1921– .

9 Bateson, F. W., ed. The Cambridge Bibliography of English Literature. Cambridge, Cambridge University Press, 1941-57. 5 vols.

10 Gohsh, J. C., and E. G. Withycombe, comps. Annals of English Literature, 1475-1950. Oxford, Clarendon Press, 1961.

11 Harlow, G., and J. Redmond, eds. The Year's Work in English Studies. London, English Association, 1921– . Annual.

12 Howard-Hill, T. H. Bibliography of British Literary Bibliographies. Oxford, Clarendon Press, 1969.

13 Kennedy, A. G., and G. B. Sands, comps. A Concise Bibliography for Students of English. 4th ed. Stanford, Stanford University Press, 1960.

14 Modern Language Association of America International Bibliography of Books and Articles on the Modern Languages and Literatures. New York, New York University Press, 1921– . Annual.

15 Northup, C. S. Register of Bibliographies of the English Language and Literature. New Haven, Yale University Press, 1925.

16 Van Patten, N. Index to Bibliographies and Bibliographical Contributions Relating to the Works of American and British Authors, 1923-1932. Stanford, Stanford University Press, 1934; repr. New York, Johnson, 1969.

17 Watson, G., ed. The Concise Cambridge Bibliography of English Literature, 600-1950. 2d ed. Cambridge, Cambridge University Press, 1965.

18 _____ . The New Cambridge Bibliography of English Literature. Cambridge, Cambridge University Press, 1971.

DICTIONARIES AND ENCYCLOPEDIAS

19 Abrams, M. H. A Glossary of Literary Terms. New York, Holt, 1957.

20 Beckson, K. E., and A. Ganz, eds. A Reader's Guide to Literary Terms. London, Thames & Hudson, 1961.

21 Benét, W. R., ed. The Reader's Encyclopedia. 2d ed. New York, Crowell, 1966.

22 Chamber's Cyclopaedia of English Literature. New ed. by D. Patrick and J. L. Geddie. London, Chambers, 1922-1938. 3 vols.

23 Fleischmann, W. B. Encyclopedia of World Literature in the Twentieth Century. New York, Ungar, 1969. 3 vols.

24 Harvey, P., comp. and ed. The Oxford Companion to English Literature. 4th ed. Oxford, Clarendon Press, 1967.

25 _____ . Concise Oxford Dictionary of English Literature. 2d ed. New York, Oxford University Press, 1970.

26 Lanham, R. A. A Handlist of Rhetorical Terms: A Guide for Students of English Literature. Berkeley, University of California Press, 1968.

27 Magill, F. N., ed. Cyclopedia of Literary Characters. New York, Harper & Row, 1963.

28 Myers, R., ed. A Dictionary of Literature in the English Language from Chaucer to 1940. New York, Pergamon, 1970. 2 vols.

29 New Century Handbook of English Literature. Ed. by C. L. Bernhart and W. D. Halsey. New York, Appleton, 1956.

30 Norton, D. S., and P. Rushton, eds. A Glossary of Literary Terms. New York, Holt, 1941.

31 Scott, A. F. Current Literary Terms: A Concise Dictionary of their Origins. London, Macmillan, 1965.

32 Shipley, J. T. A Dictionary of World Literature: Criticism—Forms— Technique. New York, Philosophical Library, 1943; rev. ed. Boston, Writer, 1970.

33 Steinberg, S. H., ed. Cassell's Encyclopaedia of World Literature. London, Funk & Wagnalls, 1953. 2 vols.

LITERARY CRITICISM

34 Allen, C. W., and H. H. Clark, eds. Literary Criticism: Pope to Croce. New York, American Book Co., 1941.

35 Altick, R. D. The Art of Literary Research. New York, Norton, 1963.

36 Atkins, J. W. H. English Literary Criticism. Cambridge, Cambridge University Press, 1943-1951. 3 vols.

37 Bate, W. J., ed. Criticism: The Major Texts. New York, Harcourt, 1952.

38 Beardsley, M. C. Aesthetics from Classical Greece to the Present: A Short History. New York, Macmillan, 1966.

39 Beaurdine, L. A., ed. A Mirror for Modern Scholars: Essays in Methods of Research in Literature. New York, Odyssey Press, 1966.

40 Beckson, K. E., ed. Great Theories of Literary Criticism. New York, Farrar, Straus, 1963.

41 Collingwood, R. G. Principles of Art. Oxford, Clarendon Press, 1947.

42 Crane, R. S., et al. Critics and Criticism, Ancient and Modern. Chicago, University of Chicago Press, 1952.

43 Daiches, D. Critical Approaches to Literature. Englewood Cliffs, N.J., Prentice-Hall, 1956.

44 Edel, L., ed. Literary History and Literary Criticism. New York, New York University Press, 1964.

45 Eliot, T. S. To Criticize the Critic. New York, Farrar, Straus, Giroux, 1965.

46 Frye, N. The Anatomy of Criticism. Princeton, Princeton University Press, 1957.

47 _____ . The Well-Tempered Critic. Bloomington, Indiana University Press, 1963.

48 Gilbert, A. H. Literary Criticism: Plato to Dryden. New York, American Books, 1940.

49 Guerin, W. L., et al. A Handbook of Critical Approaches to Literature. New York, Harper & Row, 1966.

50 Hall, V., Jr. A Short History of Literary Criticism. New York, New York University Press, 1965.

51 Hyman, S. E. The Armed Vision: A Study in the Methods of Modern Literary Criticism. New York, Knopf, 1948.

52 Jones, E. D. English Literary Essays, 16th–18th Centuries; English Critical Essays of the 19th Century. Oxford, World Classics, 1930.

53 Levin, H., ed. Perspectives of Criticism. Cambridge, Mass., Harvard University Press, 1950.

54 Lewis, C. S. An Experiment in Criticism. Cambridge, Cambridge University Press, 1961.

55 Miller, G. M. The Historical Point of View in English Literary Criticism from 1570-1770. Amsterdam, Swets & Zeitlinger, 1967.

56 Saintsbury, G. A History of Criticism and Literary Taste in Europe. Edinburgh, Blackwood, 1900-1904; repr. 1949.

57 Sesonske, A., ed. What is Art: Aesthetic Theory from Plato to Tolstoy. New York, Oxford University Press, 1965.

58 Smith, J. H., and E. W. Parks, eds. The Great Critics: An Anthology of Literary Criticism. New York, Norton, 1932.

59 Watson, G. The Literary Critics: A Study of English Descriptive Criticism. Harmondsworth, England, Penguin, 1962.

60 Wellek, R. Concepts of Criticism. New Haven, Conn., Yale University Press, 1963.

61 _____ . A History of Modern Criticism. I: Later 18th Century; II: The Romantic Age; III: The Age of Transition; IV: The Later 19th Century. New Haven, Conn., Yale University Press, 1966.

62 Wellek, R. The Rise of English Literary History. New York, McGraw-Hill, 1966.

63 _____ , and A. Warren, eds. Theory of Literature. New York, Harcourt, 1949.

64 Wimsatt, W. K., and C. Brooks. Literary Criticism: A Short History. New York, Knopf, 1957.

ENGLISH LITERARY HISTORIES

65 Armour, R. English Literature Relit: A Short History of English Literature from the Precursors to the Pre-Raphaelites and a Little After. New York, McGraw-Hill, 1969.

66 Baugh, E. C., et al. A Literary History of England. New York, Appleton, 1948.

67 Craig, H. A History of English Literature. New York, Oxford University Press, 1950.

68 Daiches, D. A Critical History of English Literature. 2d ed. New York, Ronald Press, 1970. 2 vols.

69 _____ . English Literature. Englewood Cliffs, N. J., Prentice-Hall, 1964.

70 Day, M. S., ed. History of English Literature. I: History of English Literature to 1660; II: History of English Literature 1660-1837; III: History of English Literature 1837 to the Present. Garden City, N. Y., Doubleday, 1968-1969.

71 Dobrée, B. Introduction to English Literature. London, Barrie & Rockliff Cresse Press, 1950-1958. 4 vols.

72 Elton, O. A Survey of English Literature, 1730-1880. London, St. Martin's, 1963. 6 vols.

73 Hornstein, L. H., et al., eds. The Reader's Companion to World Literature. New York, Holt, 1956.

74 Hyde, D. A Literary History of Ireland. From Earliest Times to the Present Day. 1889. Rev. New York, Barnes & Noble, 1967.

75 Moody, W. V., and R. M. Lovett. A History of English Literature. 7th ed. by F. B. Millett. New York, Scribner's, 1943.

76 O'Connor, F. A Short History of Irish Literature: A Backward Look. London, Putnam, 1967.

77 Osgood, C. G. The Voice of England: A History of English Literature. 2d ed. New York, Harper & Row, 1952.

78 Oxford History of English Literature. Ed. by F. P. Wilson and B.
    Dobrée. Oxford, Clarendon Press, 1945-1963. 12 vols.
    Vol. 2, part 1. Chaucer and the Fifteenth Century. By H. S.
    Bennett. Oxford, Oxford University Press, 1947.
    Vol. 2, part 2. English Literature at the Close of the Middle
    Ages. By E. K. Chambers. Oxford, Oxford University Press, 1945.
    Vol. 3. English Literature in the Sixteenth Century, Excluding
    Drama. By C. S. Lewis. Oxford, Oxford University Press, 1954.
    Vol. 5. English Literature in the Earlier Seventeenth Century,
    1600-1660. By D. Bush. Oxford, Oxford University Press, 1945.
    Vol. 7. English Literature in the Early Eighteenth Century, 1700-
    1740. By B. Dobrée. Oxford, Oxford University Press, 1959.
    Vol. 9. English Literature: 1789-1815. By W. L. Renwick. Ox-
    ford, Oxford University Press, 1963.
    Vol. 10. English Literature, 1815-1832. By I. Jack. Oxford,
    Oxford University Press, 1963.
    Vol. 12. Eight Modern Writers. Oxford, Oxford University
    Press, 1963.

79 Sampson, G. The Concise Cambridge History of English Literature.
    3d ed. Cambridge, Cambridge University Press, 1970.

80 Ward, A. C. Illustrated History of English Literature. New York,
    McKay, 1953-1955. 3 vols.

81 Ward, A. W., and A. R. Waller. The Cambridge History of English
    Literature. Cambridge, Cambridge University Press, 1907-1927.
    14 vols.

BOOKS ON LITERATURE IN GENERAL
(A Highly Selective List)

82 Abrams, M. H., ed. The Norton Anthology of English Literature.
    New York, Norton, 1962.

83 Auerbach, E. Mimesis: The Presentation of Reality in Western
    Literature. Trans. by W. Trask. New York, Doubleday, 1957.

84 Baugh, A. C., and G. W. McClelland. English Literature: A Period
    Anthology. New York, Meredith, 1954.

85 Buck, P. M., Jr., and H. S. Albertson. An Anthology of World
    Literature. New York, Macmillan, 1934.

86 Carter, P. J., and G. K. Smart, eds. Literature and Society, 1961-
    1965: A Selective Bibliography. Coral Gables, Fla., University of
    Miami Press, 1967.

87 Cunningham, C. C. Literature as Fine Art: Analysis and Interpretation. Chapel Hill, University of North Carolina Press, 1941.

88 Frazer, Sir J. G. The Golden Bough: A Study of Magic and Religion. London, St. Martin's, 1952.

89 Grierson, Sir H. The Background of English Literature, Classical and Romantic and Other Collected Essays and Addresses. New York, Barnes & Noble, 1960.

90 Harrison, G. B., W. J. Bate, et al., eds. Major British Writers. New York, Harcourt, 1954. 2 vols.

91 Highet, G. The Classical Tradition: Greek and Roman Influences on Western Literature. Oxford, Oxford University Press, 1949.

92 _____ . The Anatomy of Satire. Princeton, Princeton University Press, 1962.

93 Lincoln, E. T., ed. Pastoral and Romance: Modern Essays in Criticism. Englewood Cliffs, N.J., Prentice-Hall, 1969.

94 Lovejoy, A. O. The Great Chain of Being: A Study of the History of an Idea. Cambridge, Mass., Harvard University Press, 1936.

95 _____ . Essays in the Histories of Ideas. Baltimore, Johns Hopkins Press, 1948.

96 Mercier, V. The Irish Comic Tradition. Oxford, Clarendon Press, 1962.

97 Ogilvie, R. M. Latin and Greek: A History of the Influence of the Classics on the English Life from 1600 to 1918. Hamden, Conn., Archon, 1964.

98 Saymour, St. J. D. Anglo-Irish Literature, 1200-1582. Cambridge, Cambridge University Press, 1929.

99 Thomson, J. A. K. The Classical Background of English Literature. New York, Barnes & Noble, 1948.

100 Wilson, J. D. The Strength to Dream: Literature and Imagination. Boston, Houghton, 1962.

DRAMA—BIBLIOGRAPHIES

101 Arnott, J. F., and J. W. Robinson. English Theatrical Literature, 1559-1900. A Bibliography. London, Society for Research Theatre, 1970.

102 Baker, B. M. Theatre and Allied Arts: A Guide to Books Dealing with the History, Criticism, Technique of the Drama and Theatre and Related Arts and Crafts. New York, Blom, 1966.

103 Bergquist, G. W., ed. Three Centuries of English and American Plays: A Checklist. England: 1500-1800; United States: 1714-1830. New York, Hafner, 1963.

104 Cheshire, D. F. Theatre: A Reader's Guide. Hamden, Conn., Archon, 1967.

105 Greg, W. W. A Bibliography of the English Printed Drama to the Restoration. London: Oxford University Press, 1939-1959. 4 vols.

106 Harbage, A. B. Annals of English Drama, 975-1700. An Analytical Record of All the Plays, Extant or Lost, Chronologically Arranged and Indexed by Authors, Titles, Dramatic Companies, etc. Rev. by S. Schoenbaum. London, Methuen, 1964.

107 Lowe, C. J. A Guide to Reference and Bibliography for Theatre Research. Columbus, Office of Educational Services, Ohio State University Libraries, 1971.

108 Stratman, C. J., comp. Bibliography of English Printed Tragedy, 1565-1900. Carbondale, Southern Illinois University Press, 1966.

DRAMA—TEXTS

109 Bentley, G. E., ed. The Development of English Drama. New York, Appleton, 1950.

110 Felheim, M., ed. Comedy: Plays, Theory and Criticism. New York, Harcourt, 1966.

111 Heilman, R. B., ed. An Anthology of English Drama, Before Shakespeare. New York, Rinehart, 1952.

112 Spencer, T. J. B., S. Wells, et al., eds. A Book of Masques: In Honour of Alardyce Nicoll. Cambridge, Cambridge University Press, 1967.

113 Venezky, A. S., ed. Living Theatre: An Anthology of Great Plays. New York, Twayne, 1953.

DRAMA—CRITICISM

114 Bentley, G. E. The Playwright as Thinker. New York, Harcourt, 1967.

115 _____ . In Search of Theatre. New York, Random, 1953.

116 _____ . The Life of the Drama. New York, Atheneum, 1965.

117 Boulton, M. The Anatomy of Drama. New York, Hillary House, 1961.

118 Bowman, W. P., and R. H. Ball, eds. Theatre Language: A Dictionary of Terms in English of the Drama and Stage from Medieval to Modern Times. New York, Theatre Arts Books, 1961.

119 Bradbrook, M. C. English Dramatic Form: A History of Its Development. London, Chatto & Windus, 1965.

120 Cheney, S. The Theatre: Three Thousand Years of Drama, Acting and Stagecraft. New York, McKay, 1930.

121 Cheshire, D. F. Theatre: History, Criticism and Reference. Hamden, Conn., Archon, 1967.

122 Clunes, A. The British Theatre. London, Cassell, 1964.

123 Cole, T., ed. Playwrights on Playwriting. New York, Hill & Wang, 1960.

124 Coleman, A., and G. R. Tyler. Drama Criticism. Denver, Swallow, 1966.

125 Cook, A. The Dark Voyage and the Golden Mean: A Philosophy of Comedy. Cambridge, Mass., Harvard University Press, 1949.

126 Downer, A. S. The British Drama. A Handbook and Brief Chronicle. New York, Appleton, 1950.

127 Elliott, R. C. The Power of Satire: Magic, Ritual, Art. Princeton, Princeton University Press, 1960.

128 Ellis-Fermor, U. M. The Irish Dramatic Movement. 2d ed. London, Methuen, 1967.

129 _____ . The Frontiers of Drama. London, Methuen, 1945.

130 Ferguson, F. The Idea of a Theatre, A Study of Ten Plays: The Art of Drama in Changing Perspective. Princeton, Doubleday, 1949.

131 Gassner, J., and E. Quinn, eds. The Reader's Encyclopedia of World Drama. New York, Crowell, 1969.

132 Herrick, M. T. Tragicomedy: Its Origins and Development in Italy, France, and England. Urbana, University of Illinois Press, 1962.

133 Highet, G. The Anatomy of Satire. Princeton, Princeton University Press, 1962.

134 Hunningher, B. The Origins of the Theatre. New York, Hill & Wang, 1961.

135 Hunt, H. The Live Theatre. New York, Oxford University Press, 1962.

136 Kerr, W. Tragedy and Comedy. New York, Simon & Schuster, 1967.

137 Knight, G. W. The Golden Labyrinth: A Study of British Drama. London, Phoenix House, 1962.

138 Kronenberger, L. The Thread of Laughter. Chapters on English Stage Comedy from Jonson to Maugham. New York, Knopf, 1952.

139 Macgowan, K., and W. Melnitz. The Living Stage: A History of the World Theatre. Englewood Cliffs, N. J., Prentice-Hall, 1955.

140 Millett, F. B., and G. E. Bentley. The Art of the Drama. New York, Appleton, 1935.

141 Müller, H. J. The Spirit of Tragedy. New York, Knopf, 1956.

142 Myers, H. A. Tragedy: A View of Life. Ithaca, N. Y., Cornell University Press, 1956.

143 Nicoll, A. British Drama. London, Barnes & Noble, 1925.

144 _____ . A History of English Drama, 1660-1900. Cambridge, Cambridge University Press, 1952-1959. 6 vols.

145 _____ . The World of Harlequin: A Critical Study of the Commedia Dell' Arte. Cambridge, Cambridge University Press, 1963.

146 _____ . The Development of the Theatre: A Study of Theatrical Art from the Beginnings to the Present Day. 5th ed. New York, Harcourt, 1967.

147 _____ . English Drama: A Modern Viewpoint. New York, Barnes & Noble, 1968.

148 Russell, J., and A. Brown. Satire: A Critical Anthology. Cleveland, World Publishing Company.

149 Tennyson, G. B. An Introduction to Drama. New York, Holt, 1967.

150 Thompson, A. R. The Anatomy of Drama. Berkeley, University of California Press, 1942.

151 _____ . The Dry Mock: A Study of Irony in Drama. Berkeley, University of California Press, 1948.

152 Vos, N. The Drama of Comedy: Victim and Victor. Richmond, John Knox, 1967.

153 Wimsatt, W. K., ed. The Idea of Comedy: Essays in Prose and Verse, Ben Jonson to Meredith. Englewood Cliffs, N. J., Prentice-Hall, 1969.

154 Worcester, D. The Art of Satire. Cambridge, Mass., Harvard University Press, 1940.

POETRY—BIBLIOGRAPHIES

155 Case, A. E. A Bibliography of English Poetical Miscellanies, 1521-1750. London, Bibliographical Society, 1935.

156 Crum, M., ed. First-Line Index of English Poetry, 1500-1800: In Manuscripts of the Bodleian Library. Oxford: Modern Language Association, 1969. 2 vols.

POETRY—TEXTS

157 Auden, W. H., ed. The Oxford Book of Light Verse. Oxford, Oxford University Press, 1938.

158 _____ , and H. Pearson, eds. Poets of the English Language. New York, Viking Press, 1951. 5 vols.

159 Benèt, W. R., ed. An Anthology of Famous English and American Poetry. New York, Simon & Schuster, 1959.

160 Brooks, C., and R. P. Warren, eds. Understanding Poetry. New York, Holt, 1938.

161 Coffin, C. M., ed. The Major Poets: English and American from Chaucer to Dylan Thomas. New York, Harcourt, 1954.

162 Cole, W., ed. The Fire-Side Book of Humorous Poetry. New York, Simon & Schuster, 1959.

163 Crane, R. S., ed. A Collection of English Poems, 1600-1800. New York, Harper, 1932.

164 Hollander, J., and H. Bloom, eds. The Wind and the Rain: An Anthology of Poems. New York, Doubleday, 1967.

165 Kinghorn, A. M., ed. The Middle Scots Poets. Evanston: Northwestern University Press, 1970.

166 Kinsley, J., ed. The Oxford Book of Ballads. New ed. Oxford, Clarendon Press, 1969.

167 Lowry, H. F., and W. Thorp, eds. The Oxford Anthology of English Poetry. Oxford, Oxford University Press, 1935.

168 McDonagh, D., and L. Robinson, eds. The Oxford Book of Irish Verse: Seventeenth to Twentieth Century. Oxford, Oxford University Press, 1958.

169 McQueen, J., and T. Scott, eds. The Oxford Book of Scottish Verse. Oxford, Oxford University Press, 1967.

170 Nicholson, D. H. S., and A. H. E. Lee, eds. The Oxford Book of English Mythical Verse. Oxford, Oxford University Press, 1917.

171 Norman, C., ed. Come Live With Me: Five Centuries of Romantic Poetry. New York, McKay, 1966.

172 Parry, T., ed. The Oxford Book of Welsh Verse. Oxford, Oxford University Press, 1962.

173 Peacock, W., ed. English Verse. London, Oxford University Press, 1928-1931.

174 Pinto, V. de Sola, and A. E. Rodway, eds. The Common Muse: An Anthology of Popular British Ballad Poetry, XVth to XXth Century. New York, Philosophical Library, 1957.

175 Reeves, J., ed. The Everlasting Circle: English Traditional Verse. London, Heinemann, 1960.

176 Winters, Y., and K. Fields, eds. Quest for Reality. An Anthology of Short Poems in English. Denver, Swallow, 1969.

POETRY—CRITICISM

177 Bate, W. J. The Burden of the Past and the English Poet. Cambridge, Mass., Harvard University Press, 1970.

178 Bateson, F. W. English Poetry: A Critical Introduction. New York, Barnes & Noble, 1966.

179 Beaty, J., and W. H. Matchett. Poetry: From Statement to Meaning. New York, Oxford University Press, 1965.

180 Boulton, M. The Anatomy of Poetry. London, Routledge & K. Paul, 1953.

181 Bowra, C. M. Heroic Poetry. New York, St. Martin's, 1961.

182 Bronowski, J. The Poet's Defence: The Concept of Poetry from Sidney to Yeats. Cleveland, World Publishing Company, 1966.

183 Brook, C. The Well Wrought Urn: Studies in the Structure of Poetry. New York, Harcourt, 1947.

184 Bush, D. Pagan Myth and Christian Tradition in English Poetry. Philadelphia, American Philosophical Society, 1968.

185 _____ . English Poetry: The Main Currents from Chaucer to the Present. New York, Peter Smith, 1952.

186 Davie, D. Purity of Diction in English Verse. London, Routledge & K. Paul, 1967.

187 Davies, H. S., ed. Poets and Their Critics. London, Hutchinson, 1943-1962. 2 vols.

188 Day, L. C. The Lyric Impulse. Oxford, Oxford University Press, 1954.

189 Drew, E. Poetry: A Modern Guide to Its Understanding and Enjoy-
     ment. New York, Norton, 1959.

190 Eliot, T. S. Selected Essays. New York, Harcourt, 1932.

191 Foerster, D. M. The Fortunes of Epic Poetry: A Study in English
     and American Criticism, 1750-1950. Washington, Catholic University
     Press, 1962.

192 Frye, N. Fables of Identity: Studies in Poetic Mythology. New
     York, Harcourt, 1963.

193 Goldin, F. The Mirror of Narcissus in the Courtly Love Lyric.
     Ithaca, N. Y., Cornell University Press, 1967.

194 Grierson, Sir H., and J. C. Smith. A Critical History of English
     Poetry. Oxford, Oxford University Press, 1946.

195 Hall, D., and S. Spender. Concise Encyclopedia of English and
     American Poets and Poetry. New York, Hawthorne Books, 1963.

196 Highet, G. The Powers of Poetry. New York, Oxford University
     Press, 1960.

197 Hopkins, K. English Poetry: A Short History. Philadelphia,
     Lippincott, 1962.

198 Hyman, S. E. Poetry and Criticism: Four Revolutions in Literary
     Taste. New York, Atheneum, 1961.

199 Kennedy, X. J. An Introduction to Poetry. Boston, Little, Brown,
     1966.

200 Kitto, H. D. F. Poiesis: Structure and Thought. Berkeley, University
     of California Press, 1966.

201 Linenthal, M. Aspects of Poetry: Modern Perspectives. Boston,
     Little, Brown, 1963.

202 MacKail, J. W. The Springs of Helicon: A Study in the Progress of
     English Poetry from Chaucer to Milton. Lincoln, University of
     Nebraska Press, 1962.

203 Nemerov, H., ed. Poets on Poetry. New York, Basic Books,
     1966-1967.

204 Pottle, F. A. The Idiom of Poetry. Rev. ed. Ithaca, N. Y., Cornell
     University Press, 1946.

205 Preminger, A., F. Warnke, and O. B. Hardison, eds. Encyclopedia of
     Poetry and Poetics. Princeton, Princeton University Press, 1965.

206 Reeves, J. A Short History of English Poetry, 1340-1940. London, Heinemann, 1961.

207 _____ . Understanding Poetry. New York, Barnes & Noble, 1966.

208 Seymour-Smith, M. Poets Through Their Letters. New York, Holt, 1969.

209 Tillyard, E. M. W. The English Epic Tradition and Its Background. Oxford, Galaxy Books, 1954.

210 Untermeyer, L. Lives of the Poets: The Story of One Thousand Years of English and American Poetry. New York, Simon & Schuster, 1959.

211 _____ . The Pursuit of Poetry: A Guide to Its Understanding and Appreciation with an Explanation of its Forms and a Dictionary of Poetic Terms. New York, Simon & Schuster, 1969.

212 Van Doren, M. The Noble Voice: A Study of Ten Great Poems. New York, Holt, 1946.

213 Vickers, B. Classical Rhetoric in English Poetry. London, St. Martin's, 1970.

214 Vries, J. P. M. L. de. Heroic Songs and Heroic Legend. New York, Oxford University Press, 1963.

215 Walcutt, C. C., and J. E. Whitesell. The Explicator Cyclopedia. Vol. I. Chicago, Quadrangle Books, 1966.

216 Warton, T. History of English Poetry. New York, Haskell House, 1970. 4 vols.

217 Wheeler, C. B. The Design of Poetry. New York, Norton, 1966.

PROSE—BIBLIOGRAPHIES

218 Baker, E. A. Guide to Historical Fiction. London, Routledge & K. Paul, 1914. Repr. New York, Burt Franklin, 1969.

219 Bonheim, H. The English Novel Before Richardson: A Checklist of Texts and Criticism to 1970. Metuchen, N. J., Scarecrow, 1971.

220 Brown, S. J. M. Ireland in Fiction. A Guide to Irish Novels, Tales, Romances, and Folklore. Vol. I. 2d ed. Dublin, Irish University Press, 1919. Repr. New York, Barnes & Noble, 1969.

221 Cotton, G. B., and H. M. McGill. Fiction Guides. General: British and American. London, Clive Bingley, 1967.

222 Hagen, O. A., comp. Who Done It: An Encyclopedic Guide to Detective, Mystery, and Suspense Fiction. New York, Bowker, 1969.

223 Kerr, E. M. Bibliography of the Sequence Novel. Minneapolis, University of Minnesota Press, 1950.

224 Matthews, W., ed. British Diaries: An Annotated Bibliography of British Diaries Written Between 1442 and 1942. Berkeley, University of California Press, 1950.

225 _____ . ed. British Autobiographies: An Annotated Bibliography of British Autobiographies Published or Written Before 1951. Hamden, Conn., Archon, 1968.

226 O'Dell, S. A Chronological List of Prose Fiction in English Printed in England and Other Countries, 1475-1600. New York, Kraus, 1969.

PROSE—TEXTS

227 Connolly, C., ed. Great English Short Novels. New York, Apollo, 1962.

228 Edwards, S. L., ed. Anthology of English Prose: Bede to Stevenson. New York, Dutton, 1953.

229 Graecen, R., ed. Irish Harvest: An Anthology of Prose and Poetry. Dublin, Irish University Press, 1946.

230 Mercier, V., and H. Greene, eds. 1000 Years of Irish Prose: The Literary Revival Anthology. New York, Devin-Adair, 1953.

231 Quiller-Couch, A., ed. The Oxford Book of English Prose. Oxford, Oxford University Press, 1925.

PROSE—CRITICISM

232 Allen, W. The English Novel: A Short Critical History. New York, Dutton, 1957.

233 Allott, M., ed. Novelists on the Novel. New York, Columbia University Press, 1959.

234 Baker, E. A. The History of the English Novel. New York, Barnes & Noble, 1924-1957. 18 vols.

235 Beachcroft, T. O. The English Short Story. London, Longmans, Green, 1963.

236 Bell, I. F., and D. Baird. The English Novel: 1578-1956. A Checklist of Twentieth Century Criticism. Denver, Swallow, 1959.

237 Booth, W. The Rhetoric of Fiction. Chicago, University of Chicago Press, 1961.

238 Boulton, M. The Anatomy of Prose. London, Routledge & K. Paul, 1954.

239 Forster, E. M. Aspects of the Novel. New York, Harcourt, 1947.

240 Gordon, I. A. The Movement of English Prose. Bloomington, University of Indiana Press, 1967.

241 Grabo, C. H. The Technique of the Novel. Brooklyn, Gordian Press, 1964.

242 Graham, K. English Criticism of the Novel, 1865-1900. Oxford, Oxford University Press, 1965.

243 James, H. The Art of the Novel. Ed. by R. P. Blackmur. New York, Scribner's, 1934.

244 Kearney, E. H., and L. S. Fitzgerald. The Continental Novel: A Checklist of Criticism in English, 1900-1966. Metuchen, N.J., Scarecrow, 1968.

245 Kettle, A. An Introduction to the English Novel. New York, Harper, 1960. 2 vols.

246 Kronenberger, L., ed. Novelists on Novelists: An Anthology. New York, Doubleday, 1962.

247 Leavis, F. R. The Great Tradition. New York, G. W. Stewart, 1948.

248 Lubbock, P. The Craft of Fiction. New York, Viking Press, 1957.

249 Lucács, G. The Historical Novel. Trans. by H. and S. Mitchell. London, Humanities Press, 1963.

250 McCullough, B. W. Representative English Novelists, Defoe to Conrad. New York, Harper, 1946.

251 Magill, F. N., ed. Cyclopedia of Literary Characters. New York, Harper, 1963.

252 Morgan, C. The Rise of the Novel of Manners. New York, Columbia University Press, 1911.

253 Muir, E. The Structure of the Novel. New York, Harcourt, 1929.

254 O'Connor, F. The Lonely Voice: A Study of the Short Story. Cleveland, World Publishing Company, 1963.

255 Romberg, B. Studies in the Narrative Technique of the First-Person Novel. Stockholm, Almqvist & Wiksell, 1962.

256 Schlauch, M. Antecedents of the English Novel, 1400-1600: From Chaucer to Deloney. Warsaw, Polish Scientific Publications, 1963.

257 Scholes, R. Approaches to the Novel. San Francisco, Chandler, 1965.

258 _____ , and R. Kellogg. The Nature of Narrative. New York, Oxford University Press, 1966.

259 Shapiro, C., ed. Twelve Original Essays on Great English Novels. Detroit, Wayne State University Press, 1960.

260 Stevenson, L. The English Novel: A Panorama. Boston, Houghton, 1960.

261 Symons, J. The Detective Story in Britain. London, Longmans, Green, 1962.

262 Van Ghent, D. The English Novel: Form and Function. New York, Harper, 1961.

263 Verschoyle, D., ed. The English Novelists; a Survey of the Novel by Twenty Contemporary Novelists. New York, Harcourt, 1936.

264 Walsh, W. S. Heroes and Heroines of Fiction. Philadelphia, Lippincott, 1914-1915.

265 Watt, I. The Rise of the Novel. London, Chatto & Windus, 1957.

PERIODICALS

266 American Journal of Philology. Baltimore, Johns Hopkins Press, 1880– . Quarterly.

267 Antioch Review. Yellowsprings, Ohio, Antioch Press, 1941– . Quarterly.

268 Blake Studies. Tulsa, University of Oklahoma Press, 1968– . Two issues yearly.

269 The Browning Newsletter. Waco, Texas, Baylor University Press, 1968– . Two issues yearly.

270 Chaucer Review. University Park, Pennsylvania State University Press, 1966– . Quarterly.

271 Conradiana. Abilene, Texas, McMurry College, 1967– . Three times yearly.

272 Critical Quarterly. Manchester, University of Manchester Press, 1959– . Quarterly.

273 Criticism. Detroit, Wayne State University Press, 1959— . Quarterly.

274 The D. H. Lawrence Review. Fayteville, University of Arkansas Press, 1968— . Three times yearly.

275 English Association. London, Humanities Press, 1963— . Annual.

276 English Journal. Honolulu, University of Hawaii Press, 1911— . Monthly.

277 English Language Notes. Boulder, University of Colorado, 1963— . Quarterly.

278 English Studies. Amsterdam, Swets & Zeitlinger, 1919— . Six issues yearly.

279 Essays in Criticism. Brill, Aylesbury, England. 1951— . Quarterly.

280 Harvard Library Bulletin. Cambridge, Mass., Harvard University Press, 1947— . Quarterly.

281 Huntington Library Quarterly. San Marino, Calif., Huntington Library, 1937— . Quarterly.

282 James Joyce Quarterly. Tulsa, University of Oklahoma Press, 1963— . Quarterly.

283 Johnsonian Newsletter. New York, Columbia University Press, 1940— . Quarterly.

284 Journal of English and Germanic Philology. Urbana, University of Illinois Press, 1897— . Quarterly.

285 Keats-Shelley Journal. Cambridge, Mass., Harvard University Press, 1951— . Annual.

286 Medieval Studies. Ontario, University of Toronto Press, 1939— . Annual.

287 Medium Aevum. Cambridge, University of Cambridge Press, 1932— . Three times a year.

288 Milton Quarterly. Athens, Ohio University Press, 1967— . Quarterly.

289 Milton Studies. Pittsburgh, University of Pittsburgh Press, 1969— . Annual.

290 Modern Fiction Studies. Lafayette, Ind., Purdue University Press, 1955— . Quarterly.

291 Modern Language Journal. Milwaukee, University of Wisconsin Press, 1916— . Eight times a year.

292 Modern Language Notes. Baltimore, Johns Hopkins Press, 1886— . Six issues yearly.

293 Modern Language Quarterly. Seattle, University of Washington Press, 1940— . Quarterly.

294 Modern Language Review. Cambridge, Douning College, 1905— . Quarterly.

295 Modern Philology. Chicago, University of Chicago Press, 1903— . Quarterly.

296 Nineteenth Century Fiction. Los Angeles, University of California Press, 1945— . Quarterly.

297 Notes and Queries. London, Oxford University Press, 1849— . Monthly.

298 Old English Newsletter. Columbus, Ohio State University Press, 1966— . Semiannual.

299 Philological Quarterly. Iowa City, University of Iowa Press, 1922— . Quarterly.

300 Publications of the Modern Language Association of America. New York, Modern Language Association of America, 1883— . Quarterly.

301 Renaissance Quarterly. New York, Renaissance Society of America, 1954— . Quarterly.

302 Review of English Studies. Oxford, Oxford University Press, 1925— . Quarterly.

303 Scrutiny. Cambridge, Cambridge University Press, 1932-1953. Quarterly.

304 Seventeenth Century News. New York, University of New York Press, 1942— . Quarterly.

305 Shakespeare Newsletter. Chicago, University of Illinois Press, 1951— . Six issues yearly.

306 Shakespeare Quarterly. Chevy Chase, Md, 1950— . Quarterly.

307 Shakespeare Studies. Nashville, Tenn., Vanderbilt University Press, 1965— . Annual.

308 Shakespeare Survey. Cambridge, Cambridge University Press, 1948— . Annual.

309 Shaw Review. University Park, Pennsylvania State University Press, 1951— . Three issues yearly.

310 Spenser Newsletter. Ontario, University of Western Ontario Press, 1970— . Three issues yearly.

311 Studies in English Literature. Houston, Texas, Rice University
     Press, 1960— . Quarterly.

312 Studies in Philology. Chapel Hill, University of North Carolina
     Press, 1906— . Quarterly.

313 Studies in Romanticism. Boston, Boston University Press, 1961— .
     Quarterly.

314 The Victorian Newsletter. New York, University of New York Press,
     1953— . Semiannual.

315 Victorian Studies. Bloomington, Indiana University Press, 1957— .
     Quarterly.

OLD ENGLISH LITERATURE
ANGLO-SAXON TO 1100

GENERAL WORKS—BIBLIOGRAPHIES

316 Bonser, W. Anglosaxon and Celtic Bibliography, 450-1087. Oxford, B. Blackwell, 1957. 2 vols.

317 Heusinkveld, A. H., and E. J. Basche, eds. A Bibliographical Guide to Old English: A Selective Bibliography of the Language, Literature and History of the Anglo-Saxons. Iowa City, University of Iowa Press, 1931.

318 Ker, N. R. Catalogue of Manuscripts Containing Anglo-Saxon. Oxford, Clarendon Press, 1957.

319 Robinson, F. C. Old English Literature: A Select Bibliography. Toronto, University of Toronto Press, 1970.

320 Zesmer, D. M. A Guide to English Literature: From Beowulf Through Chaucer and Medieval Drama. New York, Barnes & Noble, 1961.

GENERAL WORKS—TEXTS

321 Bolton, W. F., ed. An Old English Anthology. London, E. Arnold, 1963.

322 Funke, O., and K. Jost, eds. An Old English Reader. Berne, A. Franke, 1942.

323 Magoun, F. P., and J. A. Walker, eds. An Old-English Anthology: Translations of Old English Prose and Verse. Dubuque, Iowa, W. C. Brown, 1950.

324 Whitelock, D., ed. Sweet's Anglo-Saxon Reader in Prose and Verse. 15th ed. Oxford, Oxford University Press, 1967.

325 Williams, M., ed. Word-Hoard: Passages from Old English Literature from the Sixth to the Eleventh Centuries. New York, Sheed & Ward, 1940.

GENERAL WORKS—CRITICISM

326 Albertson, C. S. J. Anglo-Saxon Saints and Heroes. Bronx, N.Y., Fordham University Press, 1967.

327 Anderson, G. K. The Literature of the Anglosaxons. Princeton, Princeton University Press, 1966.

328 Bouman, A. C. Patterns in Old English and Old Icelandic Literature. Leiden, Leiden University Press, 1962.

329 Greenfield, S. B. A Critical History of Old English Literature. New York, New York University Press, 1965.

330 Matthews, W. Old and Middle English Literature. New York, Appleton, 1968.

331 Poole, A. L. From Doomsday Book to Magna Carta. 2d ed. Oxford, Clarendon Press, 1955.

332 Stanley, E. G. Continuations and Beginnings: Studies in Old English Literature. London, Nelson, 1966.

333 Stevens, M., and J. Mandell, eds. Old English Literature: Twenty-Two Analytical Essays. Lincoln, University of Nebraska Press, 1968.

334 Wrenn, C. L. A Study of Old English Literature. London, Harrap, 1967.

POETRY—TEXTS

335 Campbell, J. J., and J. L. Rosier, eds. Poems in Old English. New York, Harper, 1962.

336 Crossley-Holland, K., ed. The Battle of Maldon and Other Old English Poems. Ed. by B. Mitchell. London, Macmillan, 1965.

337 Dobbie, E. V. K., ed. The Anglo-Saxon Minor Poems. New York, Columbia University Press, 1942.

338 Fowler, R., ed. Old English Prose and Verse: An Annotated Selection. London, Routledge & K. Paul, 1966.

339 Gordon, R. K., trans. Anglo-Saxon Poetry, 650-1000. New York, Dutton, 1926.

340 Kennedy, C. W., ed. The Earliest English Poetry: A Critical Survey of the Poetry Written before the Norman Conquest, with Illustrative Translations. New York, Oxford University Press, 1943.

341 _____ . An Anthology of Old English Poetry, Translated into Alliterative Verse. New York, Oxford University Press, 1960.

342 Pope, J. C., ed. Seven Old English Poems. Indianapolis, Bobbs-Merrill, 1966.

POETRY—CRITICISM

343 Bessinger, J. B. A Short Dictionary of Anglo-Saxon Poetry. Toronto, University of Toronto Press, 1960.

344 _____ , and S. J. Kahrl. Essential Articles for the Study of Old English Poetry. Hamden, Conn., Archon Books, 1968.

345 Greenfield, S. B. The Exile-Wanderer in Anglo-Saxon Poetry. Berkeley, University of California Press, 1950.

346 Huppé, B. F. Doctrine and Poetry: Augustine's Influence on Old English Poetry. Albany, State University of New York, 1959.

347 Jackson, K. Studies in Early Celtic Nature Poetry. Cambridge, Harvard University Press, 1936.

348 Lord, A. B. The Singer of Tales. Cambridge, Harvard University Press, 1960.

349 Sisam, K. Studies in the History of Old English Literature. Oxford, Oxford University Press, 1953.

EPIC POETRY

Beowulf (10th Century)

BIBLIOGRAPHIES

350 Fry, D. K. Beowulf and the Fight at Finnsburg: A Bibliography. Charlottesville, University of Virginia Press, 1969.

351 Tinker, C. B. The Translations of Beowulf: A Critical Bibliography. New Haven, Conn., Yale University Press, 1963.

TEXTS

352 Collins, R. L., ed. Beowulf. Bloomington, Indiana University Press, 1965.

353 Davis, N., ed. Beowulf. London, Oxford University Press, 1960.

354 Dobbie, E. V. K., ed. Beowulf and Judith. New York, Columbia University Press, 1953.

355 Donaldson, E. T., ed. and trans. Beowulf. New York, Norton, 1966.

356 Hall, R. C., trans. Beowulf and the Finnsburg Fragment. Introduction with Notes by C. L. Wrenn. New York, Barnes & Noble, 1958.

357 Hieatt, C. B., ed. Beowulf and Other Old English Poems. New York, Odyssey Press, 1967.

358 Kennedy, C. W., ed. Beowulf, the Oldest English Epic, Translated into Alliterative Verse. New York, Oxford University Press, 1940.

359 Klaeber, F., ed. Beowulf, and the Fight at Finnsburg. 3d ed. Boston, Heath, 1950.

360 Malone, K., ed. The Thorkelin Transcripts of Beowulf. Baltimore, Johns Hopkins Press, 1951.

CRITICISM

361 Bessinger, J., Jr., ed. A Concordance to Beowulf. Ithaca, N.Y., Cornell University Press, 1969.

362 Bliss, A. J. The Metre of Beowulf. Oxford, B. Blackwell, 1958.

363 Brodeur, A. G. The Art of Beowulf. Berkeley, University of California Press, 1959.

364 Fry, D. K. The Beowulf Poet: A Collection of Critical Essays. Englewood Cliffs, N.J., Prentice-Hall, 1968.

365 Irving, E. B., Jr. Introduction to Beowulf. Englewood Cliffs, N.J., Prentice-Hall, 1969.

366 _____ . A Reading of Beowulf. New Haven, Conn., Yale University Press, 1968.

367 Lawrence, W. W. Beowulf and Epic Tradition. New York, Hafner, 1961.

368 Nicholson, L. E., ed. An Anthology of Beowulf Criticism. Notre Dame, Ind., University of Notre Dame Press, 1963.

369 Pope, J. C. The Rhythm of Beowulf: An Interpretation of the Normal and Hypermetric Verse-Forms in Old English Poetry. New Haven, Conn., Yale University Press, 1942.

370 Sisam, K. The Structure of Beowulf. Oxford, Clarendon Press, 1964.

371 Whitelock, D. The Audience of Beowulf. Oxford, Clarendon Press, 1951.

Miscellaneous Epic Poetry

TEXTS

372 Bone, G., ed. Anglo-Saxon Poetry. Oxford, Oxford University Press, 1943.

373 Dobbie, E. V. K., ed. The Anglo-Saxon Minor Poems. New York, Columbia University Press, 1942.

374 Hieatt, C. B., trans. Beowulf and Other Old English Poems. New York, Odyssey Press, 1967.

375 Krapp, G. P., and E. V. K. Dobbie, eds. The Exeter Book. New York, Columbia University Press, 1936.

376 Malone, K., ed. Widsith. Rev. ed. Copenhagen, Rosenkilde & Bagger, 1962.

377 Smyser, H. M., and F. P. Magoun, eds. Survivals in Old Norwegian of Medieval English, French and German Literature, Together with the Latin Version of the Heroic Legend of Walter of Aquitaine. Baltimore, Johns Hopkins Press, 1941.

CRITICISM

378 Brady, C. A. The Legends of Ermanaric. Berkeley, University of California Press, 1943.

379 Chambers, R. W. Widsith: A Study in Old English Heroic Legend. New York, Russell & Russell, 1965.

380 Magoun, F. P., and H. M. Smyser. Walter of Aquitaine: Materials for the Study of his Legend. New London, Conn., Connecticut College, 1950.

ELEGIES

TEXTS

381 Bone, G. Anglo-Saxon Poetry. Oxford, Oxford University Press, 1943.

382 Dunning, T. P., and A. J. Bliss, eds. The Wanderer. New York, Appleton, 1969.

383 Gordon, I. L., ed. The Seafarer. London, Methuen, 1960.

384 Hieatt, C. B. Beowulf and Other Old English Poems. New York, Odyssey Press, 1967.

385 Kennedy, C. W., ed. Old English Elegies. Princeton, Princeton University Press, 1936.

386 Krapp, G. P., and E. V. K. Dobbie, eds. The Exeter Book. New York, Columbia University Press, 1936.

387 Leslie, R. F., ed. Three Old English Elegies: The Wife's Lament, The Husband's Message, The Ruin. Manchester, University of Manchester Press, 1961.

388 _____ , ed. The Wanderer. Manchester, University of Manchester Press, 1966.

389 Malone, K., ed. Ten Old English Poems. Baltimore, Johns Hopkins
     Press, 1941.

CRITICISM

390 Hotchner, C. A. Wessex and Old English Poetry with Special Con-
     sideration of the Ruin. New York, New York University Press, 1939.

RELIGIOUS POETRY

School of Caedmon

WORKS

391 Genesis, n.d.   393 Daniel, n.d.
392 Exodus, n.d.   394 Dream of the Rood, n.d.

TEXTS

395 The Caedmon MS of Anglo-Saxon Biblical Poetry. Oxford, Oxford
     University Press, 1927.

396 Gordon, R. K., ed. Anglo-Saxon Poetry, 650-1000. New York,
     Dutton, 1926.

397 Irving, E. B., trans. The Old English Exodus. New Haven, Conn.,
     Yale University Press, 1953.

398 Kennedy, C. W., ed. Early English Christian Poetry. New York,
     Oxford University Press, 1952.

399 _____ , trans. The Caedmon Poems. London, P. Smith,
     1916.

400 Krapp, G. P., ed. The Junius Manuscript. New York, Columbia
     University Press, 1931.

401 _____ , and E. V. K. Dobbie, eds. The Exeter Book. New
     York, Columbia University Press, 1936.

CRITICISM

402 Wrenn, C. L. The Poetry of Caedmon. London, British Academy,
     1947.

School of Cynewulf

WORKS

403 Elene, n.d.   405 The Ascension, n.d.
404 The Fates of the Apostles,   406 Christ, n.d.
     n.d.   407 Juliana, n.d.

TEXTS

408   Blake, N. F., ed. The Phoenix. Manchester, University of Manchester Press, 1964.

409   Bone, G., ed. Anglo-Saxon Poetry. Oxford, Oxford University Press, 1943.

410   Brooks, K. R., ed. Andreas and the Fates of the Apostles. Oxford, Clarendon Press, 1961.

411   Dobbie, E. V. K., ed. Beowulf and Judith. New York, Columbia University Press, 1953.

412   Hieatt, C. B., trans. Beowulf and Other Old English Poems. New York, Odyssey Press, 1967.

413   Kennedy, C. W., ed. Early English Christian Poetry. New York, Oxford University Press, 1952.

414   Krapp, G. P., ed. The Vercelli Book. New York, Columbia University Press, 1932.

415   _____ , and E. V. K. Dobbie, eds. The Exeter Book. New York, Columbia University Press, 1936.

CRITICISM

416   Gradon, P. O. E. Cynewulf's Elene. London, Methuen, 1958.

417   Schaar, C. Critical Studies in the Cynewulf Group. Lund, Lund University Press, 1949.

418   Sisam, K. Cynewulf and his Poetry. London, British Academy, 1932.

PROSE—TEXTS

419   Fowler, R., ed. Old English Prose and Verse: An Annotated Selection. London, Routledge & K. Paul, 1966.

420   Jones, C. W., ed. Saints Lives and Chronicles in Early England. Ithaca, N. Y., Cornell University Press, 1947.

421   Sweet, H., ed. Anglo-Saxon Primer. Rev. by N. Davis. (First ed. 1882) Oxford, Clarendon Press, 1953.

PROSE—CRITICISM

422   Wright, C. E. The Cultivation of Saga in Anglo-Saxon England. Edinburgh, Oliver & Boyd, 1939.

PROSE—INDIVIDUAL AUTHORS

Aelfric's Prose

WORKS

423 Catholic Homilies, n.d.   427 Life of Saint Aethelwold, n.d.
424 Bede's De Temproibus, n.d.   428 Regularis Concordia, n.d.
425 Latin Grammar, n.d.   429 Treatise on the Old and the
426 Saints' Lives, n.d.   New Testament, n.d.

TEXTS

430 Crawford, S. J., ed. The Old English Version of the Heptateuch, Aelfric's Treatise on the Old and New Testament and his Preface to Genesis. EETS 160 (1921). Repr. 1968.

431 Henel, H., ed. Aelfric's De Temporibus Anni. EETS 213 (1940).

432 Pope, J. C., ed. Homilies of Aelfric. London, Oxford University Press, 1967.

433 Skeat, W. W., ed. Aelfric's Lives of Saints. EETS 76, 82, 94, 114 (1881-1900). Repr. in 2 vols., 1966.

CRITICISM

434 Cross, J. E. Aelfric and the Medieval Homiliary—Objection and Contribution. Lund, University of Lund Press, 1961-1962.

435 White, C. L. Aelfric: A New Study of his Life and Writings. Boston, Houghton, 1898.

Alfred's Prose

WORKS

436 St. Augustine's Soliloquies, n.d.   439 Gregory's Pastoral Care, n.d.
437 Selections from Bede, n.d.   440 Orosius, n.d.
438 Translation of Boethius' De
     Consolatione Philosophiae, n.d.

TEXTS

441 Browne, G. F., ed. King Alfred's Books by the Right Reverend Bishop G. F. Browne. New York, Macmillan, 1920.

442 Campbell, A., ed. The Tollemache Orosius. Copenhagen, Rosenkilde & Bagger, 1953.

443 Carnicelli, T. A., ed. King Alfred's Version of St. Augustine's Soliloquies. Cambridge, Mass., Harvard University Press, 1969.

444 Dobbie, E. V. K., ed. The Metrical Preface and Epilogue of the Pastoral Care. New York, Columbia University Press, 1942.

445 Ker, N. R., ed. The Pastoral Care: King Alfred's Translation of St. Gregory's Regula Pastoralis. Copenhagen, Rosenkilde & Bagger, 1956.

446 Krapp, G. P., ed. The Paris Psalter and the Meters of Boethius. New York, Columbia University Press, 1933.

447 Sweet, H., ed. King Alfred's Orosius. EETS 79 (1883).

448 _____ , ed. King Alfred's West-Saxon Version of Gregory's Pastoral Care. EETS 45, 50 (1871-1872). Repr. 1958.

449 Whitelock, D., ed. The Old English Prose and Verse Prefaces to King Alfred's Translation of Gregory's Pastoral Care. London, Oxford University Press, 1967.

CRITICISM

450 Duckett, E. S. Alfred the Great. Chicago, University of Chicago Press, 1956.

451 Payne, F. A. King Alfred and Boethius. Madison, University of Wisconsin Press, 1968.

CHRONICLES
TEXTS

452 Ashdown, M., ed. The Anglo-Saxon Chronicle (C), Annals 978-1017. In English and Norse Documents Relating to the Reign of Ethelred the Unready. Cambridge, Cambridge University Press, 1930.

453 Clark, C., ed. The Peterborough Chronicle, 1070-1154. London, Oxford University Press, 1958.

454 Garmonsway, G. N., ed. The Anglo-Saxon Chronicle. New York, Dutton, 1954.

455 Rositzke, H. A., ed. The C—Text of the Old English Chronicles. Repr. New York, Johnson, 1967.

456 Whitelock, D., D. C. Douglas, and S. I. Tucker, eds. The Anglo-Saxon Chronicle: A New Translation. London, Eyre & Spottiswoode, 1962.

WRITINGS IN LATIN
CRITICISM

457 Messenger, R. E. Ethical Teaching in the Latin Hymns of Medieval England. New York, Columbia University Press, 1930.

458 Raby, F. J. E. A History of Christian Latin Poetry from the Beginnings to the End of the Middle Ages. 2d ed. Oxford, Clarendon Press, 1953.

Alcuin (d. 804)

TEXTS

459 Howell, W. S., ed. The Rhetoric of Alcuin and Charlemagne. Princeton, Princeton University Press, 1941.

460 Widding, O., ed. Alcuin. Copenhagen, Rosenkilde & Bagger, 1960.

CRITICISM

461 Duckett, E. S. Alcuin, Friend of Charlemagne: His World and his Work. New York, Macmillan, 1951.

462 Ellard, G. Master Alcuin, Liturgist: A Partner of our Piety. Chicago, Loyola University Press, 1956.

Bede (673-735)

WORKS

463 Historia Ecclesiastica Gentis   464 History of the Abbots, 734
     Anglorum, 731

TEXTS

465 Jones, C. W., ed. Opera de Temporibus. Cambridge, Medieval Academy of American Publications, 1943.

466 _____ , ed. Bedae Pseudepigrapha: Scientific Writings Falsely Attributed to Bede. Ithaca, N.Y., Cornell University Press, 1939.

467 Laistner, M. L. W., ed. Expositio Actuum Apostolorum et Retractatio. Cambridge, Mass., Harvard University Press, 1939.

468 Miller, T., ed. The Old English Version of Bede's Ecclesiastical History of the English People. EETS 95, 96, 110, 111 (1890-1898). Repr. 1963.

CRITICISM

469 Blair, P. Hunter. The Moore Bede. Copenhagen, Rosenkilde & Bagger, 1959.

470 _____ . The World of Bede. London, Secker & Warburg, 1970.

471 Carroll, Sister M. The Venerable Bede: His Spiritual Teachings. Washington, Catholic University Press, 1946.

MEDIEVAL LITERATURE
1100-1500

GENERAL WORKS—BIBLIOGRAPHIES

472 Farrar, C. P., and A. P. Evans, eds. Bibliography of English Translations from Medieval Sources. New York, Columbia University Press,
1946.

473 Loomis, R. S., ed. Introduction to Medieval Literature Chiefly in
England: A Reading List and Bibliography. New York, Columbia
University Press, 1948.

474 Ogden, M.S., et al., eds. A Bibliography of Middle English Texts.
Ann Arbor, University of Michigan Press, 1954.

475 Severs, J. B., ed. A Manual of the Writings in Middle English, 1050-
1550. New Haven, Conn., Shoe String Press, 1967.

476 Wells, J. E., et al., eds. A Manual of the Writings in Middle English,
1050-1400. New Haven, Conn., Yale University Press, 1916.

GENERAL WORKS—TEXTS

477 Dickins, B., and R. M. Wilson, eds. Early Middle English Texts.
Cambridge, Bowes and Bowes, 1951.

478 Funke, O., ed. A Middle English Reader: Texts from the Twelfth
and the Fourteenth Centuries. Berne, A. Francke, 1944.

479 Haskell, A. S., ed. A Middle English Anthology. New York, Doubleday, 1969.

480 Jones, C. W., ed. Medieval Literature in Translation. New York,
Longmans, Green, 1950.

481 Loomis, R. S., and R. Willard, eds. Medieval English Verse and Prose
in Modernized Versions. New York, Appleton, 1948.

482 Ross, J. B., and M. M. McLaughlin, eds. The Portable Medieval
Reader. New York, Viking, 1949.

483 Williams, M., ed. Glee-Wood: Passages from Middle English Literature from the Eleventh Century to the Fifteenth. New York, Sheed
& Wood, 1949.

GENERAL WORKS—CRITICISM

484 Ackerman, R. Backgrounds to Medieval English Literature. New York, Random House, 1966.

485 Artz, F. B. The Mind of the Middle Ages: A.D. 200-1500, A Historical Survey. New York, Knopf, 1953.

486 Atkins, J. W. H. English Literary Criticism: The Medieval Phase. Cambridge, Cambridge University Press, 1943.

487 Baldwin, C. S. Three Medieval Centuries of Literature in England, 1100-1400. Boston, Little, Brown, 1932.

488 Bernheimer, R. Wild Men in the Middle Ages: A Study in Art, Sentiment and Demonology. Cambridge, Mass., Harvard University Press, 1952.

489 Boas, G. Essays on Primitivism and Related Ideas in the Middle Ages. Baltimore, Johns Hopkins Press, 1948.

490 Broomfield, M. W. The Seven Deadly Sins: An Introduction to the History of Religious Concept with Special Reference to Medieval English Literature. East Lansing, Michigan State University Press, 1952.

491 Coulton, G. G. Medieval Panorama: The English Scene from Conquest to Reformation. Cambridge, Cambridge University Press, 1938.

492 Evans, J., ed. The Flowering of the Middle Ages. London, Thames & Hudson, 1966.

493 Everrett, D. Essays in Middle English Literature. Oxford, Clarendon Press, 1966.

494 Ford, B., et al., eds. The Age of Chaucer. Baltimore, Penguin, 1969.

495 Hays, D., ed. Europe in the Fourteenth Century. London, Longmans, 1966.

496 Howard, D. R. The Three Temptations: Medieval Man in Search of the World. Princeton, Princeton University Press, 1966.

497 Lewis, C. S. The Allegory of Love: A Study in Medieval Tradition. Oxford, Oxford University Press, 1936.

498 McKisack, M. The Fourteenth Century, 1307-1399. Oxford, Clarendon Press, 1959.

499 Moore, A. K. Studies in a Medieval Prejudice: Antifeminism. Nashville, Tenn., Vanderbilt University Press, 1945.

500 Patch, H. R. The Other World According to Descriptions in Medieval Literature. Cambridge, Mass., Harvard University Press, 1950.

501 Powicke, Sir M. The Thirteenth Century, 1216-1307. 2d ed. Oxford, Clarendon Press, 1962.

502 Purdy, R. R. The Platonic Tradition in Middle English Literature. Nashville, Tenn., Vanderbilt University Press, 1949.

503 Schlauch, M. English Medieval Literature and its Social Foundations. Warsaw, Polish Scientific Publications, 1956.

504 Vasta, E. Middle English Survey: Critical Essays. Notre Dame, Ind., University of Notre Dame Press, 1965.

505 Wilson, R. M. Early Middle English Literature. 3d ed. London, Methuen, 1968.

506 _____ . The Lost Literature of Medieval England. 2d rev. ed. London, Methuen, 1970.

DRAMA—BIBLIOGRAPHIES

507 Stratman, C. J. Bibliography of Medieval Drama. Berkeley, University of California Press, 1954.

DRAMA—TEXTS

508 Dodsley, R., ed. A Select Collection of Old English Plays. New York, Blom, 1964.

509 Franklin, A., ed. Seven Miracle Plays. London, Oxford University Press, 1963.

510 Greenberg, N., ed. The Play of Daniel: A Thirteenth Century Musical Drama. New York, Oxford University Press, 1959.

511 Heilman, R. B., ed. An Anthology of English Drama Before Shakespeare. New York, Holt, 1952.

512 Hopper, V. F., and G. B. Latey, eds. Medieval Mysteries, Moralities, and Interludes. Woodbury, N.Y., Barron's, 1962.

513 Pollard, A. W., ed. English Miracle Plays, Moralities and Interludes. 8th ed. Oxford, Clarendon Press, 1927.

514 Rose, M., ed. The Wakefield Mystery Plays. London, Evan Bros, 1961.

515 Thomas, R. G., ed. Ten Miracle Plays. Evanston, Ill., Northwestern University Press, 1966.

516 Wilson, F. P. The English Drama, 1485-1585. Ed. with a Bibliography by G. K. Hunter. Oxford, Oxford University Press, 1969.

517 Young, K., ed. The Drama of the Medieval Church. Oxford, Clarendon Press, 1933. 2 vols.

DRAMA—CRITICISM

518 Anderson, M. D. Drama and Imagery in English Medieval Churches. Cambridge, Cambridge University Press, 1963.

519 Chambers, E. K. The Medieval Stage. Oxford, Clarendon Press, 1903. 2 vols.

520 Chauvin, Sister M. J. of Carmel. The Role of Mary Magdalene in Medieval Drama. Washington, Catholic University Press, 1951.

521 Craig, H. English Religious Drama of the Middle Ages. Oxford, Oxford University Press, 1955.

522 Gardiner, H. C. Mysteries' End: An Investigation of the Last Days of the Medieval Religious Stage. New Haven, Conn., Yale University Press, 1946.

523 Hardison, O. B., Jr. Christian Rite and Christian Drama in the Middle Ages: Essays in the Origin and Early History of Modern Drama. Baltimore, Johns Hopkins Press, 1965.

524 Prosser, E. A. Drama and Religion in the English Mystery Plays: A Re-Evaluation. Stanford, Stanford University Press, 1961.

525 Reinhard, J. R. Medieval Pageant. New York, Harcourt, 1939.

526 Rossiter, A. P. English Drama from Early Times to the Elizabethans. London, Hutchinson University Library, 1950.

527 Williams, A. The Drama of Medieval England. East Lansing, Michigan State University Press, 1961.

POETRY—TEXTS

528 Alexander, M., trans. The Earliest English Poems. Berkeley, University of California Press, 1970.

529 Bennett, J. A., and G. V. Smithers, eds. Early Middle English Verse and Prose. Oxford, Clarendon Press, 1966.

530 Bowers, R. H., ed. Three Middle English Religious Poems. Gainesville, University of Florida Press, 1963.

531 Brown, C., ed. Religious Lyrics of the Fourteenth Century. Oxford, Clarendon Press, 1924.

532 Brown, C., ed. English Lyrics of the Thirteenth Century. Oxford, Clarendon Press, 1932.

533 Loomis, R. S., and R. Willard, eds. Medieval English Verse and Prose in Modernized Versions. New York, Appleton, 1948.

534 Moore, A. K., ed. Secular Lyric in Middle English. Lexington, University of Kentucky Press, 1951.

535 Owen, L. J., and Nancy H. Owen, eds. Middle English Poetry, An Anthology. Boston, Bobbs-Merrill, 1971.

536 Person, H. A., ed. Cambridge Middle English Lyrics. 2d ed. Seattle, University of Washington Press, 1962.

537 Pinto, V. de Sola, and A. E. Rodway, eds. The Common Muse: An Anthology of Popular British Ballad Poetry, Fifteenth to Twentieth Century. New York, Philosophical Library, 1957.

538 Robbins, R. H., ed. Secular Lyrics of the Fourteenth and Fifteenth Centuries. New York, Columbia University Press, 1958.

539 Sisam, C., and K. Sisam, eds. The Oxford Book of Medieval English Verse. Oxford, Oxford University Press, 1970.

540 Stevick, R. D., ed. One Hundred Middle English Lyrics. Indianapolis, Bobbs-Merrill, 1964.

541 Stone, B., ed. and trans. Medieval English Verse. Baltimore, Johns Hopkins Press, 1964.

542 Weston, J. L., ed. Chief Middle English Poets. Boston, Houghton, 1944.

POETRY—CRITICISM

543 Bronson, B. H. The Ballad as Song. Berkeley, University of California Press, 1970.

544 Damon, P. Modes of Analogy in Ancient and Medieval Verse. Berkeley, University of California Press, 1961.

545 Davies, R. T., ed. Medieval English Lyrics: A Critical Anthology. London, Faber & Faber, 1963.

546 Dronke, P. The Medieval Lyric. London, Hutchinson University Library, 1968.

547 Green, R. H. Biblical Symbolism in the Latin Poetry of the Twelfth Century. Berkeley, University of California Press, 1950.

548 Kane, G. Middle English Literature: A Critical Study of the Romances, the Religious Lyrics, Piers Plowman. London, Methuen, 1951.

549 Pecheux, Mother M. Christopher. Aspects of the Treatment of Death in Middle English Poetry. Washington, Catholic University Press, 1951.

550 Speirs, J. Medieval English Poetry: The Non-Chaucerian Tradition. New York, Hillary House, 1957.

551 Weber, S. A. Theology and Poetry in the Middle English Lyric: A Study of Sacred History and Aesthetic Form. Columbus, Ohio State University, 1969.

552 Woolf, R. The English Religious Lyric in the Middle Ages. Oxford, Clarendon Press, 1968.

INDIVIDUAL POETS AND POEMS

Ancren Riwle (late 12th century)

TEXTS

553 Baugh, A. C., ed. The English Text of the Ancren Riwle. London, Early English Texts Society, 1956.

554 Mack, F. M., ed. The English Text of the Ancrene Riwle. London, Oxford University Press, 1963.

555 Tolkien, J. R. R., ed. The English Text of the Ancren Riwle. London, Oxford University Press, 1962.

CRITICISM

556 Darwin, F. D. The English Medieval Recluse. London, Society for Promoting Christian Knowledge, 1944.

Geoffrey Chaucer (1340-1400)

WORKS

557 The Book of Duchess, 1369
558 The House of Fame, 1382
559 The Parliament of Fowles, 1383

560 Troilus and Criseyde, 1385
561 The Legend of Good Women, 1386
562 Canterbury Tales, 1387

BIBLIOGRAPHIES

563 Baugh, A. C., comp. Chaucer. New York, Appleton, 1968.

564 Bowden, M. A Reader's Guide to Geoffrey Chaucer. New York, Farrar, 1964.

565 Crawford, W. R. Bibliography of Chaucer, 1954-1963. Seattle, University of Washington Press, 1967.

566 Griffith, D. Bibliography of Chaucer, 1908-1953. Seattle, University of Washington Press, 1955.

567 Hammond, E. P. Chaucer: A Bibliographical Manual. New York, Macmillan, 1908. Repr. New York, P. Smith, 1933.

568 Martin, W. E., Jr. A Chaucer Bibliography, 1925-1933. Durham, N.C., Duke University Press, 1935.

TEXTS

569 Baugh, A. C., ed. Chaucer's Major Poetry. New York, Appleton, 1963.

570 Donaldson, E. T., ed. Chaucer's Poetry: An Anthology for the Modern Reader. New York, Ronald, 1958.

571 Dunn, C. W., ed. A Chaucer Reader. New York, Harcourt, 1952.

572 Kee, K., ed. Chaucer: A Selection of his Works. Toronto, Macmillan, 1966.

573 Morrison, T., ed. The Portable Chaucer. New York, Viking, 1949.

574 Pratt, R. A., ed. Selection from the Tales of Canterbury. Boston, Houghton, 1933.

575 Robinson, F. N., ed. The Complete Works of Geoffrey Chaucer. Boston, Houghton, 1957.

576 Tatlock, J. S. P., and P. McKay, eds. The Modern Reader's Chaucer: His Complete Poetical Works. New York, Macmillan, 1912. Reissue, 1966.

CRITICISM

577 Baum, P. F. Chaucer, A Critical Appreciation. Durham, N.C., Duke University Press, 1957.

578 Brewer, D. S. Chaucer in his Time. London, T. Nelson, 1963.

579 _____ , ed. Chaucer and Chaucerians: Critical Studies in Middle English Literature. London, T. Nelson, 1966.

580 Bronson, B. H. In Appreciation of Chaucer's Parlement. Berkeley, University of California Press, 1935.

581 Brooks, H. F. Chaucer's Pilgrims: The Artistic Order of the Portraits in the Prologue. London, Methuen, 1962.

582 Bryan, W. F., and G. Dempster, eds. Sources and Analogues of Chaucer's Canterbury Tales. Chicago, University of Chicago Press, 1941.

583 Cawley, A. C., ed. Chaucer's Mind and Art. New York, Barnes & Noble, 1970.

584 Chute, M. Chaucer of England. New York, Dutton, 1958.

585 Clemen, W. Chaucer's Early Poetry. New York, Barnes & Noble, 1963.

586 Corsa, H. S. Chaucer, Poet of Mirth and Morality. Notre Dame, Ind., University of Notre Dame Press, 1964.

587 Coulton, G. G. Chaucer and his England. New York, Russell & Russell, 1957.

588 Craik, T. W. The Comic Tales of Chaucer. London, Methuen, 1964.

589 Curry, W. C. Chaucer and the Medieval Sciences. New York, Barnes & Noble, 1926.

590 Gerould, G. H. Chaucerian Essays. New York, Russell & Russell, 1968.

591 Gordon, I. L. The Double Sorrow of Troilus: A Study of Ambiguities in Troilus & Creseyde. Oxford, Oxford University Press, 1970.

592 Halliday, F. E. Chaucer and his World. London, Thames & Hudson, 1968.

593 Hieatt, C. B. The Realism of Dream Vision. The Poetic Exploitation of the Dream Experience in Chaucer and his Contemporaries. The Hague, Mouton, 1967.

594 Kirby, T. A. Chaucer's Troilus: A Study in Courtly Love. Baton Rouge, La., La Salle University Press, 1940.

595 Lawrence, W. W. Chaucer and the Canterbury Tales. New York, Columbia University Press, 1950.

596 Lowes, J. L. Geoffrey Chaucer. Bloomington, Indiana University Press, 1958.

597 Makerewicz, Sister M. R. The Patristic Influence in Chaucer. Washington, Catholic University Press, 1953.

598 Malone, K. Chapters on Chaucer. Baltimore, Johns Hopkins Press, 1951.

599 Marckwardt, A. H. Characterization in Chaucer's Knight's Tale. Ann Arbor, University of Michigan Press, 1947.

600 Mogan, J. J., Jr. Chaucer and the Theme of Mutability. The Hague, Mouton, 1969.

601 Newstead, H., ed. Chaucer and his Contemporaries: Essays on Medieval Literature and Thought. Greenwich, Conn., Fawcett, 1968.

602 Rowland, B., ed. Companion to Chaucer Studies. Toronto, Oxford University Press, 1968.

603 Schoeck, R. J., and J. Taylor, eds. Chaucer Criticism, The Canterbury Tales: An Anthology. Notre Dame, Ind., University of Notre Dame Press, 1960.

604 _____ , eds. Chaucer Criticism, Vol. 2: Troilus and Cressida and the Minor Poems. Notre Dame, Ind., University of Notre Dame Press, 1962.

605 Severs, J. B. The Literary Relationship of Chaucer's Clerke's Tale. New Haven, Conn., Yale University Press, 1942.

606 Slaughter, E. E. Love and the Virtues and Vices in Chaucer. Nashville, Tenn., Vanderbilt University Press, 1946.

607 Speirs, J. Chaucer the Maker. 2d ed. London, Faber & Faber, 1960.

608 Spurgeon, F. E. Five Hundred Years of Chaucer Criticism and Allusion, 1357-1900. London, Cambridge University Press, 1925. 3 vols.

609 Wagenknecht, E. C., ed. Chaucer: Modern Essays in Criticism. New York, Oxford University Press, 1959.

610 Williams, G. A New View of Chaucer. Durham, N.C., Duke University Press, 1965.

611 Wimsatt, J. Chaucer and the French Love Poets: The Literary Background of the Book of the Duchess. Chapel Hill, University of North Carolina Press, 1968.

The Owl and the Nightingale (c. 1200)

TEXTS

612 Ker, N. R., ed. The Owl and the Nightingale. London, Oxford University Press, 1963.

613 Stanley, E. G., ed. The Owl and the Nightingale. London, T. Nelson, 1960.

The Pearl (14th century)

TEXTS

614 DeFord, S., ed. The Pearl. New York, Appleton, 1967.

615 Gardner, J., trans. The Complete Works of the Gawain-Poet. Chicago, University of Chicago Press, 1965.

616 Hillman, Sister M. V., ed. The Pearl. Convent Station, N.J., College of St. Elizabeth Press, 1961.

617 Williams, M., ed. The Pearl-Poet: His Complete Works. New York, Random House, 1967.

CRITICISM

618 Bishop, I. Pearl in its Setting: A Critical Study of the Structure and Meaning of the Middle English Poem. London, B. Blackwell, 1968.

619 Kean, P. M. The Pearl: An Interpretation. New York, Barnes & Noble, 1967.

620 Oakden, J. P. Alliterative Poetry in Middle English. Manchester, University of Manchester Press, 1930-1935. 2 vols.

Vision Concerning Piers Plowman (c. 1362)

TEXTS

621 Donaldson, E. T., ed. Piers Plowman, the C—Text and its Poet. New Haven, Conn., Yale University Press, 1949.

622 Goodridge, J. F., ed. Piers the Ploughman. Baltimore, Penguin, 1959.

623 Kane, G., ed. Piers the Plowman: The A—Version. Will's Vision of Piers Plowman and Do-Well. London, Athlone Press, 1960.

624 Knott, T. A., and D. C. Fowler, eds. Piers the Plowman: A Critical Edition of the A—Version. Baltimore, Johns Hopkins Press, 1952.

CRITICISM

625 Blanch, R. J., ed. Style and Symbolism in Piers Plowman: A Modern Critical Anthology. Knoxville, University of Tennessee Press, 1969.

626 Fowler, D. C. Piers the Plowman: Literary Relations of the A— and B—Texts. Seattle, University of Washington Press, 1961.

627 Hussey, S. S., ed. Piers Plowman: Critical Approaches. London, Methuen, 1970.

628 Kane, G. Piers Plowman: The Evidence for Authorship. London, Athlone Press, 1965.

629 _____ . Middle English Literature: A Critical Study of the Romance, the Religious Lyrics and Piers Plowman. London, Methuen, 1951.

630 Lawler, J. Piers Plowman: An Essay in Criticism. London, E. Arnold, 1962.

631 Robertson, D. W., and B. F. Huppé. Piers Plowman and Scriptural Tradition. Princeton, Princeton University Press, 1951.

632 Salter, E. Piers Plowman: An Introduction. Cambridge, Mass., Harvard University Press, 1962.

633 Smith, B. H., Jr. Traditional Imagery of Charity in Piers Plowman. The Hague, Mouton, 1966.

634 Vasta, E. The Spiritual Basis of Piers Plowman. The Hague, Mouton, 1965.

635 _____ , ed. Interpretations of Piers Plowman. Notre Dame, Ind., University of Notre Dame Press, 1968.

PROSE—TEXTS

636 Bennett, J. A., and G. V. Smithers, eds. Early Middle English Verse and Prose. Oxford, Clarendon Press, 1966.

637 Colledge, E., ed. The Medieval Mystics of England. New York, Scribner's, 1961.

638 Stevick, R. D., ed. Five Middle English Narratives. Indianapolis, Bobbs-Merrill, 1967.

PROSE—CRITICISM

639 Knowles, D. The English Mystical Tradition. London, Burns & Oates, 1961.

640 Pepler, C. The English Religious Heritage. London, Blackfriars, 1958.

PROSE—INDIVIDUAL AUTHORS

Geoffrey of Monmouth (d. c. 1152)

TEXTS

641 Hammer, J., ed. Historia Regum Britanniae: A Variant Version. Cambridge, Mass., Harvard University Press, 1951.

642 Thorpe, L., trans. The History of the Kings of Britain. Harmondsworth, Penguin, 1966.

CRITICISM

643 Keeler, L. Geoffrey of Monmouth and the Late Latin Chronicles, 1300-1500. Berkeley, University of California Press, 1946.

644 Tatlock, J. S. P. The Legendary History of Britain: Geoffrey of Monmouth's Historia and its Early Vernacular Versions. Berkeley, University of California Press, 1950.

ROMANCES—TEXTS

645 French, W. H., and C. B. Hale, eds. Middle English Metrical Romances. New York, Russell & Russell, 1964.

646 Gibbs, A. C., ed. Middle English Romances. Evanston, Ill., Northwestern University Press, 1966.

647 Loomis, R. S., and L. H. Loomis, eds. Medieval Romances. New York, Random House, 1957.

648 Sands, D. B., ed. Middle English Verse Romances. New York, Holt, 1966.

ROMANCES—CRITICISM

649 Bordman, G. Motif-Index of the English Metrical Romances. Helsinki, STA, 1963.

650 Dinkins, P. Human Relationships in the Medieval Romances. Nashville, Tenn., Vanderbilt University Press, 1944.

651 Fisher, F. Narrative Art in Medieval Romances. Cleveland, World Publishing Company, 1939.

652 Kane, G. Middle English Literature: A Critical Study of the Romances, the Religious Lyrics and Piers Plowman. London, Methuen, 1951.

653 Lanham, M. Chastity: A Study of Sexual Morality in the English Medieval Romances. Nashville, Tenn., Vanderbilt University Press, 1947.

654 Mehl, D. The Middle English Romances of the Thirteenth and Fourteenth Centuries. New York, Barnes & Noble, 1969.

655 Van de Voort, D. Love and Marriage in the English Medieval Romance. Nashville, Tenn., Vanderbilt University Press, 1938.

INDIVIDUAL ROMANCES

Arthurian Romances (14th century)

TEXTS

656 Brengle, R. L., ed. Arthur, King of Britain: History, Romance, Chronicle and Criticism. New York, Appleton, 1964.

CRITICISM

657 Barber, R. W. Arthur of Albion: An Introduction to the Arthurian Literature and Legends of England. London, Barrie & Rockliff, 1961.

658 Cosman, M. P. The Education of the Hero in Arthurian Romance. Chapel Hill, University of North Carolina Press, 1966.

659 Loomis, R. S. Arthurian Literature in the Middle Ages: A Collaborative History. London, Oxford University Press, 1938.

660 _____ . The Grail: From Celtic Myth to Christian Symbol. Cardiff, University of Wales Press, 1963.

661 _____ . The Development of Arthurian Romance. London, Hutchinson University Library, 1963.

662 Nitze, W. A. Perceval and the Holy Grail. Berkeley, University of California Press, 1949.

663 Owen, D. D. R. The Evolution of the Grail Legend. Edinburgh, Oliver & Boyd, 1968.

664 Reid, M. J. C. The Arthurian Legend: Comparison of Treatment in Modern and Medieval Literature: A Study in the Literary Value of Myth and Legend. New York, Barnes & Noble, 1970.

665 Traherne, R. F. The Glastonbury Legends: Joseph of Arimathea, The Holy Grail, and King Arthur. London, Cresset, 1967.

666 Waite, A. E. The Holy Grail: The Galahad Quest in the Arthurian Literature. New Hyde Park, N. Y., University Books, 1961.

Richard Coeur de Lyon (14th century)

TEXTS

667 Broughton, B. B., ed. and trans. Richard the Lion-Hearted, and Other Medieval English Romances. New York, Dutton, 1966.

CRITICISM

668 Broughton, B. B. The Legends of King Richard I, Coeur de Lion: A Study of Sources and Variations to the Year 1600. The Hague, Mouton, 1966.

Sir Gawain and the Greene Knight (c. 1390)

TEXTS

669 Barroff, M., trans. Sir Gawain and the Green Knight. New York, Norton, 1967.

670 Gardner, J., ed. The Complete Works of the Gawain-Poet. Chicago, University of Chicago Press, 1965.

671 Kreuzer, J. R., ed. Sir Gawain and the Green Knight. Trans. by J. L. Rosenberg. New York, Rinehart, 1959.

CRITICISM

672 Barroff, M. Sir Gawain and the Green Knight: A Stylistic and Metrical Study, New Haven, Conn., Yale University Press, 1962.

673 Fox, D., ed. Twentieth Century Interpretations of Sir Gawain and the Green Knight: A Collection of Critical Essays. Englewood Cliffs, N. J., Prentice-Hall, 1968.

674 Howard, D. R., and C. K. Zacher, eds. Critical Studies of Sir Gawain and the Green Knight. Notre Dame, University of Notre Dame Press, 1968.

675 Savage, H. L. The Gawain Poet: Studies in his Personality and Background. Chapel Hill, University of North Carolina Press, 1956.

676 Schnyder, H. Sir Gawain and the Green Knight: An Essay in Interpretation. Bern, Franke, 1961.

677 Spearing, A. C. The Gawain-Poet: A Critical Study. Cambridge, Cambridge University Press, 1971.

Tristan (13th century)

TEXTS

678 The Romance of Tristran and Iseult. Trans. by H. Belloc and P. Rosenfeld. New York, Heritage, 1960.

679 The Romance of Tristran and Iseult. New York, Pantheon, 1945.

680 Tristran and Isolde. Trans. S. Robb. New York, Dutton, 1965.

CRITICISM

681 Eisner, S. The Tristan Legend: A Study in Sources. Evanston, Ill., Northwestern University Press, 1969.

682 Loomis, R. S. The Romance of Tristram and Ysolt by Thomas of Britain. New York, Columbia University Press, 1931.

683 Zeydel, E. H. The Tristram and Isolde of Gottfried von Strassburg. Princeton, Princeton University Press, 1948.

15TH CENTURY LITERATURE—TEXTS

684 Brown, C., ed. Religious Lyrics of the Fifteenth Century. Oxford, Clarendon Press, 1939.

15TH CENTURY LITERATURE—CRITICISM

685 McMahon, C. P. Education in Fifteenth Century England. Baltimore, Johns Hopkins, 1947.

686 Workman, S. K. Fifteenth-Century Translations as an Influence on English Prose. Princeton, Princeton University Press, 1940.

15TH CENTURY POETRY—INDIVIDUAL AUTHORS

John Lydgate (1370-1450)

WORKS

687 The Fall of Princis, 1494
688 The Siege of Thebes, 1500

689 The Governaunce of Kynges and Prynces, 1511
690 The Historye, Sege and Dys-truccyon of Troy, 1513

TEXTS

691 Lauritis, J. A., R. A. Klinefelter, and V. F. Gallagher, eds. A Critical Edition of John Lydgate's Life of Our Lady. Pittsburgh, Duquesne University Press, 1961.

692 Lydgate's Fall of Princes. 4 vols. by H. Bergen. London, Oxford University Press, 1924-1927.

693 Lydgate's Minor Poems. ed. O. Glauning. London, K. Paul, Trench, Trübner, 1900.

CRITICISM

694 Schirmer, W. F. John Lydgate: A Study in the Culture of the Fifteenth Century. Berkeley, University of California Press, 1961.

15TH CENTURY PROSE—INDIVIDUAL AUTHORS

William Caxton (1421-1491)

WORKS

695 The Recuyell of the Histories of Troye, 1469
696 The Game and Playe of the Chesse, 1475

697 The Myrrour of the World, 1481

TEXTS

698 The Game and Playe of the Chesse. English Books, 1475-1640.

699 Lenagham, R. T., ed. Caxton's Aesop. Cambridge, Mass., Harvard University Press, 1967.

700 Prior, O. H., ed. Caxton's Mirror of the World. London, Oxford University Press, 1966.

701 The Recuyell of the Histories of Troye. English Books, 1475-1640.

CRITICISM

702 Kaplan, M. Ovid and Fifteenth Century Literature with Special Reference to Caxton's Translation. New York, New York University Press, 1950.

703 Winship, G. P. William Caxton. Berkeley, University of California Press, 1937.

Sir Thomas Malory (d. 1471)

WORKS

704 Le Morte Darthur, 1485

TEXTS

705 Davies, R. T., ed. King Arthur and His Knights: A Selection From What Has Been Known as Le Morte Darthur. London, Faber & Faber, 1967.

706 Sanders, C. R., and C. E. Ward, eds. Le Morte d'Arthur. New York, Dutton, 1962.

707 Vinaver, E., ed. The Works of Sir Thomas Malory. 2d ed. Oxford, Clarendon Press, 1971.

CRITICISM

708 Bennett, J. A. W., ed. Essays on Malory. Oxford, Oxford University Press, 1963.

709 Bradbrook, M. C. Sir Thomas Malory. London, Longmans, Green, 1958.

710 Field, P. J. C. Romance and Chronicle: A Study of Malory's Prose Style. Bloomington, Indiana University Press, 1971.

711 Hicks, E. Sir Thomas Malory: His Turbulent Career: A Biography. New York, Octagon, 1970.

712 Lumiansky, R. M., ed. Malory's Originality: A Critical Study of Le Morte Darthur. Baltimore: Johns Hopkins Press, 1964.

713 Matthews, W. The Ill-Framed Knight: A Skeptical Inquiry Into the Identity of Sir Thomas Malory. Berkeley, University of California Press, 1966.

714 Moorman, C. The Book of Kyng Arthur: The Unity of Malory's Morte Darthur. Lexington, University of Kentucky Press, 1965.

715 Reiss, E. Sir Thomas Malory. New York, Twayne, 1966.

716 Vinaver, E. Malory. Oxford, Oxford University Press, 1970.

LITERATURE OF THE RENAISSANCE
1500-1660

GENERAL WORKS—BIBLIOGRAPHIES

717 Lievsay, J. L., comp. The Sixteenth Century: Skelton Through Hooker. New York, Appleton, 1968.

718 Tannenbaum, S. A., and R. D. Elizabethan Bibliographies. New York, The Authors, 1937—.

GENERAL WORKS—CRITICISM

719 Allen, D. C. The Star-Crossed Renaissance: The Quarrel About Astrology and its Influence in England. Durham, N. C., Duke University Press, 1941.

720 Ashley, M. Life in Stuart England. London, Batsford, 1964.

721 Babb, L. The Elizabethan Malady: A Study of Melancholia in Elizabethan Literature from 1580 to 1642. East Lansing, Michigan State University Press, 1951.

722 Baker, H. The Wars of Truth: Studies in the Decay of Christian Humanism in the Earlier Seventeenth Century. Cambridge, Mass., Harvard University Press, 1952.

723 Brinkley, R. F. Arthurian Legend in Seventeenth Century. Baltimore, Johns Hopkins Press, 1932.

724 Burton, E. The Jacobean at Home. London: Secker & Warburg, 1962.

725 Bush, D. The Renaissance and English Humanism. Toronto: Toronto University Press, 1956.

726 _____ . Mythology and the Renaissance Tradition. Minneapolis, University of Minnesota Press, 1932. Repr. New York, Norton, 1963.

727 _____ . English Literature in the Earlier Seventeenth Century, 1600-1660. Oxford, Clarendon Press, 1945.

728 Caspari, F. Humanism and the Social Order in Tudor England. Chicago, University of Chicago Press, 1954.

729 Chew, S. C. The Pilgrimage of Life: An Exploration Into the Renaissance Mind. New Haven, Conn., Yale University Press, 1962.

730 Craig, H. The Enchanted Glass: The Renaissance Mind in English Literature. New York, Oxford University Press, 1936.

731 Crane, W. G. Wit and Rhetoric in the Renaissance. New York, Columbia University Press, 1937.

732 Davis, H., and H. Gardner, eds. Elizabethan and Jacobean Studies; Presented to Frank Percy Wilson in Honor of His 70th Birthday. Oxford, Oxford University Press, 1970.

733 Ferguson, A. B. The Articulate Citizen and the English Renaissance. Durham, N. C., Duke University Press, 1965.

734 Ford B., et. al, ed. The Age of Shakespeare. Baltimore, Penguin, 1969.

735 Grierson, H. J. C. Cross Currents in English Literature of the Seventeenth Century. Harmondsworth, Penguin, 1929.

736 Herrick, M. T. Comic Theory in the Sixteenth Century. Urbana, University of Illinois Press, 1950.

737 Hoopes, R. Right Reason in the English Renaissance. Cambridge, Mass., Harvard University Press, 1962.

738 Johnson, F. R. Astronomical Thought in Renaissance England. Baltimore, Johns Hopkins Press, 1937.

739 Kocher, P. H. Science and Religion in Elizabethan England. San Marino, Huntington Library, 1953.

740 Lechner, J. M. Renaissance Concepts of the Common Places. New York, Pageant Press, 1962.

741 Levin, H. The Myth of the Golden Age in the Renaissance. Bloomington, Indiana University Press, 1969.

742 Lewis, C. S. English Literature of the Sixteenth Century, Excluding Drama. Oxford, Oxford University Press, 1954.

743 Lovejoy, A. O. The Great Chain of Being: A Study of the History of an Idea. Cambridge, Mass., Harvard University Press, 1936.

744 Matthiesen, F. O. Translation, an Elizabethan Art. Cambridge, Mass., Harvard University Press, 1931.

745 Muir, K. Introduction to Elizabethan Literature. New York, Random House, 1967.

746 O'Connor, J. J. Amadis de Gaule and Its Influence on Elizabethan Literature. New Brunswick, N. J., Rutgers University Press, 1970.

747 Pearson, L. E. Elizabethan Love Conventions. New York, Barnes & Noble, 1967.

748 Praz, M. Studies in Seventeenth Century Imagery. Roma, Edizioni di Storia e Literatura, 1964.

749 Sellery, G. C. The Renaissance: Its Nature and Origins. Madison, University of Wisconsin Press, 1950.

750 Simon, J. Education and Society in Tudor England. Cambridge, Cambridge University Press, 1966.

751 Tayler, E. W. Nature and Art in Renaissance Literature. New York, Columbia University Press, 1964.

752 Tillyard, E. M. W. The Elizabethan World Picture. London, 1943. Repr. Harmondsworth, Penguin, 1966:

753 Tuve, R. Elizabethan and Metaphysical Imagery: Renaissance Poetic and Twentieth Century Critics. Chicago, University of Chicago Press, 1947.

754 Van Gelder, H. A. Enno. The Two Reformations in the Sixteenth Century: A Study of the Religious Aspects and Consequences of Renaissance and Humanism. The Hague, Mouton, 1961.

755 Wedgwood, C. V. Seventeenth Century English Literature. New York, Oxford University Press, 1961.

756 Willey, B. The Seventeenth Century Background. Harmondsworth, Penguin, 1934.

757 Williams, P. Life in Tudor England. London, Putnam, 1965.

758 Wright, L. B. Middle Class Culture in Elizabethan England. Ithaca, N. Y., Cornell University Press, 1963.

DRAMA—BIBLIOGRAPHIES

759 Greg, W. W., ed. A Bibliography of English Printed Drama to the Restoration. London, Oxford University Press, 1939-1959. 4 vols.

760 _____ , ed. A List of English Plays Written Before 1643 and Printed Before 1700. London, Bibliographical Society, 1900. Repr. New York, Haskell House, 1969.

761 Stratman, C. J. Bibliography of English Printed Drama. 1565-1900. Carbondale, Southern Illinois University Press, 1966.

DRAMA—CRITICISM

762 Adams, H. H. English Domestic and Homiletic Tragedy, 1575-1642. New York, Blom, 1965.

763 Bevington, D. M. From Mankind to Marlowe: Growth of Structure in the Popular Drama of Tudor England. Cambridge, Mass., Harvard University Press, 1962.

764 Kernan, A. B. The Cankered Muse: Satire of the English Renaissance. New Haven, Conn., Yale University Press, 1962.

765 Margeson, J. M. R. The Origins of the English Tragedy. Oxford, Clarendon Press, 1967.

766 Powell, A. F. The Melting Mood: A Study of the Function of Pathos in English Tragedy Through Shakespeare. Nashville, Tenn., Vanderbilt University Press, 1949.

767 Robbins, E. W. Theories of Characterization in Commentaries on Terrence Before 1600. Urbana, University of Illinois Press, 1948.

TUDOR AND ELIZABETHAN DRAMA
TEXTS

768 Adams, J. Q., ed. Chief Pre-Shakesperian Drama. Boston, Houghton, 1924.

769 Armstrong, W. A., ed. Elizabethan History Plays. London, Oxford University Press, 1965.

770 Bald, R. C., ed. Six Elizabethan Plays. Boston, Houghton, 1963.

771 Boas, F. S., ed. Five Pre-Shakespearean Comedies. Oxford, World's Classics, 1934.

772 Creeth, E., ed. Tudor Plays: An Anthology of Early English Drama. Garden City, N. Y., Doubleday, 1966.

773 Cunliffe, J. W., ed. Early English Classical Tragedies. Oxford, Clarendon Press, 1912.

774 Gassner, J., ed. Medieval and Tudor Drama. New York, Bantam, 1963.

775 _____ , ed. Elizabethan Drama. New York, Bantam, 1967.

776 Heilman, R. B., ed. An Anthology of English Drama Before Shakespeare. New York, Holt, 1952.

777 Huston, J. D., and A. B. Kernan, eds. Classics of the Renaissance Theatre: Seven English Plays. New York, Harcourt, 1969.

778 Nethercot, A. H., et al., eds. Elizabethan Plays. Rev. ed. New York, Holt, 1971.

779 Wine, M. L., ed. Drama of the English Renaissance. New York, Modern Library, 1969.

CRITICISM

780 Bernard, J. E. The Prosody of the Tudor Interlude. New Haven, Conn., Yale University Press, 1939.

781 Bevington, D. M. Fron Mankind to Marlowe: Growth of Structure in the Popular Drama of Tudor England. Cambridge, Mass., Harvard University Press, 1962.

782 Bowers, F. T. Elizabethan Revenge Tragedy, 1587-1642. Gloucester, Mass., P. Smith, 1959.

783 Bradbrook, M. C. Themes and Conventions of Elizabethan Tragedy. Cambridge, Cambridge University Press, 1957.

784 _____ . The Growth and Structure of Elizabethan Comedy. London, Chatto & Windus, 1955.

785 _____ . The Rise of Common Player: A Study of Actor and Society in Shakespeare's England. London, Chatto & Windus, 1962.

786 Brooke, C. F. T. Tudor Drama: A History of English National Drama to the Retirement of Shakespeare. New York, Haskell, 1967.

787 Carpenter, F. I. Metaphor and Simile in the Minor Elizabethan Drama. New York, Phaeton, 1967.

788 Chambers, E. K. Elizabethan Stage. Oxford, Oxford University Press, 1923. 4 vols.

789 Craik, T. W. The Tudor Interlude: Stage, Costume and Acting. Leicester, Leicester University Press, 1958.

790 Cunningham, J. E. Elizabethan and Early Stuart Drama. London, Evans, 1965.

791 Doran, M. Endeavors of Art: A Study of Form in Elizabethan Drama. Madison, University of Wisconsin Press, 1954.

792 Eliot, T. S. Essays on Elizabethan Drama. New York, Harcourt, 1956.

793 Farnham, W. The Medieval Heritage of Elizabethan Tragedy. Berkeley, University of California Press, 1936.

794 Freeburg, V. O. Disguise Plots in Elizabethan Drama: A Study in Stage Tradition. New York, Blom, 1966.

795 Greg, W. W. Dramatic Documents from the Elizabethan Playhouses; Stage Plots; Actors Parts. Oxford, Prompt Books, 1969.

796 Harbage, A. Cavalier Drama: An Historical and Critical Supplement to the Study of the Elizabethan and the Restoration Stage. New York, Russell & Russell, 1964.

797 Harrison, G. B. Elizabethan Plays and Players. Ann Arbor, University of Michigan Press, 1956.

798 Kaufmann, R. J., ed. Elizabethan Drama: Modern Essays in Criticism. New York, Oxford University Press, 1961.

799 Klein, D. The Elizabethan Dramatists as Critics. New York, Philosophical Library, 1963.

800 Klemen, W. English Tragedy Before Shakespeare: The Development of Dramatic Speech. New York, Barnes & Noble, 1961.

801 Mehl, D. The Elizabethan Dumb Show. Cambridge, Mass., Harvard University Press, 1967.

802 Parrott, T. M., and R. H. Ball. A Short View of Elizabethan Drama. New York, Scribner's, 1943.

803 Ribner, I. The English History Play in the Age of Shakespeare. Rev. ed. New York, Barnes & Noble, 1965.

804 _____ . Tudor and Stuart Drama. New York, Appleton, 1966.

805 Spencer, T. Death and Elizabethan Tragedy: A Study of Convention and Opinion in the Elizabethan Drama. Cambridge, Mass., Harvard University Press, 1936.

806 Stroup, T. B. Microcosmos: The Shape of the Elizabethan Play. Lexington, University of Kentucky Press, 1965.

807 Tomlinson, T. B. A Study of Elizabethan and Jacobean Tragedy. Cambridge, Cambridge University Press, 1964.

Francis Beaumont (1585-1616) and John Fletcher (1579-1625)

WORKS

808 The Knight of the Burning Pestle, 1607

809 The Faithful Shepherdes, 1608-9

810 Philaster, 1608-10

811 The Maid's Tragedy, 1608-11

812 A King and No King, 1611

BIBLIOGRAPHIES

813 Pennel, C. A., and W. P. Williams, comps. Elizabethan Bibliographies Supplements VIII: Francis Beaumont, John Fletcher, Philip Massinger 1937-1965, John Ford 1940-1965, James Shirley 1945-1965. London, Nether Press, 1968.

814 Tannenbaum, S. A., and R. Dorothy. Supplement to Beaumont and Fletcher, a Concise Bibliography. New York, Privately Published, 1946.

TEXTS

815 Baker, G. P., ed. Selected Plays. New York, Dutton, 1966.

816 Bowers, F. T., gen. ed. The Dramatic Works in the Beaumont and Fletcher Canon. Vol. I. Cambridge, Cambridge University Press, 1966.

CRITICISM

817 Appleton, W. W. Beaumont and Fletcher: A Critical Study. Fair Lawn, N. J., Essential Books, 1956.

818 McKeithan, D. M. The Debt of Shakespeare in the Beaumont and Fletcher Plays. Austin, University of Texas Press, 1938.

819 Maxwell, W. B. Studies in Beaumont, Fletcher and Massinger. Chapel Hill, University of North Carolina Press, 1939.

Robert Greene (1558-1592)

WORKS

820 Pandosto, 1588
821 Tullie's Love, 1589
822 Menaphon, 1589
823 Greene's Vision, 1590
824 The Scottish History of James the Fourth, 1590-91

825 The Honorable History of Frier Bacon and Frier Bongay, 1591
826 Repentance of Robert Greene, Maister of Artes, 1592

BIBLIOGRAPHY

827 Hayashi, T. Robert Greene Criticism: A Comprehensive Bibliography. Metuchen, N. J., Scarecrow, 1971.

TEXTS

828 Grosart, A. B., ed. The Life and Complete Works in Prose and Verse. 1881-1886. Rev. ed. New York, Russell & Russell, 1964. 15 vols.

CRITICISM

829 Jordan, J. C. Robert Greene. New York, Columbia University Press, 1915.

Thomas Kyd (1558-1594)

WORKS

830 The Rare Triumphs of Love and Fortune, 1589
831 The Spanish Tragedy, 1592
832 Cornelia, 1594
833 Pompey the Great, 1595
834 The Tragedie of Solimon and Perseda, 1599
835 A Warning for Faire Women, 1599
836 The True Chronicle Historie of King Leir, 1605

BIBLIOGRAPHIES

837 Johnson, R. C., comp. Elizabethan Bibliographies Suppliements IX: Minor Elizabethans: Roger Ascham 1946-1966, George Gascoigne 1941-1966, Thomas Kyd 1940-1966, Anthony Munday 1941-1966. London, Nether Press, 1968.

838 Tannenbaum, S. A. Thomas Kyd, A Concise Bibliography. New York, Privately Published, 1941.

TEXTS

839 Boas, F. S., ed. The Works of Thomas Kyd. Oxford, Oxford University Press, 1955.

CRITICISM

840 Baker, H. Induction to Tragedy. Baton Rouge, La., La Salle University Press, 1939.

841 Edwards, P. Thomas Kyd and Early Elizabethan Tragedy. London, Longmans, Green, 1966.

842 Freeman, A. Thomas Kyd: Facts and Problems. Oxford, Clarendon Press, 1967.

Christopher Marlowe (1564-1593)

WORKS

843 Tamburlaine, 1590
844 Hero and Leander, 1598
845 Dr. Faustus, 1604
846 The Jew of Malta, 1633

BIBLIOGRAPHIES

847 Johnson, R. C., comp. Elizabethan Bibliographies Supplements VI: Christopher Marlowe 1946-1965. London, Nether Press, 1967.

TEXTS

848 Brooke, T., ed. Works. Oxford, Oxford University Press, 1910.

849 Case, R. H., ed. The Works of Christopher Marlowe. London, Methuen, 1930-1933.

850 McLure, M., ed. The Poems of Christopher Marlow. London, Methuen, 1968.

851 Ribner, I., ed. Complete Plays of Christopher Marlowe. New York, Odyssey Press, 1963.

CRITICISM

852 Armstrong, W. A. Marlowe's Tamburlaine: The Image and the Stage. Hull, Hull University Press, 1966.

853 Bakeless, J. The Tragicall History of Christopher Marlowe. Cambridge, Mass., Harvard University Press, 1942. 2 vols.

854 Battenhouse, R. W. Marlowe's Tamburlaine: A Study in Renaissance Moral Philosophy. Nashville, Tenn., Vanderbilt University Press, 1941.

855 Boas, F. S. Marlowe: A Biographical and Critical Study. Oxford, Oxford University Press, 1940.

856 Cole, D. Suffering and Evil in the Plays of Chrisopher Marlowe. Princeton, Princeton University Press, 1962.

857 Farnham, W., ed. Twentieth Century Interpretations of Doctor Faustus: A Collection of Critical Essays. Englewood Cliffs, N.J., Prentice-Hall, 1969.

858 Jump, J. D., ed. Marlowe: Dr. Faustus. A Casebook. London, Macmillan, 1969.

859 Knoll, J. D. Christopher Marlowe. New York, Twayne, 1969.

860 Kocher, P. H. Christopher Marlowe: A Study of His Thought, Learning, and Character. Chapel Hill, University of North Carolina Press, 1946.

861 Leech, C., ed. Marlowe: A Collection of Critical Essays. Englewood Cliffs, N. J., Prentice-Hall, 1964.

862 Levin, H. The Overreacher: A Study of Marlowe. Cambridge, Mass., Harvard University Press, 1952.

863 Norman, C. The Muses' Darling: The Life of Christopher Marlowe. New York, Macmillan, 1946.

864 Rowse, A. L. Christopher Marlowe: His Life and Works. New York, Harper, 1964.

865 Steane, J. B. Marlowe: A Critical Study. Cambridge, Cambridge University Press, 1964.

866 Wilson, F. P. Marlowe and the Early Shakespeare. Oxford, Oxford University Press, 1952.

867 Wraight, A. D. In Search of Christopher Marlowe: A Pictorial Biography. London, Macdonald, 1965.

George Peele (1557-1596)

WORKS

868 The Araygnement of Paris, 1584
869 The Famous Chronicle of King Edwarde, 1593
870 The Battell of Alcazar, 1594
871 The Old Wives Tale, 1595

TEXTS

872 Hook, F. S., and J. Yoklavich, eds. The Dramatic Works of George Peele. Edward I. ed. by F. S. Hook. The Battle of Alcazar. Ed. by J. Yoklavich. New Haven, Conn., Yale University Press, 1961.

873 Horne, D. H., ed. The Life and Minor Works of George Peele. New Haven, Conn., Yale University Press, 1952.

874 Prouty, C. T., ed. Life and Works of Peele. Vol. I. New Haven, Conn., Yale University Press, 1952.

CRITICISM

875 Hunter, G. K. Lyly and Peele. London, Longmans, Green, 1968.

William Shakespeare (1564-1616)

WORKS

876 Henry IV, 1591-92, 1592-93
877 Venus and Adonis, 1593
878 Lucrece, 1594
879 Romeo and Juliet, 1595-96
880 Love's Labour Lost, 1595-96
881 Midsummer Night's Dream, 1596-97
882 Merchant of Venice, 1597-98
883 Much Ado About Nothing, 1599-1600
884 Julius Caesar, 1600-01
885 As You Like It, 1600-01
886 Twelfth Night, 1600-01
887 Hamlet, 1601-02
888 Troilus and Cressida, 1602-03
889 Othello, 1605-06
890 Macbeth, 1606-07
891 King Lear, 1606-07
892 Anthony and Cleopatra, 1607-08
893 Tempest, 1612-13

BIBLIOGRAPHIES

894 Bate, J. How to Find Out About Shakespeare. New York, Pergamon Press, 1968.

895 Berman, R. A Reader's Guide to Shakespeare's Plays: A Discursive Bibliography. Chicago, Scott, Foresman, 1965.

896 Ebisch, W., and L. L. Schücking. A Shakespeare Bibliography. Supplement for the Years 1930-1935. New York, Blom, 1937.

897 Howard-Hill, T. H. Shakespeare Bibliography and Textual Criticism: A Bibliography. Oxford, Clarendon Press, 1971.

898 Smith, G. R. A Classified Shakespeare Bibliography, 1936-1958. University Park, Pennsylvania State University Press, 1963.

899 Wilson, F. P. Shakespeare and the New Bibliography. Ed. by H. Gardner, Oxford, Clarendon Press, 1970.

TEXTS

900 Alexander, P., ed. The Complete Works. New York, Random, 1951.

901 Campbell, O. J., ed. The Living Shakespeare: Twenty-Two Plays and the Sonnets. New York, Macmillan, 1949.

902 _____ , ed. The Complete Sonnets, Songs and Poems of Shakespeare. New York, Schocken, 1965.

903 Craig, H., ed. Shakespeare: An Historical and Critical Study with Annotated Texts of Twenty-One Plays. Chicago, University of Chicago Press, 1931.

904 _____ , ed. The Complete Works of Shakespeare. Chicago, Scott, Foresman, 1951.

905 Harrison, G. B. Shakespeare: Twenty-Three Plays and the Sonnets. New York, Oxford University Press, 1952.

906 _____ , ed. Shakespeare: The Major Plays and the Sonnets. New York, Harcourt, 1948.

907 _____ , ed. Shakespeare: The Complete Works. New York, Harcourt, 1948.

908 Hubler, E., ed. Shakespeare's Songs and Poems. New York, McGraw-Hill, 1959.

909 Kittredge, G. L., ed. The Complete Works of William Shakespeare. New York, Crowell, 1966.

910 Kökeritz, H., ed. Mr. William Shakespeare's Comedies, Histories and Tragedies. New Haven, Conn., Yale University Press, 1954.

911 Neilson, W. A., and C. J. Hill, eds. Complete Plays and Poems of William Shakespeare. Boston, Houghton, 1942.

912 Ribner, I., and G. L. Kittredge, eds. The Complete Works of Shakespeare. Boston, Ginn, 1970.

913 Rollins, H. E., ed. The Sonnets. New York, Appleton, 1944. 2 vols.

914 Sisson, C. J., ed. The Complete Works. New York, Harper, 1954.

915 Wilson, J. D., ed. The New Cambridge Shakespeare. Cambridge, Cambridge University Press, 1952.

916 _____ , ed. The Sonnets. Cambridge, Cambridge University Press, 1966.

CRITICISM

917 Alexander, P. Shakespeare's Life and Art. New York, New York University Press, 1961.

918 Baker, A. E. A Shakespeare Commentary. New York, Ungar, 1957. 2 vols.

919 Baldwin, T. W. Shakespeare's Petty School. Urbana, University of Illinois Press, 1943.

920 _____ . Shakespeare's Small Latine and Lesse Greeke. Urbana, University of Illinois Press, 1944. 2 vols.

921 Barber, C. L. Shakespeare's Festive Comedy: A Study of Dramatic Form and Its Relation to Social Custom. Princeton, Princeton University Press, 1959.

922 Barnet, S., ed. Twentieth Century Interpretations of the Merchant of Venice: A Collection of Critical Essays. Englewood Cliffs, N.J., Prentice-Hall, 1970.

923 Bentley, G. E. Shakespeare and Jonson: Their Reputation in the Seventeenth Century Compared. Chicago, Chicago University Press, 1945. 2 vols.

924 _____ . Shakespeare and His Theatre. Lincoln, University of Nebraska Press, 1964.

925 _____ . Shakespeare: A Biographical Handbook. New Haven, Conn., Yale University Press, 1961.

926 Berman, R., ed. Twentieth Century Interpretations of Henry V: A Collection of Critical Essays. Englewood Cliffs, N. J., Prentice-Hall, 1968.

927 Bevington, D. M., ed. Twentieth Century Interpretations of Hamlet: A Collection of Critical Essays. Englewood Cliffs, N. J., Prentice-Hall, 1968.

928 Bradbrook, M. C. Shakespeare and Elizabethan Poetry. Oxford, Oxford University Press, 1951.

929 _____ . Elizabethan Stage Conditions: A Study of Their Place in the Interpretation of Shakespeare's Plays. London, Cambridge University Press, 1968.

930 Bradley, A. C. Shakespearean Tragedy. London, St. Martin's, 1952.

931 Brooke, C. F. T. Essays on Shakespeare and Other Elizabethans. New Haven, Conn., Yale University Press, 1948.

932 Brown, J. R. Shakespeare's Dramatic Style: Romeo and Juliet, As You Like It, Twelfth Night, Julius Caesar, Macbeth. New York, Barnes & Noble, 1971.

933 Bucknill, J. C. The Mad Folk of Shakespeare: Psychological Essays. New York, B. Franklin, 1969.

934 Bullough, G. Narrative and Dramatic Sources of Shakespeare. Vol. V. The Roman Plays. New York, Columbia University Press, 1964.

935 _____ . Narrative and Dramatic Sources of Shakespeare. Vol. VI: Other Classical Plays. New York, Columbia University Press, 1966.

936 Campbell, L. B. Shakespeare's 'Histories' Mirrors of Elizabethan Policy. San Marino, Calif., Huntington Library, 1947.

937 Campbell, O. J. Comical Satire and Shakespeare's Troilus and Cressida. San Marino, Calif., Huntington Library, 1938.

938 _____ . Shakespeare's Satire. Oxford, Oxford University Press, 1943.

939 _____ , and E. G. Quinn, eds. The Reader's Encyclopedia of Shakespeare. New York, Crowell, 1966.

940 Champion, L. S. The Evolution of Shakespeare's Comedy: A Study in Dramatic Perspective. Cambridge, Mass., Harvard University Press, 1970.

941 Chapman, G. W., ed. Essays on Shakespeare. Princeton, Princeton University Press, 1965.

942 Charney, M., ed. Discussions of Shakespeare's Roman Plays. Boston, Heath, 1964.

943 Charney, M. Shakespeare's Roman Plays: The Function of Imagery in the Drama. Cambridge, Mass., Harvard University Press, 1961.

944 Chute, M. Shakespeare of London. New York, Dutton, 1949.

945 Clemen, W. The Development of Shakespeare's Imagery. Cambridge, Mass., Harvard University Press, 1951.

946 Coe, C. N. Demi-Devils: The Character of Shakespeare's Villains. New York, Bookman Associates, 1962.

947 Cole, D., comp. Twentieth Century Interpretations of Romeo and Juliet: A Collection of Critical Essays. Englewood Cliffs, N.J., Prentice-Hall, 1970.

948 Conklin, P. S. A History of Hamlet in Criticism, 1601-1821. New York, Humanities Press, 1957.

949 Corder, J. W., ed. Shakespeare 1964. Fort Worth, Tex., Christian University Press, 1965.

950 Craig, H. An Interpretation of Shakespeare. New York, Dryden Press, 1948.

951 Crane, M. Shakespeare's Prose. Chicago, University of Chicago Press, 1951.

952 Cutts, J. P. Rich and Strange: A Study of Shakespeare's Last Plays. Pullman, Washington State University Press, 1968.

953 _____ . The Shattered Glass: A Dramatic Pattern in Shakespeare's Early Plays. Detroit, Wayne State University Press, 1968.

954 Dales, J. S. Shakespeare and the English Classic Drama. Lincoln, University of Nebraska Press, 1934.

955 Danby, J. F. Shakespeare's Doctrine of Nature: A Study of King Lear. New York, Hillary House, 1949.

956 Dean, L. F., ed. Shakespeare: Modern Essays in Criticism. New York, Oxford University Press, 1967.

957 _____ , ed. Twentieth Century Interpretations of Julius Caesar. Englewood Cliffs, N. J., Prentice-Hall, 1968.

958 Dowden, E. Shakespeare: A Critical Study of His Mind and Art. 3d ed. New York, Barnes & Noble, 1962.

959 Draper, J. W. The Humors and Shakespeare's Characters. Durham, N. C., Duke University Press, 1945.

960 Driver, T. S. The Sense of History in Greek and Shakespearean Drama. New York, Columbia University Press, 1960.

961 Eastman, A. M. A Short History of Shakespearian Criticism. New York, Random House, 1968.

962 _____ , and G. B. Harrison, eds. Shakespeare's Critics from Jonson to Auden: A Medley of Judgments. Ann Arbor, University of Michigan Press, 1964.

963 Eccles, M. Shakespeare in Warwickshire. Madison, University of Wisconsin Press, 1961.

964 Elliott, G. R. Flaming Minister: A Study of Othello as Tragedy of Love and Hate. Durham, N. C., Duke University Press, 1953.

965 _____ . Dramatic Providence in Macbeth: A Study of Shakespeare's Tragic Theme of Humanity and Grace. Princeton, Princeton University Press, 1960.

966 Ellis-Fermor, U. M. Some Recent Research in Shakespeare's Imagery. Oxford, Oxford University Press, 1937.

967 Evans, B. Shakespeare's Comedies. Oxford, Clarendon Press, 1960.

968 Farnham, W. Shakespeare's Tragic Frontier: The World of His Final Tragedies. Berkeley, University of California Press, 1950.

969 Frost, D. L. The School of Shakespeare: The Influence of Shakespeare on English Drama, 1600-1642. Cambridge, Cambridge University Press, 1968.

970 Frye, N. Fools of Time: Studies in Shakespearean Tragedy. Toronto, Toronto University Press, 1967.

971 _____ . A Natural Perspective: The Development of Shakespearean Comedy and Romance. New York, Columbia University Press, 1965.

972 Frye, R. M. Shakespeare's Life and Times: A Pictorial Record. Princeton, Princeton University Press, 1967.

973 Goddard, H. C. The Meaning of Shakespeare. Chicago, University of Chicago Press, 1951.

974 Goldsmith, R. H. Wise Fools in Shakespeare. Ann Arbor, University of Michigan Press, 1963.

975 Granville-Barker, H., and G. B. Harrison, eds. A Companion to Shakespeare Studies, Garden City, N. Y., Anchor Books, 1960.

976 Halio, J. L., ed. Twentieth Century Interpretations of As You Like It: A Collection of Critical Essays. Englewood Cliffs: Prentice-Hall, 1968.

977 Halliday, F. E. Shakespeare and His Critics. New York, Schocken, 1949.

978 _____ . Shakespeare, the Tragedies: A Collection of Critical Essays. Englewood Cliffs, N. J., Prentice-Hall, 1964.

979 _____ . A Shakespeare Companion, 1564-1964. New York, Schocken, 1965.

980 _____ . Shakespeare: A Pictorial Biography. New York, Crowell, 1957.

981 Harbage, A. Shakespeare's Audience. New York, Columbia University Press, 1941.

982 _____ . As They Liked It: An Essay on Shakespeare and Morality. New York, Harper, 1947.

983 _____ . Shakespeare and the Rival Traditions. New York, Barnes & Noble, 1968.

984 Harrison, G. B., ed. Julius Caesar in Shakespeare, Shaw, and the Ancients. New York, Harcourt, 1960.

985 Hart, A. Shakespeare and the Homilies and Other Pieces of Research into the Elizabethan Drama. New York, Octagon, 1970.

986 Heilman, R. B. This Great Stage: Image and Structure in King Lear. Baton Rouge, La., La Salle University Press, 1948.

987 Holloway, J. The Story of the Night: Studies in Shakespeare's Major Tragedies. London, Routledge & K. Paul, 1961.

988 Hubler, K. The Sense of Shakespeare's Sonnets. Princeton, Hill & Wang, 1952.

989 _____ , et al. The Riddle of Shakespeare's Sonnets. New York, Basic Books, 1962.

990 Hunter, G. K. William Shakespeare: The Late Comedies. New York, Longmans, Green, 1962.

991 Hunter, R. G. Shakespeare and the Comedy of Forgiveness. New York, Columbia University Press, 1965.

992 Hyman, S. E. Iago: Some Approaches to the Illusion of His Motivation. New York, Atheneum, 1970.

993 King, W. N., ed. Twentieth Century Interpretations of Twelfth Night: A Collection of Critical Essays. Englewood Cliffs, N.J., Prentice-Hall, 1968.

994 Klein, D. Milestones to Shakespeare: A Study of the Dramatic Forms and Pageantry that were the Prelude to Shakespeare. New York, Twayne, 1970.

995 Knight, G. Wilson. The Wheel of Fire. New York, Barnes & Noble, 1930.

996 _____ . The Imperial Theme. Oxford, Methuen, 1931.

997 _____ . Shakespeare and Religion: Essays of Forty Years. London, Routledge & K. Paul, 1967.

998 _____ . The Olive and the Sword: A Study of Shakespeare's England. Oxford, Oxford University Press, 1944.

999 _____ . The Crown of Life: Essays in Interpretation of Shakespeare's Final Plays. New York, Barnes & Noble, 1947.

1000 _____ . The Mutual Flame. New York, Barnes & Noble, 1955.

1001 Knights, L. C. Some Shakespearean Themes. London, Chatto & Windus, 1959.

1002 _____ . Henry V. London, Longmans, Green, 1962.

1003 _____ . An Approach to Hamlet. Stanford, Stanford University Press, 1961.

1004 Landry, H. Interpretations in Shakespeare's Sonnets. Berkeley, University of California Press, 1963.

1005 Lawrence, W. W. Shakespeare's Problem Comedies. New York, Ungar, 1931.

1006 Leech, C., ed. Shakespeare, The Tragedies: A Collection of Critical Essays. Chicago, University of Chicago Press, 1965.

1007 Leishman, J. B. Themes and Variations in Shakespeare's Sonnets. New York, Harper, 1966.

1008 Lerner, L., ed. Shakespeare's Comedies: An Anthology of Modern Criticism. Harmondsworth, Penguin, 1967.

1009 MacCallum, M. W. Shakespeare's Roman Plays and their Background. Rev. ed. New York, Russell & Russell, 1967.

1010 Mason, H. A. Shakespeare's Tragedies of Love: An Examination of the Possibility of Common Readings of Romeo and Juliet, Othello, King Lear, and Anthony and Cleopatra, New York, Barnes & Noble, 1971.

1011 Muir, K. Shakespeare: The Great Tragedies. London, Longmans, Green, 1961.

1012 _____ . Shakespeare's Sources. New York, Barnes & Noble, 1957. 2 vols.

1013 _____ . Shakespeare, the Comedies: A Collection of Critical Essays. Englewood Cliffs, N. J., Prentice-Hall, 1965.

1014 _____ , and S. Schoenbaum, eds. A New Companion to Shakespeare Studies. Cambridge, Cambridge University Press, 1971.

1015 Nicoll, A. Shakespeare. An Introduction. Oxford, Oxford University Press, 1952.

1016 _____ ., ed. Shakespeare Survey: An Annual Survey of Shakespearian Study and Productions. Vol. XIV. Cambridge, Cambridge University Press, 1961.

1017 Pearson, H. A Life of Shakespeare. New York, Walker, 1961.

1018 Pettet, E. C. Shakespeare and the Romantic Tradition. London, Staples Press, 1950.

1019 Proser, M. N. The Heroic Image in Five Shakespearean Tragedies. Princeton, Princeton University Press, 1965.

1020 Quennell, P. Shakespeare: A Biography. Cleveland, World Publishing Company, 1963.

1021 Rabkin, N., ed. Approaches to Shakespeare. New York, McGraw-Hill, 1964.

1022 Reese, M. M. Shakespeare: His World and His Work. London, St. Martin's, 1953.

1023 Ribner, I. William Shakespeare: An Introduction to His Life, Times, and Theatre. Waltham, Mass., Blaisdell, 1969.

1024 _____ . Patterns in Shakespearian Tragedy. New York, Barnes & Noble. 1960.

1025 Ridler, A., ed. Shakespeare Criticism, 1935-1960. London, Oxford University Press, 1963.

1026 Rosen, W. Shakespeare and the Craft of Tragedy. Cambridge, Mass., Harvard University Press, 1960.

1027 Rowse, A. L. William Shakespeare: A Biography. New York, Harper, 1963.

1028 Schanzer, E. The Problem Plays of Shakespeare: A Study of Julius Caesar, Measure for Measure, Anthony and Cleopatra. London, Routledge & K. Paul, 1963.

1029 Schoenbaum, S. Shakespeare's Lives. Oxford, Oxford University Press, 1970.

1030 Sisson, C. J. Shakespeare's Tragic Justice. London, Methuen, 1962.

1031 Smith, G. R., ed. Essays on Shakespeare. University Park, Pennsylvania State University Press, 1965.

1032 Speaight, R. Nature in Shakespearian Tragedy. New York, Collier, 1955.

1033 Spencer, T. Shakespeare and the Nature of Man. New York, Macmillan, 1942.

1034 Spencer, T. J. B., ed. Shakespeare: A Celebration, 1564-1964. Harmondsworth, Penguin, 1964.

1035 Sprague, A. C. Shakespeare and the Audience: A Study in the Technique of Exposition. Cambridge, Mass., Harvard University Press, 1935.

1036 _____ . Shakespearian Players and Performances. Cambridge, Mass., Harvard University Press, 1953.

1037 Spurgeon, C. Shakespeare's Imagery and What It Tells Us. Rev. ed. Boston, Beacon Press, 1958.

1038 Stewart, J. I. M. Character and Motive in Shakespeare: Some Recent Appraisals Examined. New York, Barnes & Noble, 1949.

1039 Stoll, E. E. Art and Artifice in Shakespeare: A Study in Dramatic Contrast and Illusion. New York, Barnes & Noble, 1962.

1040 Tillyard, E. M. W. Shakespeare's Last Plays. 6th ed. New York, Barnes & Noble, 1964.

1041 _____ . Shakespeare's History Plays. 2d ed. New York, Barnes & Noble, 1964.

1042 _____ . Shakespeare's Early Comedies. London, Chatto & Windus, 1965.

1043 Traci, P. J. The Love Play of Anthony and Cleopatra: A Critical Study of Shakespeare's Play. The Hague, Mouton, 1970.

1044 Traversi, D. A. An Approach to Shakespeare. New York, Hollis & Carter, 1968.

1045 _____ . Shakespeare: The Last Phase. Stanford, Stanford University Press, 1954.

1046 _____ . William Shakespeare: The Early Comedies. London, Longmans, Green, 1960.

1047 Ure, P. William Shakespeare: The Problem Plays. London, Long-mans, Green, 1961.

1048 Van Doren, M. Shakespeare. New York, Doubleday, 1939.

1049 Velz, J. W. Shakespeare and the Classical Tradition: A Critical Guide to Commentary, 1660-1960. Minneapolis, University of Minnesota Press, 1968.

1050 Wagner, B. M., ed. The Appreciation of Shakespeare: A Collection of Criticism. Washington, Georgetown University Press, 1949.

1051 Watson, C. B. Shakespeare and the Renaissance Concept of Honor. Princeton, Princeton University Press, 1960.

1052 Webster, M. Shakespeare Without Tears. Cleveland, World Publishing Company, 1955.

1053 Whitaker, V. K. Shakespeare's Use of Learning: An Inquiry Into the Growth of His Mind and Art. San Marino, Calif., Huntington Library, 1953.

1054 _____ . The Mirror Up to Nature: The Techniques of Shakespeare's Tragedies. San Marino, Calif., Huntington Library, 1965.

1055 Wickham, G. W. Shakespeare's Dramatic Heritage: Selected Studies in Medieval, Tudor and Shakespearean Drama. New York, Barnes & Noble, 1969.

1056 Wilson, J. D. The Essential Shakespeare: A Biographical Adventure. Cambridge, Cambridge University Press, 1932.

1057 _____ . Shakespeare's Happy Comedies. Evanston, Ill., Northwestern University Press, 1963.

1058 Wright, L. B. Shakespeare Celebrated: Anniversary Lectures Delivered at the Folger Library. Ithaca, N. Y., Cornell University Press, 1966.

1059 _____ & V. A. LaMar. The Folger Guide to Shakespeare. New York, Washington Square, 1969.

JACOBEAN AND STUART DRAMA

TEXTS

1060 Bald, R. C., ed. Six Elizabethan Plays. Boston, Houghton, 1963.

1061 Harrier, R. C., ed. The Anchor Anthology of Jacobean Drama. Garden City, N. Y., Doubleday, 1963. 2 vols.

1062 Huston, J. D., and A. B. Kernan, eds. Classics of the Renaissance Theatre: Seven English Plays. New York, Harcourt, 1969.

1063 Knowland, A. S., ed. Six Caroline Plays. London, Oxford University Press, 1962.

1064 McIlwraith, A. K., ed. Five Stuart Tragedies. Oxford, World's Classics, 1953.

1065 Wine, M. L., ed. Drama of the English Renaissance. New York, Modern Library, 1969.

CRITICISM

1066 Baskervill, C. R. Elizabethan and Stuart Plays. New York, Holt, 1963.

1067 Bauer, R. V. The Use of Humors in Comedy by Ben Jonson and His Contemporaries. Urbana, University of Illinois Press, 1948.

1068 Bentley, G. E. The Seventeenth Century Stage: A Collection of Critical Essays. Chicago, University of Chicago Press, 1968.

1069 _____ . Jacobean and Caroline Stage: Dramatic Companies and Players. Oxford, Oxford University Press, 1941-56. 6 vols.

1070 Boas, F. S. An Introduction to Stuart Drama. Oxford, Oxford University Press, 1946.

1071 Cunningham, J. E. Elizabethan and Early Stuart Drama. London, Evans, 1965.

1072 Ellis-Fermor, U. M. The Jacobean Drama: An Interpretation. London, Methuen, 1936.

1073 McDonald, C. O. The Rhetoric of Tragedy: Form in Stuart Drama. Amherst, University of Massachusetts Press, 1957.

1074 Ornstein, R. The Moral Vision of Jacobean Tragedy. Madison, University of Wisconsin Press, 1960.

1075 Ribner, I. Jacobean Tragedy: The Quest for Moral Order. New York, Barnes & Noble, 1962.

1076 _____ . Tudor and Stuart Drama. New York, Appleton, 1966.

1077 Tomlinson, T. B. A Study of Elizabethan and Jacobean Tragedy. Cambridge, Cambridge University Press, 1964.

George Chapman (1559-1634)

WORKS

1078 Bussy d' Ambois, 1607   1080 The Widow's Tears, 1612
1079 The Conspiracy and Tragedy
      of Charles Duke of Byron,
      1608

BIBLIOGRAPHIES

1081 Tannenbaum, S. A., and R. Dorothy, eds. Supplement to George
      Chapman, a Concise Bibliography. New York, Privately Published,
      1946.

TEXTS

1082 Barlett, R. B., ed. The Poems of George Chapman, New York, MLA
      Gen. Series XII, 1941.

1083 McIlwraith, A. K., ed. Five Stuart Tragedies. Oxford, World's
      Classics, 1953.

1084 Nicoll, A., ed. Homeric Translations. New York, Pantheon Books,
      1956. 2 vols.

1085 Parrott, T. M., ed. George Chapman: The Plays. New York, Russell
      & Russell, 1910-14. 2 vols.

CRITICISM

1086 Kreider, P. V. Elizabethan Comic Character Conventions as
      Revealed in the Comedies of George Chapman. Ann Arbor, Uni-
      versity of Michigan Press, 1935.

1087 MacLure, M. George Chapman: A Critical Study. Toronto, Toronto
      University Press, 1966.

1088 Wieler, J. W. George Chapman: The Effect of Stoicism Upon His
      Tragedies. New York, Crown Press, 1949.

Sir William Davenant (1606-1668)

WORKS

1089 The Wits, 1634   1092 The Temple of Love, 1638
1090 Love and Honour, 1634   1093 Gondibert, 1651
1091 Madagascar, 1638   1094 The Siege of Rhodes, 1656

TEXTS

1095 Bush, D., ed. Select Poems of Sir William Davenant. Cambridge,
      Mass., Willow Press, 1943.

1096 Spencer, C. Davenant's Macbeth from the Yale Ms.: An Edition with a Discussion of the Relation of Davenant's Text to Shakespeare's. New Haven, Conn., Yale University Press, 1961.

1097 Works. London, 1673. In Three Centuries of Drama: English, 1642-1700.

CRITICISM

1098 Collins, H. S. The Comedy of Sir William Davenant. The Hague, Mouton, 1967.

1099 Nethercot, A. H. Sir William D'Avenant: Poet Laurete and Playright-Manager. New York, Russell & Russell, 1967.

Thomas Dekker (1572-1632)
WORKS

1100 The Shoemaker's Holiday, 1600
1101 Satiromastix, 1601
1102 The Wonderful Year, 1603
1103 The Bellman of London, 1608
1104 Characters, 1616

BIBLIOGRAPHIES

1105 Tannenbaum, S. A., and R. Dorothy, eds. Supplement to Thomas Dekker, a Concise Bibliography. New York, Privately Published, 1945.

TEXTS

1106 Bowers, F. T., ed. The Dramatic Works of Thomas Dekker. Cambridge, University of Cambridge Press, 1953-1960. 4 vols.

1107 Grosart, A. B., ed. The Non-Dramatic Works. New York, Russell & Russell, 1963. 5 vols.

1108 Pendry, E. D., ed. Thomas Dekker: The Wonderful Year; The Gull's Horn Book; Penny-Wise, Pound-Foolish; English Villainies Discovered by Lauteres and Candle Light, and Selected Writings. London, E. Arnold, 1967.

CRITICISM

1109 Davies, P. C. The Shoemaker's Holiday. Berkeley, University of California Press, 1968.

1110 Hunt, M. Thomas Dekker: A Study. New York, Columbia University Press, 1911.

Ben Jonson (1572-1637)

WORKS

1111 Every Man in His Humor, 1598	1116 Epicoene, 1609
1112 Every Man Out of His Humour, 1600	1117 The Alchemist, 1610
	1118 Bartholomew Fair, 1614
1113 Sejanus, 1605	1119 Epigrams, 1616
1114 Volpone, 1606	1120 Under-Woods, 1640
1115 Masques and Entertainments, 1606-40	1121 Timber, 1640

BIBLIOGRAPHIES

1122 Tannenbaum, S. A, and R. Dorothy, eds. Supplement to a Bibliography of Ben Jonson. New York, Privately Published, 1947.

TEXTS

1123 Greg, W. W., ed. Jonson's Masque of Gipsies in the Burley, Belvoir, and Windsor Versions: An Attempt at Reconstruction. Oxford, Oxford University Press, 1952.

1124 Herford, C. H., and P., and E. M. Simpson, eds. Ben Jonson. Oxford, Oxford University Press, 1925-1952. 11 vols.

1125 Hunter, W. B., ed. The Complete Poetry of Ben Jonson. Garden City, Doubleday, 1963.

1126 Nicholson, Brinsly, and C. H. Herford, eds. Ben Jonson. New York, Hill & Wang, 1957.

1127 Redwine, J. D., Jr., ed. Ben Jonson's Literary Criticism. Lincoln, University of Nebraska Press, 1970.

1128 Schelling, F. E., ed. Complete Plays of Ben Jonson. New York, Dutton, 1960. 2 vols.

1129 Walker, R. S., ed. Ben Jonson's Timber or Discoveries. Syracuse, N. Y., Syracuse University Press, 1953.

CRITICISM

1130 Bamborough, J. B. Ben Jonson. London, Longmans, Green, 1959.

1131 Barish, J. A. Ben Jonson and the Language of Prose Comedy. Cambridge, Mass., Harvard University Press, 1960.

1132 _____ , ed. Ben Jonson: A Collection of Critical Essays. Englewood Cliffs, N. J., Prentice-Hall, 1963.

1133 Baum, H. W. The Satiric and the Didactic in Ben Jonson's Comedies. Chapel Hill, University of North Carolina Press, 1947.

1134 Bentley, G. E. Shakespeare and Jonson: Their Reputation in the Seventeenth Century Compared. Chicago, University of Chicago Press, 1945. 2 vols.

1135 Boughner, D. C. The Devil's Disciple: Ben Jonson's Debt to Machiavelli. New York, Philosophical Library, 1968.

1136 Bradley, J. F., and J. Q. Adams, eds. The Jonson Allusion-Book. New Haven, Conn., Yale University Press, 1922.

1137 Chute, M. Ben Jonson of Westminster. New York, Dutton, 1953.

1138 Davis, J. L. The Sons of Ben: Jonsonian Comedy in Caroline England. Detroit, Wayne State University Press, 1967.

1139 Dessen, Allan C. Jonson's Moral Comedy. Evanston, Ill., Northwestern University Press, 1971.

1140 Enck, J. J. Jonson and the Comic Truth. Madison, University of Wisconsin Press, 1957.

1141 Gum, C. The Aristophanic Comedies of Ben Jonson. The Hague, Mouton, 1969.

1142 Herford, C. H., and P. Simpson. Ben Jonson: The Man and his Work. Vol. 1 and 2 of Complete Works. Oxford, Oxford University Press, 1928.

1143 Knights, L. C. Drama and Society in the Age of Jonson. New York, Barnes & Noble, 1957.

1144 Knoll, R. E. Ben Jonson's Plays: An Introduction. Lincoln, University of Nebraska Press, 1964.

1145 McEuen, K. A. Classical Influence Upon the Tribe of Ben. New York, Octagon, 1968.

1146 Nichols, J. G. The Poetry of Ben Jonson. New York, Barnes & Noble, 1969.

1147 Partridge, A. C. The Broken Compass. London, Chatto & Windus, 1958.

1148 Steel, B. O Rare Ben Jonson. New York, Knopf, 1928.

1149 Townsend, F. L. Apologie for Bartholomew Fayre: The Art of Jonson's Comedies. London, Oxford University Press, 1947.

1150 Trimpi, W. Ben Jonson's Poems: A Study of the Plain Style. Stanford, Stanford University Press, 1962.

1151 Wimsatt, W. K., ed. The Idea of Comedy: Essays in Prose and Verse, Ben Jonson to George Meredith. Englewood Cliffs, N. J., Prentice-Hall, 1969.

John Marston (1575-1634)

WORKS

1152	The Scourge of Villanie, 1598	1155	Parasitaster, 1606
1153	Antonio and Mellida, 1602	1156	Sophonisba, 1606
1154	The Malcontent, 1604	1157	What You Will, 1607

TEXTS

1158 Davenport, A., ed. The Poems of John Marston. Liverpool, University of Liverpool Press, 1961.

1159 Wood, H. H., ed. The Plays of Marston. Edinburgh, Oliver & Boyd, 1934-39. 3 vols.

CRITICISM

1160 Burke, Brother F. Metrical Roughness in Marston's Formal Satire. Washington, Catholic University Press, 1957.

1161 Caputi, A. John Marston, Satirist. Ithaca, N. Y., Cornell University Press, 1961.

1162 Finkelpearl, P. J. John Marston of the Middle Temple: An English Dramatist in His Social Setting. Cambridge, Mass., Harvard University Press, 1969.

Philip Massinger (1583-1648)

WORKS

1163	The Duke of Millaine, 1623	1165	A New Way to Pay Old Debts,
1164	The Maid of Honour, 1632		1633
		1166	The City Madam, 1658

BIBLIOGRAPHIES

1167 Pennel, C. A., and W. P. Williams, comps. Elizabethan Bibliographies Supplements VIII: Francis Beaumont, John Fletcher, Philip Massinger 1937-1965, John Ford 1940-1965, James Shirley 1945-1965. London, Nether Press, 1968.

TEXTS

1168 Byrne, M. St. C., ed. A New Way to Pay Old Debts. London, London University Press, 1956.

1169 Dramatic Works of Massinger and Ford. London, E. Moxon, 1840.

1170 Kirk, R., ed. The City Madam. Princeton, University of Princeton Press, 1934.

1171 Philip Massinger. ed., A. Symons. London, Unwin, 1887-1889. 2 vol.

1172 The Plays of Philip Massinger. Ed. W. Gifford. New York, Ames Press, 1966. 4 vols.

1173 The Poems of Philip Massinger. Ed. D. S. Lawless. Muncie, Ind., Ball State University, 1968.

CRITICISM

1174 Dunn, T. A. Philip Massinger: The Man and the Playwright. London, Nelson, 1957.

Thomas Middleton (1580-1627)

WORKS

1175 The Honest Whore, 1604

1176 A Tricke to Catch the Old One, 1608

1177 A Mad World, My Masters, 1608

1178 The Roaring Girl, 1611

1179 A Game at Chesse, 1625

1180 The Changeling, 1653

1181 The Spanish Gipsie, 1653

BIBLIOGRAPHIES

1182 Tannenbaum, S. A., ed. Thomas Middleton, A Concise Bibliography. New York, Privately Published, 1940.

TEXTS

1183 Bawcutt, N. W., ed. The Changeling. London, Methuen, 1958.

1184 Henning, S., ed. A Mad World, My Masters. Lincoln, University of Nebraska Press, 1965.

1185 Thomas Middleton. By A. C. Swinburne. London, Vizetelly, 1887-1890. 2 vols.

1186 Thomson, P., ed. The Changeling. London, E. Benn, 1964.

1187 Works of Thomas Middleton. Ed. A. H. Bullen. London, J. C. Nimmo, 1885-1886. 8 vols.

CRITICISM

1188 Barker, R. H. Thomas Middleton. New York, Columbia University Press, 1957.

1189 Schoenbaum, S. Middleton's Tragedies: A Critical Study. New York, Columbia University Press, 1955.

Cyril Tourneur (1575-1626)

WORKS

1190 The Revenger's Tragedy, 1607   1192 The Atheist's Tragedy, 1611
1191 The Transformed Metamor-   1193 The Noble Man, 1612
      phosis, 1609

BIBLIOGRAPHIES

1194 Tannenbaum, S. A., and R. Dorothy, eds. Cyril Tourneur, A Concise
      Bibliography. New York, Privately Published, 1946.

TEXTS

1195 Nicoll, A. Complete Works of Cyril Tourneur, Rev. ed. New York,
      Russell & Russell, 1963.

1196 Ribner, I., ed. Atheist's Tragedy. Cambridge, Mass., Harvard Univer-
      sity Press, 1964.

CRITICISM

1197 Peter, J. Complaint and Satire. Oxford, Clarendon Press, 1956.

John Webster (1580-1625)

WORKS

1198 The White Devil, 1612   1200 The Devil's Law-Case, 1623
1199 The Duchess of Malfi, 1623   1201 A Cure for a Cuckold, 1661

BIBLIOGRAPHIES

1202 Tannenbaum, S. A. John Webster, A Concise Bibliography. New
      York, Privately Published, 1941.

TEXTS

1203 Lucas, F. L., ed. The Complete Works of John Webster. London,
      Chatto & Windus, 1966. 4 vols.

CRITICISM

1204 Bogard, T. The Tragic Satire of Webster. Berkeley, University of
      California Press, 1955.

1205 Boklund, G. The Sources of the White Devil. Uppsala, Lundequist-
      ska Bokhandeln, 1957.

1206 Brooke, R. John Webster and the Elizabethan Drama. New York,
      Russell & Russell, 1916.

1207 Dent, R. W. Webster's Borrowings. Berkeley, University of Cali-
      fornia Press, 1960.

1208 Hunter, G. K., and S. K. John, eds. Webster: A Critical Anthology. Baltimore, Penguin, 1969.

1209 Leech, C. John Webster, The Duchess of Malfi. London, E. Arnold, 1963.

1210 Moore, D. D. John Webster and His Critics, 1617-1964. Baton Rouge, La., La Salle University Press, 1966.

1211 Rabkin, N., ed. Twentieth Century Interpretations of the Duchess of Malfi: A Collection of Critical Essays. Englewood Cliffs, N. J., Prentice-Hall, 1968.

POETRY—CRITICISM

1212 Brook, C. The Well-Wrought Urn: Studies in the Structure of Poetry. New York, Harcourt, 1947.

1213 Bush, D. Mythology and the Renaissance Tradition in English Poetry. Minneapolis, University of Minnesota Press, 1933.

1214 Cullen, P. Spenser, Marvell, and Renaissance Pastoral. Cambridge, Mass., Harvard University Press, 1970.

1215 Evans, M. English Poetry in the Sixteenth Century. London, Hutchinson, 1967.

1216 Ford, B. et al., eds. From Donne to Marvell. Baltimore, Penguin, 1969.

1217 Peterson, D. L. The English Lyric from Wyatt to Donne: A History of the Plain and Eloquent Styles. Princeton, Princeton University Press, 1967.

TUDOR AND ELIZABETHAN POETRY
TEXTS

1218 Alexander, N., ed. Narrative Verse. London, E. Arnold, 1967.

1219 Ault, N., ed. Elizabethan Lyrics from the Original Texts. London, Putnam, 1960.

1220 Bender, R. M., ed. Five Courtier Poets of the English Renaissance. New York, Washington Square Press, 1967.

1221 Chambers, E. K., ed. The Oxford Book of Sixteenth Century Verse. Oxford, Oxford University Press, 1932.

1222 Donno, E. S., ed. Elizabethan Minor Epics. London, Routledge & K. Paul, 1963.

1223 Hebel, J. W., and H. H. Hudson, eds. Poetry of the English Renaissance, 1509-1660. New York, Appleton, 1957.

1224 Rollins, H. E., and H. Baker, eds. The Renaissance in England. Non-Dramatic Prose and Verse. Lexington, Mass., D. C. Heath, 1954.

1225 Williams, J., ed. English Renaissance Poetry: A Collection of Shorter Poems from Skelton to Jonson. Garden City, N. Y., Doubleday, 1963.

CRITICISM

1226 Allen, Don C. Image and Meaning: Metaphoric Tradition in Renaissance Poetry. Baltimore, Johns Hopkins, 1960.

1227 Alpers, P. J., ed. Elizabethan Poetry: Modern Essays in Criticism. Oxford, Oxford University Press, 1967.

1228 Campbell, L. B. Divine Poetry and Drama in the Sixteenth Century England. Cambridge, Cambridge University Press, 1959.

1229 Fowler, Alastair. Triumphal Forms: Structural Patterns in Elizabethan Poetry. Cambridge, Cambridge University Press, 1970.

1230 Grundy, J. The Spenserian Poets: A Study in Elizabethan and Jacobean Poetry. London, St. Martin's, 1970.

1231 Hudson, H. H. The Epigram in the English Renaissance. Princeton, Princeton University Press, 1947.

1232 John, L. C. The Elizabethan Sonnet Sequences: Studies in Conventional Conceits. New York, Columbia University Press, 1938.

1233 Mazzaro, J. Transformations in the Renaissance English Lyric. Ithaca, N. Y., Cornell University Press, 1970.

1234 Muir, K., ed. Elizabethan Lyrics: A Critical Anthology. London, Harrap, 1952.

1235 Lever, J. W. The Elizabethan Love Sonnet. London, Methuen, 1956.

1236 Mason, H. A. Humanism and Poetry in the Early Tudor Period. New York, Barnes & Noble, 1959.

1237 Rubel, V. L. Poetic Diction in the English Renaissance, from Skelton through Spenser, New York, MLA Revolving Fund Series, No. 12, 1941.

1238 Smith, H. Elizabethan Poetry: A Study in Conventions, Meaning and Expression. Cambridge, Mass., Harvard University Press, 1952.

1239 Tuve, R. Elizabethan and Metaphysical Imagery: Renaissance Poetic and Twentieth Century Critics. Chicago, University of Chicago Press, 1947.

Samuel Daniel (1563-1619)

WORKS

1240 Delia, 1592
1241 The Complaint of Rosamond, 1592
1242 The Tragedie of Cleopatra, 1594
1243 The Civile Warres, 1595-1609

1244 Poeticall Essayes, 1599
1245 Defence of Ryme, 1602
1246 The Tragedie of Philotas, 1604
1247 The Queenes Arcadia, 1606
1248 The Collection of the Historie of England, 1612-18

BIBLIOGRAPHIES

1249 Guffey, G. R., comp. Elizabethan Bibliographies Supplement VII: Samuel Daniel 1942-1965, Michael Drayton 1941-1965, Sir Philip Sidney 1941-1965. London, Nether Press, 1967.

TEXTS

1250 Grosart, A. B., ed. The Complete Works in Verse and Prose of Samuel Daniel. London, Hazell, Watson & Viney, 1885-1896.

1251 Himelick, R., ed. Samuel Daniel's Musophilus. Lafayette, Ind., Purdue University Press, 1965.

1252 Michael, L., ed. The Tragedy of Philotas. New Haven, Conn., Yale University Press, 1949.

1253 _____, ed. The Civil Wars. New Haven, Conn., Yale University Press, 1958.

CRITICISM

1254 Donow, H. S., ed. A Concordance to the Sonnet Sequences of Daniel, Drayton, Shakespeare and Spenser. Carbondale, Southern Illinois University Press, 1969.

1255 Rees, J. Samuel Daniel: A Critical and Biographical Study. Liverpool, University of Liverpool Press, 1964.

George Gascoigne (1539-1577)

WORKS

1256 Jocasta, 1566
1257 Supposes, 1566
1258 A Hundreth Sundrie Flowres, 1573

1259 The Posies, 1575
1260 The Steel Glass, 1576
1261 The Complaint of Philomene, 1576

BIBLIOGRAPHIES

1262 Johnson, R. C., comp. Elizabethan Bibliographies Supplement IX: Minor Elizabethans: Roger Ascham 1946-1966, George Gascoigne 1941-1966, John Heywood 1944-1966, Thomas Kyd 1940-1966, Anthony Munday 1941-1966. London, Nether Press, 1968.

TEXTS

1263 Cunliffe, J. W., ed. Complete Works of George Gascoigne. Cambridge, Cambridge University Press, 1907-1910. 2 vols.

1264 Schelling, F. E., ed. The Life and Writings of George Gascoigne with Three Poems Heretofore not Reprinted. New York, Russell & Russell, 1967.

CRITICISM

1265 Prouty, C. T. Gascoigne: Elizabethan Courtier, Soldier, and Poet. New York, Columbia University Press, 1942.

Sir Philip Sidney (1554-1586)

WORKS

1266 Astrophel and Stella, 1591   1268 The Contesse of Pembroke's
1267 Defence of Poesie, 1595   Arcadia, 1598

BIBLIOGRAPHIES

1269 Guffey, G. R., comp. Elizabethan Bibliographies Supplement VII: Samuel Daniel 1942-1965, Michael Drayton 1941-1965, Sir Philip Sidney 1941-1965. London, Nether Press, 1967.

TEXTS

1270 Bradley, W. A., ed. The Correspondence of Philip Sidney and Hubert Languet. Boston, Merrymount, 1942.

1271 Bullett, G., ed. Silver Poets of the Sixteenth Century. London, Dent, 1960.

1272 Craik, T. W., ed. Arcadia and Other Poetry. London, Putnam, 1966.

1273 Feuillerat, A., ed. The Complete Prose Works. New York, Cambridge University Press, 1912-1926. 4 vols.

1274 Gray, W., ed. The Miscellaneous Works of Sir Philip Sidney. Boston, Burnham, 1860.

1275 Grosart, A. B., ed. The Complete Poems of Sir Philip Sidney. London, Chatto & Windus, 1877.

1276 Kimbrough, R., ed. Sir Philip Sidney. Selected Prose and Poetry. New York, Holt, 1969.

1277 Ringler, W. A., Jr., ed. The Poems of Sir Philip Sidney. Oxford, Clarendon, 1962.

1278 Shepherd, G., ed. An Apology for Poetry: Or the Defense of Poesy. New York, Barnes & Noble, 1965.

CRITICISM

1279 Boas, F. S. Sir Philip Sidney, Representative Elizabethan: His Life and Writings. London, Staples Press, 1955.

1280 Buxton, J. Sir Philip Sidney and the English Renaissance. London, St. Martin's, 1964.

1281 Cooke, P. J. The Spanish Romances in Sidney's 'Arcadia.' Urbana, University of Illinois Press, 1939.

1282 Kalstone, D. Sidney's Poetry: Contexts and Interpretations. Cambridge, Mass., Harvard University Press, 1965.

1283 Montgomery, R. L. Symmetry and Sense: The Poetry of Sir Philip Sidney. Austin, University of Texas Press, 1961.

1284 Muir, K. Sir Philip Sidney. London, Longmans, Green, 1960.

1285 Myrick, K. O. Sidney as a Literary Craftsman. Lincoln, University of Nebraska Press, 1965.

1286 Rose, M. Heroic Love: Studies in Sidney and Spenser. Cambridge, Mass., Harvard University Press, 1968.

1287 Rowe, K. T. Romantic Love and Parental Authority in Sidney's 'Arcadia.' Ann Arbor, University of Michigan Press, 1947.

1288 Thaler, A. Shakespeare and Sidney. New York, Russell & Russell, 1947.

1289 Van Dorsten, J. A. Poets, Patrons, and Professors: Sir Philip Sidney, Daniel Rogers, and the Leiden Humanists. Leiden, Leiden University Press, 1962.

1290 Wallace, M. W. The Life of Sir Philip Sidney. New York, Octagon, 1966.

John Skelton (1460-1529)

WORKS

1291 Ware the Hauke, 1504-12
1292 Phillip Sparow, 1508
1293 Ballade of the Scottyshe Kynge, 1513
1294 Magnyfycence, 1516
1295 Speke, Parrot, 1521
1296 Colin Clout, 1522
1297 Why Come Ye Nat to Court? 1522
1298 Garlande of Laurell, 1523
1299 The Duke of Albany, 1523

TEXTS

1300 Henderson, P., ed. Complete Poems of John Skelton, Laurete. London, Dent, 1948.

1301 Pinto, V. de Sola, ed. John Skelton: A Selection from His Poems. New York, Grove, 1950.

CRITICISM

1302 Fish, S. E. John Skelton's Poetry. New Haven, Conn., Yale University Press, 1965.

1303 Green, P. John Skelton. London, Longmans, Green, 1960.

1304 Heiserman, A. R. Skelton and Satire. Chicago, University of Chicago Press, 1961.

1305 Kinsman, R. S., and T. Yonge. John Skelton: Canon and Census. Darien, Conn., Monographic Press, 1967.

1306 Nelson, W. Skelton, Laurete. New York, Columbia University Press, 1939.

Edmund Spenser (1552-1599)

WORKS

1307 The Shepherdes Calendar, 1579
1308 The Faerie Queene, 1590, 1596
1309 Amoretti, 1595
1310 Epithalamion, 1595
1311 Colin Clout, 1595
1312 Prothalamion, 1596

BIBLIOGRAPHIES

1313 Atkinson, D. F. Edmund Spenser: A Bibliographical Supplement. Repr. New York, Haskell House, 1969.

1314 Carpenter, F. I. A Reference Guide to Edmund Spenser. Repr. New York, Kraus, 1969.

1315 Johnson, F. R. A Critical Bibliography of the Works of Edmund Spenser Printed Before 1700. Baltimore, Johns Hopkins, 1933.

1316 McNeir, W. F., and F. Provost. Annotated Bibliography of Edmund Spenser, 1937-1960. Pittsburgh, Duquesne University Press, 1962.

TEXTS

1317 Dodge, R. E. N., ed. The Complete Poetical Works. Boston, Houghton, 1908.

1318 Gottfried, R., ed. Spenser's Prose Works. Baltimore, Johns Hopkins, 1949.

1319 Greenlaw, E., C. G. Osgood, and Padelford, Fr. M., and R. Heffner, eds. The Works of Edmund Spenser: A Variorum Edition. Baltimore, Johns Hopkins, 1932-1949. 9 vols.

1320 Maclean, H., ed. Poetry: Authoritative Texts and Criticism. New York, Norton, 1969.

1321 Osgood, C. G., and H. G. Lotspeich, eds. The Works of Edmund Spenser: A Variorum Edition. The Minor Poems: Vol. II. Baltimore, Johns Hopkins, 1947.

CRITICISM

1322 Alpers, P. J. The Poetry of the Faerie Queene. Princeton, Princeton University Press, 1967.

1323 Berger, H. Spenser: A Collection of Critical Essays. Englewood Cliffs, N. J., Prentice-Hall, 1968.

1324 Dunseath, T. K. Spenser's Allegory of Justice in Book Five of the Faerie Queene. Princeton, Princeton University Press, 1968.

1325 Fowler, A. Spenser and the Numbers of Time. London, Routledge & K. Paul, 1964.

1326 Hough, G. Preface to the Faerie Queene. London, Duckworth, 1962.

1327 Judson, A. C. The Life of Spenser. Baltimore, Johns Hopkins, 1945.

1328 _____ . Notes on the Life of Spenser. Bloomington, University of Indiana Press, 1949.

1329 Lewis, C. S. Spenser's Images of Life. Cambridge, Cambridge University Press, 1967.

1330 Lotspeich, H. G. Classical Mythology in the Poetry of Spenser. Princeton, Princeton University Press, 1932.

1331 Meyer, S. An Interpretation of Edmund Spenser's Colin Clout. Notre Dame, Ind., University of Notre Dame Press, 1969.

1332 Mueller, W. R. Spenser's Critics: Changing Currents in Literary Taste. Syracuse, University of Syracuse Press, 1959.

1333 Nelson, W., ed. Form and Convention in the Poetry of Edmund Spenser. New York, Columbia University Press, 1961.

1334 _____ . The Poetry of Edmund Spenser: A Study. New York, Columbia University Press, 1963.

1335 Osgood, C. G. Poetry as a Means of Grace. Princeton, Princeton University Press, 1941.

1336 Rose, M. Heroic Love: Studies in Sidney and Spenser. Cambridge, Mass., Harvard University Press, 1968.

1337 Shanley, J. L. A Study of Spenser's Gentleman. Evanston, Ill., Northwestern University Press, 1940.

1338 Tillyard, E. M. W. The English Epic and Its Background. New York, Barnes & Noble, 1954.

1339 Watkins, W. B. C. Shakespeare and Spenser. Princeton, Princeton University Press, 1950.

Henry Howard, Earl of Surrey (1517-1547)

WORKS

1340 Songs and Sonnets, 1557

1341 Certain Bokes of Virgiles Aenaeis, 1557

TEXTS

1342 Bullett, G., ed. Silver Poets of the Sixteenth Century. London, Dent, 1960.

1343 Geary, D., ed. To a Lady: The Songs and Sonnets of the Earl of Surrey. London, Forbes Robertson, 1957.

1344 Jones, E., ed. Henry Howard, Earl of Surrey: Poems. Oxford, Clarendon Press, 1964.

1345 Padelford, F. M., ed. The Poems of Henry Howard, Earl of Surrey. New York, Haskell House, 1966.

CRITICISM

1346 Chapman, H. W. Two Tudor Portraits. London, J. Cape, 1960.

Sir Thomas Wyatt (1503-1542)

WORKS

1347 Trans. Plutarch, 1528   1349 Songs and Sonnets, 1557
1348 Psalms, 1549

TEXTS

1350 Bullett, G., ed. Silver Poets of the Sixteenth Century. London, Dent, 1960.

1351 Muir, K., ed. Unpublished Poems by Sir Thomas Wyatt and His Circle. Liverpool, University of Liverpool Press, 1961.

1352 _____ , ed. Life and Letters of Sir Thomas Wyatt. Liverpool, University of Liverpool Press, 1963.

1353 _____ , ed. The Collected Poems of Sir Thomas Wyatt. Cambridge, Mass., Harvard University Press, 1960.

1354 Swallow, A., ed. Some Poems of Sir Thomas Wyatt. New York, Swallow Press, 1949.

CRITICISM

1355 Southall, R. The Courtly Maker: An Essay on the Poetry of Wyatt and His Contemporaries. New York, Barnes & Noble, 1964.

1356 Thomson, P. Sir Thomas Wyatt and His Background. Stanford, Stanford University Press, 1964.

BAROQUE AND CLASSICAL POETRY OF THE EARLY 17TH CENTURY

BIBLIOGRAPHIES

1357 Berry, L. E., comp. A Bibliography of Studies in Metaphysical Poetry, 1939-1960. Madison, University of Wisconsin Press, 1964.

1358 Frank, J. Hobbled Pegasus: A Descriptive Bibliography of Minor English Poetry, 1641-1660. Albuquerque, University of New Mexico Press, 1968.

1359 Hebel, J. W., and F. A. Patterson, eds. English Seventeenth Century Literature. A Bibliography. New York, Columbia University Press, 1929.

TEXTS

1360 Bald, R. C., ed. Sevententh Century English Poetry. New York, Harrap, 1959.

1361 Boas, F. S., ed. Songs and Lyrics from the English Masques and Light Operas. London, Harrap, 1949.

1362 Brinkley, R. F., ed. English Poetry of the Seventeenth Century. Rev. ed. New York, Norton, 1942.

1363 Cutts, J. P., ed. Seventeenth Century Songs and Lyrics. Columbia, University of Missouri Press, 1959.

1364 Grierson, H. J. C., and G. Bullough, eds. The Oxford Book of Seventeenth Century Verse. Oxford, Oxford University Press, 1934.

1365 Hebel, J. W., and H. H. Hudson, eds. Poetry of the English Renaissance, 1509-1660. New York, Appleton, 1957.

1366 Kenner, H., ed. Seventeenth Century Poetry: The Schools of Donne and Jonson. New York, Holt, 1964.

1367 Martz, L. L., ed. The Meditative Poem: An Anthology of Seventeenth Century Verse. Garden City, N. Y., Doubleday, 1963.

1368 _____ , and R. S. Sylvester, eds. The Anchor Anthology of Seventeenth Century Verse. Garden City, N. Y., Doubleday, 1969. 2 vols.

1369 Nicholson, D. H. S., and A. H. E. Lee, eds. The Oxford Book of English Mystical Verse. Oxford, Oxford University Press, 1917.

1370 Shawcross, J. T., and R. D. Emma, eds. Seventeenth Century English Poetry. Philadelphia, Lippincott, 1969.

1371 White, H. C., R. C. Wallerstein, and R. Quintana, eds. Seventeenth Century Verse and Prose. Vol. I; 1600-1660. New York, Macmillan, 1951.

1372 Williams, J., ed. English Renaissance Poetry: A Collection of Shorter Poems from Skelton to Jonson. Garden City, N. Y., Doubleday, 1963.

CRITICISM

1373 Alvarez, A. The School of Donne. New York, Pantheon, 1961.

1374 Bennett, J. Four Metaphysical Poets: Donne, Herbert, Vaughan, Crashaw. Cambridge, Cambridge University Press, 1934.

1375 _____ . Five Metaphysical Poets: Donne, Herbert, Vaughan, Crashaw, Marvell. Cambridge, Cambridge University Press, 1964.

1376 Dalglish, J. English Metaphysical Poets. New York, Barnes & Noble, 1961.

1377 Gardner, H. The Metaphysical Poets. Oxford, Penguin, 1957.

1378 Halewood, W. H. The Poetry of Grace: Reformation Themes and Structures in English Seventeenth Century Poetry. New Haven, Conn., Yale University Press, 1970.

1379 Hunter, J. The Metaphysical Poets. London, Evans, 1965.

1380 Keast, W. R., ed. Seventeenth Century English Poetry: Modern Essays in Criticism. Oxford, Galaxy Books, 1962.

1381 Kermode, F., ed. The Metaphysical Poets: Key Essays on Metaphysical Poetry and the Major Metaphysical Poets. Greenwich, Conn., Fawcett, 1969.

1382 McEuen, K. A. Classical Influence Upon the Tribe of Ben. New York, Octagon, 1968.

1383 Martz, L. L. The Poetry of Meditation: A Study of English Religious Literature of the Seventeenth Century. New Haven, Conn., Yale University Press, 1954.

1384 _____ . The Wit of Love: Donne, Carew, Crashaw, Marvell. Notre Dame, Ind., University of Notre Dame Press, 1969.

1385 Nicolson, M. H. The Breaking of the Circle: Studies in the Effect of the 'New Science' on Seventeenth Century Poetry. Rev. ed. New York, Columbia University Press, 1960.

1386 Partridge, A. C., ed. The Tribe of Ben: Pre-Augustan Classical Verse in English. London, E. Arnold, 1966.

1387 Peterson, D. L. The English Lyric from Wyatt to Donne: A History of the Plain and Eloquent Styles. Princeton, Princeton University Press, 1967.

1388 Richmond, H. M. The School of Love: The Evolution of the Stuart Love Lyric. Princeton, Princeton University Press, 1964.

1389 Stewart, S. The Enclosed Garden: Tradition and Image in Seventeenth Century Poetry. Madison, University of Wisconsin Press, 1966.

1390 Tuve, R. Elizabethan and Metaphysical Imagery: Renaissance Poetic and Twentieth Century Critics. Chicago, University of Chicago Press, 1947.

1391 Wallerstein, R. C. Studies in Seventeenth Century Poetics. Madison, University of Wisconsin Press, 1950.

1392 White, H. C. The Metaphysical Poets: A Study in Religious Experience. New York, Collier, 1936.

1393 Williamson, G. Six Metaphysical Poets: A Reader's Guide. New York, Farrar, 1967.

Richard Crashaw (1612/13-1649)

WORKS

1394 Steps to the Temple with the Delights of the Muses, 1646

1395 Religious Verse, 1652

TEXTS

1396 Martin, L. C., ed. Poems, English, Latin and Greek. 2d ed. Oxford, Clarendon Press, 1957.

CRITICISM

1397 Rickey, M. E. Phyme and Meaning in Richard Crashaw. Lexington, University of Kentucky Press, 1961.

1398 Wallerstein, R. C. Richard Crashaw: A Study in Style and Poetic Development. Madison, University of Wisconsin Press, 1959.

1399 Warren, A. Crashaw: A Study in Baroque Sensibility. Baton Rouge, La., La Salle University Press, 1939.

1400 Williams, G. W. Image and Symbol in the Sacred Poetry of Richard Crashaw. Columbia, University of South Carolina Press, 1963.

1401 Willy, M. Three Metaphysical Poets. London, Longmans, Green, 1962.

John Donne (1572-1631)

WORKS

1402 Paradoxes and Problems, 1607
1403 Ignatius His Conclave, 1611
1404 Anniversaries, 1611 & 1612

1405 Divine Poems, 1612
1406 Songs and Sonnets, 1633
1407 Sermons, 1640
1408 Essays in Divinity, 1651

BIBLIOGRAPHIES

1409 Keynes, G. L. A Bibliography of Dr. John Donne. Cambridge, Cambridge University Press, 1958.

TEXTS

1410 Bennett, R. E., ed. The Complete Poems of John Donne. Chicago, University of Chicago Press, 1942.

1411 Clements, A. L., ed. John Donne's Poetry: Authoritative Texts and Criticism. New York, Norton, 1966.

1412 Coffin, C. M., ed. Complete Poetry and Selected Prose of John Donne. New York, Modern Library, 1952.

1413 Gardner, H. L., ed. The Elegies and the Songs and Sonnets. Oxford, Clarendon Press, 1965.

1414 Grierson, H. J. C., ed. Poems. Oxford, Clarendon Press, 1912. 2 vols.

1415 Hayward, J., ed. Donne: A Selection of His Poetry. New York, Random House, 1929.

1416 Healy, T. S., ed. John Donne. Ignatius His Conclave: An Edition of the Latin and English Texts. Oxford, Oxford University Press, 1970.

1417 Manley, F., ed. John Donne: The Anniversaries. Baltimore, Johns Hopkins, 1963.

1418 Milgate, W., ed. John Donne: The Satires, Epigrams and Verse Letters. Oxford, Clarendon Press, 1967.

1419 Potter, G. R., and E. M. Simpson, eds. The Sermons of John Donne. Vols. VIII. Berkeley, University of California Press, 1956.

1420 Redpath, T., ed. Songs and Sonnets. New York, Barnes & Noble, 1956.

1421 Showcross, J. T., ed. The Complete Poetry of John Donne. Garden City, N. Y., Doubleday, 1967.

CRITICISM

1422 Anderson, N. J. John Donne: Conservative Revolutionary. Princeton, Princeton University Press, 1967.

1423 Bald, R. C. John Donne: A Life. Oxford, Oxford University Press, 1970.

1424 Combs, H. C., and Z. R. Sullens. A Concordance to the English Poems of John Donne. 1940. Repr. New York, Haskell House, 1969.

1425 Gardner, H. L, ed. John Donne: A Collection of Critical Essays. Englewood Cliffs, N. J., Prentice-Hall, 1962.

1426 Gransden, K. W. John Donne. Rev. ed. New York, Archon, 1969.

1427 Hughes, R. E. The Progress of the Soul: The Interior Career of John Donne. New York, Morrow, 1969.

1428 Leishman, J. B. Donne: The Monarch of Wit. London, Hutchinson Library, 1951.

1429 Miner, E. The Metaphysical Mode of Donne and Cowley. Princeton, Princeton University Press, 1969.

1430 Moloney, M. F. John Donne: His Flight From Medievalism. Urbana, University of Illinois Press, 1944.

1431 Moses, W. R. The Metaphysical Conceit in the Poems of John Donne. Nashville, Tenn., Vanderbilt University Press, 1941.

1432 Rugolf, M. A. Donne's Imagery: A Study in Creative Sources. New York, Russell & Russell, 1962.

1433 Schleiner, W. The Imagery of John Donne's Sermons. Providence, R. I., Brown University Press, 1970.

1434 Simpson, E. M. A Study of the Prose Works. Oxford, Clarendon Press, 1924.

1435 Smith, A. J. John Donne: The Songs and Sonnets. London, E. Arnold, 1964.

1436 Stein, A. John Donne's Lyrics: The Eloquence of Action. Minneapolis, University of Minnesota Press, 1962.

1437 Summers, J. H. The Heirs of Donne and Jonson. Oxford, Oxford University Press, 1970.

1438 Unger, L. Donne's Poetry and Modern Criticism. Chicago, Regnery Press, 1950.

1439 Webber, J. Contrary Music: The Prose Style of John Donne. Madison, University of Wisconsin Press, 1963.

Michael Drayton (1563-1631)

WORKS

1440 Endymion and Phoebe, 1595
1441 England's Heroicall Epistles, 1597
1442 The Baron's Wars, 1603
1443 Poems, 1605
1444 The Man in the Moon, 1606
1445 Poems, Lyric and Pastoral, 1606
1446 Polyolbion, 1612
1447 Nymphidia, 1627
1448 Elegies Upon Sundry Occasions, 1627

BIBLIOGRAPHIES

1449 Guffey, G. R., comp. Elizabethan Bibliographies Supplement VII; Samuel Daniel 1942-1965, Michael Drayton 1941-1965, Sir Philip Sidney 1941-1965. London, Nether Press, 1967.

1450 Tannenbaum, S. A. Michael Drayton: A Concise Bibliography. New York, Privately Published, 1941.

TEXTS

1451 Buxton, J., ed. Poems. Cambridge, Mass., Harvard University Press, 1953. 2 vols.

1452 Hebel, J. W., et al., eds. The Works of Michael Drayton. Vol. II. Oxford, Clarendon Press, 1932.

CRITICISM

1453 Berthelot, J. A. Michael Drayton. New York, Twayne, 1967.

1454 Haskel, G. P. Drayton's Secondary Modes: A Critical Study. Urbana, University of Illinois Press, 1936.

George Herbert (1593-1633)

WORKS

1455 The Temple, 1633

BIBLIOGRAPHIES

1456 Tannenbaum, S. A., and R. Dorothy, eds. George Herbert, A Concise Bibliography. New York, Privately Published, 1946.

TEXTS

1457 Gardner, H., ed. The Poems. 2d ed. Oxford, World's Classics, 1961.

1458 Hutchinson, F. E., ed. Works. Oxford, Oxford University Press, 1941.

1459 McCloskey, M., and P. R. Murphy, eds. The Latin Poetry of George Herbert: A Bilingual Edition. Athens, Ohio University Press, 1965.

1460 Thomas, R. S., ed. A Choice of George Herbert's Verse. London, Faber, 1967.

CRITICISM

1461 Chute, M. The Two Gentle Men: The Lives of George Herbert and Robert Herrick. New York, Dutton, 1959.

1462 Eliot, T. S. George Herbert. London, Longmans, Green, 1962.

1463 Leishman, J. B. The Metaphysical Poets. Oxford, Clarendon Press, 1934.

1464 Martz, L. L. The Poetry of Meditation. New Haven, Conn., Yale University Press, 1955.

1465 Stein, A. George Herbert's Lyrics. Baltimore, Johns Hopkins, 1968.

1466 Summers, J. H. George Herbert. Cambridge, Mass., Harvard University Press, 1954.

Robert Herrick (1591-1674)

WORKS

1467 Hesperides, 1648   1468 Noble Numbers, 1648

TEXTS

1469 Martin, L. C., ed. Poetical Works. Oxford, Oxford English Texts, 1956.

1470 _____ , ed. Poems. Oxford, Standard Authors, 1965.

1471 Patrick, J. M., ed. The Complete Poetry of Robert Herrick. New York, Norton, 1968.

CRITICISM

1472 Chute, M. The Two Gentle Men: The Lives of George Herbert and Robert Herrick. New York, Dutton, 1959.

1473 MacLeod, M., comp. and ed. A Concordance to the Poems of Robert Herrick. 1936. Repr. New York, Haskell House, 1971.

1474 Press, J. Robert Herrick. London, Longmans, Green, 1961.

Andrew Marvell (1621-1678)

WORKS

1475 The Character of Holland, 1652-54

1477 Miscellaneous Poems by Andrew Marvell, Esq., 1681

1476 The Rehearsal, Transpos'd, 1672-73

1478 Poems on Affairs of State, 1689-1716

TEXTS

1479 Davison, D., ed. Selected Poetry and Prose. London, Harrap, 1952.

1480 Grosart, A. B., ed. Complete Works in Verse and Prose. 1872-75. 4 vols. AMS Press, 1967.

1481 Kermode, F., ed. Selected Poetry. New American Library Signet, 1967.

1482 Lord, G. de F., ed. Complete Poetry. New York, Modern Library, 1968.

1483 MacDonald, H., ed. Poems Printed from the Unique Copy in the British Museum with Some Other Poems. Cambridge, Mass., Harvard University Press, 1952.

1484 Margoliouth, H. M., ed. Poems and Letters. Oxford, Oxford University Press, 1927. 2 vols.

1485 Summers, J. H., ed. Selected Poems. New York, Dell, 1961.

1486 Winny, J., ed. Selected Poems. London, Hutchinson Library, 1962.

CRITICISM

1487 Berthoff, A. E. The Resolved Soul: A Study of Marvell's Major Poems. Princeton, Princeton University Press, 1970.

1488 Colie, R. L. "My Ecchoing Song". Andrew Marvell's Poetry of Criticism. Princeton, Princeton University Press, 1970.

1489 Cullen, P. Spenser, Marvell, and Renaissance Pastoral. Cambridge, Mass., Harvard University Press, 1970.

1490 Davison, D. The Poetry of Andrew Marvell. London, E. Arnold, 1964.

1491 Friedman, D. M. Marvell's Pastoral Art. Berkeley, University of California Press, 1970.

1492 Hyman, L. W. Andrew Marvell. New York, Twayne, 1964.

1493 Legouis, P. Andrew Marvell: Poet, Puritan, Patriot. Oxford, Clarendon Press, 1965.

1494 Leishman, J. B. The Art of Marvell's Poetry. London, Hutchinson Library, 1966.

1495 Lord, G. de F., ed. A Collection of Critical Essays. Englewood Cliffs, N. J., Prentice-Hall, 1968.

1496 Toliver, H. E. Marvell's Ironic Vision. New Haven, Conn., Yale University Press, 1965.

1497 Wallace, J. M. Destiny His Choice: The Loyalism of Andrew Marvell. Cambridge, Cambridge University Press, 1968.

Henry Vaughan (1622-1695)

WORKS

1498 Poems, 1646

1499 Silex Scintillans, 1650

1500 Olor Iscanus, 1651

1501 The Mount of Olives, 1652

BIBLIOGRAPHIES

1502 Marilla, E. L. A Comprehensive Bibliography of Henry Vaughan. Tuscaloosa, University of Alabama Press, 1948.

1503 _____ , and J. D. Simmons. Henry Vaughan: A Bibliographical Supplement, 1946-1960. Tuscaloosa, University of Alabama Press, 1963.

TEXTS

1504 Dixon, C., ed. A Selection from Henry Vaughan. London, Longmans, Green, 1967.

1505 Fogle, F., ed. The Complete Poetry of Henry Vaughan. Garden City, N. Y., Doubleday, 1964.

1506 Marilla, E. L., ed. Secular Poems of Henry Vaughan. Cambridge, Mass., Harvard University Press, 1958.

1507 Martin, L. C., ed. Poems. 2d ed. Oxford, Oxford University Press, 1957. 2 vols.

1508 _____ , ed. Henry Vaughan: Poetry and Selected Prose. London, Oxford University Press, 1963.

CRITICISM

1509 Durr, R. A. On the Mystical Poetry of Henry Vaughan. Cambridge, Mass., Harvard University Press, 1962.

1510 Garner, R. Henry Vaughan: Experience and the Tradition. Chicago, University of Chicago Press, 1959.

1511 Hutchinson, F. E. Henry Vaughan: A Life and Interpretation. Oxford, Clarendon Press, 1947.

1512 Martz, L. L. The Paradise Within: Studies in Vaughan, Traherne, and Milton. New Haven, Conn., Yale University Press, 1964.

PROSE—BIBLIOGRAPHIES

1513 Mish, C. C., ed. English Prose Fiction, 1600-1700: A Chronological Checklist. Charlottesville, Bibliographical Society, University of Virginia, 1967.

1514 O'Dell, S. Chronological List of Prose Fiction in English. Printed in England and Other Countries, 1475-1640. Cambridge, Mass., Massachusetts Institute of Technology, 1954.

PROSE—TEXTS

1515 Ashley, R., and E. M. Moseley, eds. Elizabethan Fiction. New York, Holt, 1966.

1516 Hardison, O. B., Jr., ed. English Literary Criticism: The Renaissance. New York, Appleton, 1963.

1517 Harris, V., and I. Husain, eds. English Prose, 1600-1660. New York, Longmans, Green, 1965.

1518 Henderson, P., ed. Shorter Novels: Elizabethan. London, Dent, 1929.

1519 _____ , ed. Shorter Novels: Seventeenth Century. London, Dent, 1930.

1520 Mahl, M. R., ed. Seventeenth Century English Prose. Philadelphia, Lippincott, 1968.

1521 Mish, C. C., ed. The Anchor Anthology of Short Fiction of the Seventeenth Century. Garden City, N. Y., Doubleday, 1963.

1522 _____ , ed. English Prose Fiction, 1600-1640. Charlottesville, University of Virginia Press, 1952.

1523 Nugent, E. M., ed. Thought and Culture of the English Renaissance: An Anthology of Early Tudor Prose, 1481-1555. Cambridge, Cambridge University Press, 1956.

1524 Rollins, H. E., and H. Baker, eds. The Renaissance in England. Non-Dramatic Prose and Verse. Lexington, Mass., D. C. Heath, 1954.

1525 Tayler, E. W., ed. Literary Criticism of the Seventeenth Century England. New York, Knopf, 1967.

1526 White, H. C., R. C. Wallerstein, and R. Quintana, eds. Seventeenth Century Verse and Prose. Vol. I: 1600-1660. New York, Macmillan, 1951.

1527 Winny, J., ed. Elizabethan Prose Translations. Cambridge, Cambridge University Press, 1960.

1528 Zall, P. M., ed. A Hundred Merry Tales and Other English Jest Books of the Fifteenth and Sixteenth Centuries. Lincoln, University of Nebraska Press, 1963.

PROSE—CRITICISM

1529 Atkins, J. W. H. English Literary Criticism: The Renaissance. London, Methuen, 1947.

1530 Baldwin, C. S. Renaissance Literary Theory and Practice. New York, Columbia University Press, 1939.

1531 Davis, W. R. Idea and Act in Elizabethan Fiction. Princeton, Princeton University Press, 1969.

1532 Gilbert, A. H., ed. Literary Criticism: Plato to Dryden. New York, American Books, 1940.

1533 Hall, V., Jr. Renaissance Literary Criticism: A Study of Its Social Content. Glaucester, Mass., P. Smith, 1959.

1534 Herrick, M. T. The Fusion of Horatian and Aristotelian Literary Criticism, 1531-1555. Urbana, University of Illinois Press, 1946.

1535 Schlauch, M. Antecedants of the English Novel, 1400-1600: From Chaucer to Daloney. Warsaw, Polish Scientific Publications, 1963.

1536 Spingarn, J. E. A History of Literary Criticism in the Renaissance. New York, Columbia University Press, 1899.

1537 Sypher, W. Four Stages of Renaissance Style. Garden City, N. Y., Doubleday, 1955.

1538 White, H. C. Tudor Books of Saints and Martyrs. Madison, University of Wisconsin Press, 1963.

1539 Wilson, F. P. Seventeenth Century Prose. Berkeley, University of California Press, 1960.

PROSE—INDIVIDUAL AUTHORS

Roger Ascham (1515-1568)

WORKS

1540 Toxophilus, 1545   1541 The Schoolmaster, 1568

BIBLIOGRAPHIES

1542 Johnson, R. C., comp. Elizabethan Bibliographies Supplement IX: Minor Elizabethans: Roger Ascham 1946-1966, George Gascoigne 1941-1966, John Heywood 1944-1966, Thomas Kyd 1940-1966, Anthony Munday 1941-1966. London, Nether Press, 1968.

1543 Tannenbaum, S. A., and D. R. Roger, eds. Roger Ascham, A Concise Bibliography. New York, Privately Published, 1946.

TEXTS

1544 Bennet, J., ed. English Works of Roger Ascham. London, R. & I. Dodsley & J. Newbery, 1761.

1545 Giles, Dr., ed. The Whole Works of Roger Ascham. London, Smith, 1865. 3 vols.

1546 Wright, W. A., ed. Roger Ascham. English Works: Toxophilus, Report of the Affairs and State of Germany, the Scholemaster. Cambridge, Cambridge University Press, 1970.

CRITICISM

1547 Ryan, L. Roger Ascham. Stanford, Stanford University Press, 1963.

Sir Francis Bacon (1561-1626)

WORKS

1548 Essays, 1597
1549 Advancement of Learning, 1605
1550 Novum Organum, 1620
1551 History of Henry VII, 1622
1552 Historia Ventorum, 1622
1553 Historia Vitae and Mortis, 1623

1554 Apophthegms, 1625
1555 New Atlantis, 1627
1556 The Elements of Common Laws of England, 1630
1557 The Learned Readings of Sir Francis Bacon Upon the Statute of Uses, 1642

BIBLIOGRAPHIES

1558 Gibson, R. W. Francis Bacon: A Bibliography of His Works and of Baconiana to the Year 1750. Oxford, Scrivener Press, 1950.

TEXTS

1559 Dick, H. G., ed. Selected Writings. New York, Modern Library, 1955.

1560 Johnston, A., ed. Francis Bacon. New York, Schocken, 1965.

1561 Spedding, J., R. L. Ellis, and D. D. Heath, eds. The Complete Bacon. London, Longmans, 1857-74. 14 vols.

1562 Warhaft, S., ed. Selection of His Works. London, St. Martin's, 1965.

CRITICISM

1563 Bowen, C. D. Francis Bacon: The Temper of a Man. Boston, Little, Brown, 1963.

1564 Crowther, J. G. Francis Bacon: The First Statesman of Science. London, P. Cresset, 1960.

1565 Eiseley, L. Francis Bacon and the Modern Dilemma. Lincoln, University of Nebraska Press, 1962.

1566 Green, A. W. Sir Francis Bacon: His Life and Works. Denver, Swallow, 1952.

1567 Lemmi, C. W. The Classic Deities in Bacon: A Study in Mythological Symbolism. Baltimore, Johns Hopkins, 1933.

1568 Patrick, J. M. Francis Bacon. London, Longmans, Green, 1961.

1569 Vickers, B. Francis Bacon and Renaissance Prose. Cambridge, Cambridge University Press, 1968.

Sir Thomas Browne (1605-1682)

WORKS

1570 Religio Medici, 1642

1571 Pseudodoxia Epidemica, 1646

1572 Hydriotaphia, Urne-Buriall, 1658

BIBLIOGRAPHIES

1573 Keynes, G. L. A Bibliography of Sir Thomas Browne. Oxford, Clarendon Press, 1968.

TEXTS

1574 Endicott, N., ed. The Prose of Sir Thomas Browne. New York, New York University Press, 1967.

1575 Keynes, G. L., ed. The Letters of Sir Thomas Browne. London, Faber & Faber, 1946.

1576 _____ , ed. The Works of Sir Thomas Browne. Chicago, University of Chicago Press, 1964. 4 vols.

1577 Martin, L. C., ed. Religio Medici and Other Works. Oxford, Clarendon Press, 1964.

CRITICISM

1578 Bennett, J. Sir Thomas Browne: A Man of Achievement in Literature. Cambridge, Cambridge University Press, 1962.

1579 Dunn, W. P. Browne: A Study in Religious Philosophy. Minneapolis, University of Minnesota Press, 1926.

1580 Huntley, F. L. Sir Thomas Browne: A Biographical and Critical Study. Ann Arbor, University of Michigan Press, 1962.

Robert Burton (1577-1640)

WORKS

1581 Philosophaster, 1606

1582 Anatomy of Melancholy, 1621

TEXTS

1583 Babb, L., ed. The Anatomy of Melancholy, A Selection. East Lansing, Michigan State University Press, 1965.

1584 Jackson, H., ed. The Anatomy of Melancholy. London, Dent, 1964.

1585 Mead, G. C. F., and R. C. Clift, eds. Burton the Anatomist; Being Extracts from the "Anatomy of Melancholy" Chosen to Interest the Psychologist in Every Man. London, Methuen, 1925.

1586 Rhys, E., ed. The Anatomy of Melancholy. London, Dent, 1923.

CRITICISM

1587 Babb, L. The Elizabethan Malady: A Study of Melancholy in English Literature from 1580-1642. East Lansing, Michigan State University Press, 1951.

1588 _____ . Sanity in Bedlam: A Study of Robert Burton's Anatomy of Melancholy. East Lansing, Michigan State University Press, 1959.

1589 Mueller, W. R. The Anatomy of Burton's England. Berkeley, University of California Press, 1952.

Sir Thomas Elyot (1499-1546)

WORKS

1590 The Boke Named the Governour, 1531

1591 Of the Knowledge Which Maketh a Wise Man, 1533

1592 The Bankette of Sapience, 1539

1593 The Defence of Good Women, 1540

1594 The Image of Governance Compiled of the Ashes of Alexander Severus, 1541

TEXTS

1595 Howard, E. J., ed. Of the Knowledge Which Makes a Wise Man, by Sir Thomas Elyot. Oxford, Anchor Press, 1946.

1596 Lehmberg, S. E., ed. The Book Named the Governor. New ed. London, Dent, 1963.

1597 Major, J. M., ed. Sir Thomas Elyot's The Book Named the Governor. New York, Teachers College Press, 1970.

1598 Rhys, E., ed. The Boke Named the Governour, Devised by Sir Thomas Elyot, Knight. London, Dent, 1907.

CRITICISM

1599 Hogrefe, P. The Life and Times of Sir Thomas Elyot, Englishman. Ames, Iowa State University Press, 1967.

1600 Lehmberg, S. E. Sir Thomas Elyot: Tudor Humanist. Austin, University of Texas Press, 1960.

1601 Major, J. M. Sir Thomas Elyot and Renaissance Humanism. Lincoln, University of Nebraska Press, 1964.

Thomas Lodge (1558-1625)

WORKS

1602 Defence of Poetry, 1579
1603 Rosalynde, 1590
1604 Euphues Shadow, 1592

1605 Phyllis, 1593
1606 The Wounds of Civil War, 1594

TEXTS

1607 Greg, W. W., ed. Lodge's Rosalynde Being the Original of Shakespeare's As You Like It. New York, Duffield, 1908.

1608 Harrison, G. B., ed. A Margarite of America. Oxford, B. Blackwell, 1927.

1609 Hart, H., ed. The Wounds of Civil War. London, Oxford University Press, 1910.

1610 Sisson, C. J., ed. Thomas Lodge and Other Elizabethans. New York, Octagon, 1966.

CRITICISM

1611 Paradise, N. Burton. Thomas Lodge: The History of an Elizabethan. New Haven, Conn., Yale University Press, 1931.

1612 Rae, W. D. Thomas Lodge. New York, Twayne, 1967.

1613 Ryan, P. M. Thomas Lodge, Gentlemen. Hamden, Conn., Shoe String Press, 1958.

John Lyly (1554-1606)

WORKS

1614 Euphues. The Anatomy of Wit, 1578
1615 Euphues and His England, 1580
1616 Comedie of Alexander, Campaspe, and Diogenes, 1584

1617 Endimion, 1591
1618 Gallathea, 1592
1619 Love's Metamorphosis, 1601

TEXTS

1620 Bond, R. W., ed. The Complete Works of John Lyly. Oxford, Clarendon Press, 1967. 3 vols.

1621 Warwick, R., ed. Complete Works of John Lyly. Oxford, Clarendon Press, 1902.

CRITICISM

1622　Hunter, G. K.　John Lyly: The Humanist as Courtier. London, Routledge & K. Paul, 1962.

1623　＿＿＿＿＿＿ . Lyly and Peele. London, Longmans, Green, 1968.

1624　Saccio, P.　The Court Comedies of John Lyly: A Study in Allegorical
Dramaturgy. Princeton, Princeton University Press, 1969.

Sir Thomas More (1478-1535)

WORKS

1625　History of King Richard III,
1513
1626　Utopia, 1515

1627　The Apology of Sir Thomas
More Knyght, 1533

BIBLIOGRAPHIES

1628　Gibson, R. W.　St. Thomas More: A Preliminary Bibliography of
His Works and of Moreana to the Year 1750. New Haven, Conn.,
Yale University Press, 1961.

1629　Sullivan, S., and M. Padberg.　Moreana: Materials for the Study of
Saint Thomas More. A-F. Los Angeles, Loyola University Press,
1964.

TEXTS

1630　Bradner, L., and C. A. Lynch, eds.　The Latin Epigrams of
Sir Thomas More. New York, Colonial Press, 1901.

1631　Rogers, E. F., ed.　The Correspondence of Sir Thomas More.
Princeton, Princeton University Press, 1947.

1632　Sullivan, F., ed.　The Complete Works of Saint Thomas More. Los
Angeles, Loyola University Press, 1964.

1633　Surtz, E. S. J., and J. H. Hexter, eds.　The Complete Works of
St. Thomas More. Vol. IV: Utopia. New Haven, Conn., Yale
University Press, 1965.

1634　Sylvester, R. S., ed.　The Complete Works of Sir Thomas More.
Vol. II: The History of King Richard III. New Haven, Conn., Yale
University Press, 1963.

CRITICISM

1635　Ames, R.　Citizen Thomas More and His Utopia. Princeton,
Princeton University Press, 1949.

1636　Chambers, R. W.　Thomas More. Ann Arbor, University of Michigan
Press, 1958.

1637 Gallagher, L., ed. More's Utopia and Its Critics. Chicago, Scott, Foresman, 1964.

1638 Kautzky, K. Thomas More and His Utopia. New York, Russell & Russell, 1959.

1639 Morgan, A. E. Nowhere Was Somewhere: How History Makes Utopias and How Utopias Make History. Chapel Hill, University of North Carolina Press, 1946.

1640 Nelson, W., ed. Twentieth Century Interpretations of 'Utopia'. Englewood Cliffs, N. J., Prentice-Hall, 1968.

1641 Paul, L. A. Sir Thomas More. New York, Roy, 1959.

1642 Pineas, R. Thomas More and Tudor Polemics. Bloomington, University of Indiana Press, 1968.

1643 Raynolds, E. E. The Trial of St. Thomas More. New York, P. J. Kenedy, 1964.

1644 Surtz, E. S. J. The Praise of Pleasure: Philosophy, Education and Communion in More's Utopia. Cambridge, Mass., Harvard University Press, 1957.

1645 Thompson, C. R. The Translations of Lucian by Erasmus and Sir Thomas More. Ithaca, N. Y., Cornell University Press, 1940.

Thomas Nashe (1567-1601)

WORKS

1646 Pierce Pennilesse, 1592

1648 The Terrors of Night, 1594

1647 The Unfortunate Traveller, 1594

TEXTS

1649 McKerrow, R. B., ed. The Works of Thomas Nashe. Repr. F. P. Wilson. Oxford, B. Blackwell, 1958. 5 vols.

1650 Wells, S., ed. Thomas Nashe: Selected Writings. London, E. Arnold, 1964.

CRITICISM

1651 Hibbard, G. R. Thomas Nashe: A Critical Introduction. Cambridge, Mass., Harvard University Press, 1962.

RESTORATION TO 1800

GENERAL WORKS—BIBLIOGRAPHIES

1652 Crane, R. S., et al. English Literature, 1660-1800. A Bibliography of Modern Studies. Princeton, University of Princeton Press, 1950-62.

1653 Ewen, F. Bibliography of Eighteenth Century English Literature. New York, Haskell House, 1969.

1654 Kilb, G. J., and C. A. Zimansky, eds. English Literature, 1660-1800: A Bibliography of Modern Studies. Princeton, University of Princeton Press, 1962. 4 vols.

GENERAL WORKS—CRITICISM

1655 Allen, B. S. Tides in English Taste, 1619-1800. Cambridge, Mass., Harvard University Press, 1937. 2 vols.

1656 Bate, W. J. From Classic to Romantic: Premises of Taste in Eighteenth Century England. Cambridge, Mass., Harvard University Press, 1946.

1657 Clifford, J. L., ed. Eighteenth Century English Literature: Modern Essays in Criticism. New York, Oxford University Press, 1959.

1658 Dobrée, B. English Literature in the Earlier Eighteenth Century, 1700-1740. Oxford, Clarendon Press, 1959.

1659 Fussell, P. The Rhetorical World of Augustan Humanism: Ethics and Imagery from Swift to Burke. New York, Oxford University Press, 1969.

1660 Harris, R. W. Reason and Nature in Eighteenth Century Thought. New York, Barnes & Noble, 1969.

1661 Jack, I. The Augustan Satire. Oxford, Clarendon Press, 1952.

1662 Johnson, J. W. The Formation of English Neoclassical Thought. Princeton, Princeton University Press, 1967.

1663 Jones, R. F., et al. The Seventeenth Century: Studies in the History of English Thought and Literature from Bacon to Pope. Palo Alto, Stanford University Press, 1965.

1664 Jones, R. F. Ancients and Moderns. A Study of the Rise of the Scientific Movement in Seventeenth Century England. 2d ed. St. Louis, Washington University Press, 1961.

1665 McKillop, A. D. English Literature from Dryden to Burns. New York, Appleton, 1948.

1666 Milburn, D. J. The Age of Wit, 1650-1750. New York, Macmillan, 1966.

1667 Moore, C. A. Backgrounds of English Literature, 1700-1760. Minneapolis, University of Minnesota Press, 1953.

1668 Quinlan, M. J. Victorian Prelude. A History of English Manners, 1700-1830. New York, Columbia University Press, 1941.

1669 Sutherland, J. R. English Literature of the Late Seventeenth Century. London, Oxford University Press, 1969

1670 Sutherland, W. O. S., Jr. The Art of the Satirist: Essays on the Satire of Augustan England. Austin, Humanities Research Center, University of Texas, 1965.

1671 Tillotson, G. Augustan Studies. London, London University Press, 1961.

1672 Tobin, J. E. Eighteenth Century English Literature and Its Cultural Background. New York, Fordham University Press, 1939.

1673 Watt, I., ed. The Augustan Age: Approaches to Its Literature, Life and Thought. New York, Fawcett, 1968.

1674 Weinbrot, A. D. The Formal Strain: Studies in Augustan Imitation and Satire. Chicago, University of Chicago Press, 1969.

1675 Willey, B. The Eighteenth Century Background. New York, Doubleday, 1953.

1676 _____ . The Seventeenth Century Background. New York, Doubleday, 1953.

1677 Wilson, J. H. The Court Wits of the Restoration. Princeton, Princeton University Press, 1948.

RESTORATION DRAMA—BIBLIOGRAPHIES

1678 Stratman, C. J., ed. Restoration and Eighteenth Century Theatre Research Bibliography. New York, Whitston, 1969.

1679 Summers, M. A Bibliography of the Restoration Drama. London, Fortune, 1934. Repr. New York, Russell & Russell, 1970.

RESTORATION DRAMA—TEXTS

1680 Dobrée, B., ed. Five Heroic Plays. London, Oxford University Press, 1960.

1681 Hughes, L., and A. H. Scouten, eds. Ten English Farces. Austin, University of Texas Press, 1948.

1682 Miner, E., ed. Restoration Dramatists. Englewood Cliffs, N. J., Prentice-Hall, 1966.

1683 Nettleton, G. H., and A. E. Case, eds. British Dramatists from Dryden to Sheridan. Boston, Houghton, 1939.

RESTORATION DRAMA—CRITICISM

1684 Baur-Heinhold, M. The Baroque Theatre: A Cultural History of the Seventeenth and the Eighteenth Centuries. New York, McGraw-Hill, 1967.

1685 Cunningham, J. E. Restoration Drama. London, Evans Brothers, 1968.

1686 Fujimura, T. H. The Restoration Comedy of Wit. Princeton, Princeton University Press, 1952.

1687 Loftis, J. Comedy and Society from Congreve to Fielding. Stanford, University of Stanford Press, 1959.

1688 _____ . Restoration Drama: Modern Essays in Criticism. New York, Oxford University Press, 1966.

1689 Mignon, E. Crabbed Age and Youth, the Old Men and Women in the Restoration Comedy of Manners. Durham, N. C., Duke University Press, 1947.

1690 Nicoll, A. A History of Restoration Drama, 1660-1700. Cambridge, Cambridge University Press, 1923.

1691 Rothstein, E. Restoration Tragedy: Form and the Process of Change. Madison, University of Wisconsin Press, 1967.

1692 Smith, J. H. The Gay Couple in Restoration Comedy. Cambridge, Mass., Harvard University Press, 1948.

1693 Wilson, J. H. A Preface to Restoration Drama. Boston, Houghton, 1965.

RESTORATION DRAMA—INDIVIDUAL AUTHORS

William Congreve (1670-1729)

WORKS

1694 The Double Dealer, 1693
1695 Love for Love, 1695

1696 Letters Upon Several Occasions, 1696
1697 The Way of the World, 1700

TEXTS

1698 Bentley, E., ed. Complete Plays. Chicago, Chicago University Press, 1967.

1699 Davis, H., ed. The Complete Plays of William Congreve. Chicago, Chicago University Press, 1967.

1700 Dobrée, B., ed. The Comedies. Oxford, World's Classics, 1968.

1701 Hodges, J. C., ed. William Congreve: Letters and Documents. New York, Harcourt, 1963.

1702 Summers, M., ed. William Congreve: The Complete Works. New York, Russell & Russell, 1964. 4 vols.

CRITICISM

1703 Dobrée, B. William Congreve. London, Longmans, Green, 1963.

1704 Hodges, J. C. William Congreve the Man: A Biography from New Sources. New York, Kraus, 1941.

1705 Holland, N. H. The First Modern Comedies: The Significance of Etherege, Wycherly and Congreve. Cambridge, Mass., Harvard University Press, 1959.

1706 Taylor, D. C. William Congreve. New York, Russell & Russell, 1963.

John Dryden (1631-1700)

WORKS

1707 Astrea Redux, 1660
1708 Annus Mirabilis, 1666
1709 Of Dramatic Poesie, an Essay, 1668
1710 All for Love, 1677
1711 Macflecknoe, 1678
1712 Troilus and Cressida, 1679

1713 Absalom and Achitophel, 1681
1714 Religio Laici, 1682
1715 The Hind and the Panther, 1687
1716 Satires, 1693
1717 Fables Ancient and Modern, 1700

BIBLIOGRAPHIES

1718 Macdonald, H. John Dryden: A Bibliography of Early Editions of Drydeniana. Oxford, Clarendon Press, 1939.

TEXTS

1719 Aden, J. M., ed. The Critical Opinions of John Dryden: A Dictionary. Nashville, Tenn., Vanderbilt University Press, 1963.

1720 Beaurline, L. A., and F. T. Bowers, eds. Four Comedies. Chicago, Chicago University Press, 1967.

1721 _____ , eds. Four Tragedies. Chicago, Chicago University Press, 1967.

1722 Day, C. L., ed. The Songs of John Dryden. Cambridge, Mass., Harvard University Press, 1932.

1723 Frost, W., ed. Selected Works of John Dryden. New York, Holt, 1953.

1724 Grant, G., ed. Dryden: Poetry, Prose and Plays. London, Reynard Lib., 1952.

1725 Hooker, E. N., and H. T. Swedenberg, eds. Works. Berkeley, University of California Press, 1956— . To be published in 21 vols.

1726 Kinsley, J., ed. The Poems and Fables of John Dryden. London, Oxford University Press, 1962.

1727 Noyes, G. R., ed. The Poetical Works of Dryden. Cambridge, Mass., Harvard University Press, 1909.

1728 Pendlebury, B. J., ed. The Heroic Plays. New York, Russell & Russell, 1967.

1729 Ward, C. E., ed. The Letters. Durham, N. C., AMS Press, 1942.

CRITICISM

1730 Allen, N. B. The Sources of John Dryden's Comedies. Ann Arbor, University of Michigan Press, 1935.

1731 Budick, S. Dryden and the Abyss of Light: A Study of Religio Laici and the Hind and the Panther. New Haven, Conn., Yale University Press, 1970.

1732 Eliot, T. S. John Dryden: The Poet, the Dramatist, the Critic. New York, T. & Elsa Holliday, 1932.

1733 Ford, B., et al. From Dryden to Johnson. Baltimore, Penguin, 1970.

1734 Frost, W. Dryden and the Art of Translation. New Haven, Conn., Yale University Press, 1955.

1735 Gardner, W. B. The Prologues and Epilogues of John Dryden. New York, Columbia University Press, 1951.

1736 Hoffman, A. W. John Dryden's Imagery. Gainesville, University of Florida Press, 1962.

1737 Hume, R. D. Dryden's Criticism. Ithaca, N. Y., Cornell University Press, 1970.

1738 Jensen, J. H. A Glossary of John Dryden's Critical Terms. Minneapolis, University of Minnesota Press, 1969.

1739 King, B., ed. Twentieth Century Interpretations of All For Love: A Collection of Critical Essays. Englewood Cliffs, N. J., Prentice-Hall, 1968.

1740 Kinsley, J., comp. Dryden: The Critical Heritage. New York, Barnes & Noble, 1971.

1741 Kirsch, A. C. Dryden's Heroic Drama. Princeton, Princeton University Press, 1965.

1742 Montgomery, G. Concordance to the Poetical Works of John Dryden. New York, Russell & Russell, 1967.

1743 Moore, F. H. The Nobler Pleasure: Dryden's Comedy in Theory and Practice. Chapel Hill, University of North Carolina Press, 1963.

1744 Nicoll, A. Dryden and His Poetry. New York, Russell & Russell, 1967.

1745 Ramsey, P. The Art of John Dryden. Lexington, University of Kentucky Press, 1969.

1746 Schilling, B. N. Dryden and the Conservative Myth. New Haven, Conn., Yale University Press, 1961.

1747 _____ . Dryden: A Collection of Critical Essays. Englewood Cliffs, N. J., Prentice-Hall, 1963.

1748 Swedenberg, H. T., Jr. Essential Articles for the Study of John Dryden. Hamden, Conn., Archon, 1966.

1749 Van Doren, M. Dryden: A Study of His Poetry. London, P. Smith, 1960.

1750 Ward, C. E. The Life of John Dryden. Chapel Hill, University of North Carolina Press, 1961.

1751 Zebouni, S. A. Dryden: A Study in Heroic Characterization. Baton Rouge, La., La Salle University Press, 1965.

Sir George Etherege (1635-1691)

WORKS

1752 The Comical Revenge, 1664   1754 The Man of the Mode, 1676
1753 She Wou'd If She Cou'd, 1676

TEXTS

1755 Bertt-Smith, H. F. B., ed. Plays. Oxford, B. Blackwell, 1927. 2 vols.

1756 Thorpe, J. E., ed. The Poems of Sir George Etherege. Princeton, Princeton University Press, 1963.

CRITICISM

1757 Holland, N. H. The First Modern Comedies: The Significance of Etherege, Wycherley and Congreve. Cambridge, Mass., Harvard University Press, 1959.

William Wycherley (1640-1716)

WORKS

1758 Hero and Leander, 1669   1760 The Country Wife, 1675
1759 The Gentleman Dancing   1761 The Plain Dealer, 1677
      Master, 1673

TEXTS

1762 Summers, M., ed. Complete Works. New York, Russell & Russell, 1965. 4 vols.

1763 Weales, G. C., ed. The Complete Plays of William Wycherley. New York, New York University Press, 1967.

CRITICISM

1764 Holland, N. H. The First Modern Comedies: The Significance of Etherege, Wycherley and Congreve. Cambridge, Mass., Harvard University Press, 1959.

1765 Zimbardo, R. A. Wycherley's Drama: A Link in the Development of English Satire. New Haven, Conn., Yale University Press, 1965.

18TH CENTURY DRAMA—TEXTS

1766 Booth, M. R., ed. Eighteenth Century Tragedy. London, Oxford University Press, 1965.

1767 Krutch, J. W., ed. Eighteenth Century English Drama. New York, Bantam, 1967.

1768   Quintana, R., ed. Eighteenth Century Plays. New York, Modern Library, 1952.

1769   Taylor, W. D., ed. Eighteenth Century Comedies. Oxford, World's Classics, 1950.

1770   Wilson, J. H., ed. Six Eighteenth Century Plays. Boston, Houghton, 1963.

18TH CENTURY DRAMA—CRITICISM

1771   Bernbaum, E. The Drama of Sensibility. London, P. Smith, 1958.

1772   Boas, F. S. Early Eighteenth Century Drama, 1700-1750. Cambridge, Cambridge University Press, 1952.

1773   _____ . An Introduction to Eighteenth Century Drama, 1700-1780. Oxford, Oxford University Press, 1953.

1774   Brener, C. D. Dramatization of French Short Stories in the Eighteenth Century. Berkeley, University of California Press, 1947.

1775   Evans, B. Gothic Drama from Walpole to Shelley. Berkeley, University of California Press, 1947.

1776   Gassner, J. Eighteenth Century English Drama. New York, Bantam, 1967.

1777   Green, C. C. The Neoclassic Theory of Tragedy in England During the Eighteenth Century. Cambridge, Mass, Harvard University Press, 1934.

1778   Krutch, J. W. Comedy and Conscience after the Restoration. New York, Russell & Russell, 1949.

1779   Loftis, J. Essays on the Theatre from Eighteenth Century Periodicals. Los Angeles, W. A. Clark Memorial Library, 1960.

1780   _____ . The Politics of Drama in Augustan England. Oxford, Oxford University Press, 1963.

1781   Lynch, J. J. Drama in the Theatre During the Mid-Eighteenth Century, 1737-1777. Berkeley, University of California Press, 1948.

1782   _____ . Box, Pit, and Gallery: Stage and Society in Johnson's London. Berkeley, University of California Press, 1953.

1783   Nicoll, A. A History of Early Eighteenth Century Drama, 1700-1750. Cambridge, Cambridge University Press, 1925.

1784   _____ . A History of Late Eighteenth Century Drama, 1750-1800. Cambridge, Cambridge University Press, 1927.

1785 Scouten, A. H., et al., eds. The London Stage, 1660-1800: A Calendar of Plays, Entertainments and Afterpieces, Together with Casts, Box-Receipts, and Contemporary Comments. Part III: 1729-1747. Carbondale, Southern Illinois University Press, 1961. 2 vols.

1786 Sherbo, A. English Sentimental Drama. East Lansing, Michigan State University Press, 1957.

1787 Smith, D. F. The Critics in the Audience of London Theatres from Buchingham to Sheridan: A Study of Neoclassicism in the Playhouse, 1671-1779. Albuquerque, University of New Mexico Press, 1953.

1788 Worcester, D. The Art of Satire. Cambridge, Mass., Harvard University Press, 1940.

18TH CENTURY DRAMA—INDIVIDUAL AUTHORS

John Gay (1685-1732)

WORKS

1789 Rural Sports, 1708

1790 The Shepherd's Week, 1714

1791 Fables, 1727

1792 The Beggar's Opera, 1728

TEXTS

1793 Bond, D. F., and W. E. Britton, eds. John Gay: The Present State of Wit (1711) and Excerpts from the English Theophrastus: Or the Manners of the Age (1782). Ann Arbor, University of Michigan Press, 1947.

1794 Burgess, C. F., ed. The Letters of John Gay. Oxford, Clarendon Press, 1966.

1795 _____ , ed. The Beggar's Opera and Companion Pieces. New York, Appleton, 1968.

1796 Faber, G. L., ed. Poetical Works. London, Oxford University Press, 1926.

1797 Griffith, B. W., Jr., ed. The Beggar's Opera. Great Neck, N. Y., Barron's, 1962.

1798 Smith, J. A., ed. Three Hours after Marriage. Los Angeles, W. A. Clark Memorial Library, 1961.

CRITICISM

1799 Gagey, E. M. Ballad Opera. New York, Columbia University Press, 1937.

1800 Irving, W. H. John Gay: Favorite of the Wits. New York, Russell & Russell, 1962.

1801 Schultz, W. E. The Beggar's Opera. New York, Russell & Russell, 1923.

1802 Spacks, P. M. John Gay. New York, Twayne, 1965.

1803 Warner, O. John Gay. London, Longmans, Green, 1964.

Oliver Goldsmith (1721-1774)

WORKS

1804 The Citizen of the World, 1762

1805 The Vicar of Wakefield, 1762

1806 The Deserted Village, 1770

1807 She Stoops to Conquer, 1773

TEXTS

1808 Balderston, K. C., ed. Oliver Goldsmith: She Stoops to Conquer or the Mistakes of a Night. New York, Appleton, 1951.

1809 Dobson, A., ed. Goldsmith: Four Plays. London, Hill & Wang, 1957.

1810 _____ , ed. Poems and Plays. New York, Dutton, 1968.

1811 Friedman, A., ed. Collected Works. Oxford, Oxford University Press, 1966. 5 vols.

1812 _____ , ed. She Stoops to Conquer. London, Oxford University Press, 1968.

1813 Garnett, R., ed. Selected Works. Cambridge, Mass., Harvard University Press, 1951.

1814 Hilles, F. W., ed. The Vicar of Wakefield and Other Writings. New York, Modern Library, 1968.

1815 Jeffares, A. N., ed. A Goldsmith Selection. New York, St. Martin's, 1963.

1816 Lonsdale, R. H., ed. The Poems of Thomas Gray, William Collins and Oliver Goldsmith. London, Longmans, 1969.

1817 Piggin, J. R., ed. The Vicar of Wakefield. New York, Barnes & Noble, 1969.

CRITICISM

1818 Emslie, M. Goldsmith: The Vicar of Wakefield. London, E. Arnold, 1963.

1819 Hopkins, R. H. The True Genius of Oliver Goldsmith. Baltimore, Johns Hopkins, 1969.

1820 Jeffares, A. N. Oliver Goldsmith. London, British Book Center, 1959.

1821 Lucas, F. L. The Search for Good Sense: Four Eighteenth Century Characters. New York, Macmillan, 1958.

1822 Quintana, R. Oliver Goldsmith: A Georgian Study. New York, Macmillan, 1967.

1823 Sherwin, O. Goldsmith: The Life and Times of Oliver Goldsmith. New York, Twayne, 1961.

Richard Brinsley Sheridan (1751-1816)

WORKS

1824 The Rivals, 1775   1826   The School for Scandal, 1780
1825 The Duenna, 1775

TEXTS

1827 Complete Plays. New York, Collins, 1968.

1828 Knight, J., ed. Plays. Oxford, World's Classics, 1951.

1829 Kronenberger, L., ed. Six Plays. London, Hill & Wang, 1968.

1830 Price, C., ed. The Letters of Richard Brinsley Sheridan. Oxford, Clarendon Press, 1966. 3 vols.

1831 Rhodes, R. C., ed. Plays and Poems. New York, Russell & Russell, 1962. 3 vols.

CRITICISM

1832 Foss, K. Here Lies Sheridan. New York, Dutton, 1939.

1833 Sherwin, O. Uncorking Old Sherry: The Life and Times of Richard Brinsley Sheridan. New York, Twayne, 1960.

RESTORATION POETRY—TEXTS

1834 Crane, R. S., ed. A Collection of English Poems, 1660-1800. New York, Harper, 1932.

1835 Love, H., ed. The Penguin Book of Restoration Verse. Baltimore, Penguin, 1968.

1836 Moore, C. A., ed. Restoration Literature: Poetry and Prose, 1660-1700. New York, F. S. Crofts, 1934.

1837 Pinto, V. de Sola, ed. Poetry of the Restoration, 1653-1700. New York, Barnes & Noble, 1966.

1838 Pinto, V. de Sola, ed. The Restoration Court Poets. New York, Longmans, Green, 1965.

1839 Sharp, R. L., ed. From Donne to Dryden. Durham, N. C., Duke University Press, 1940.

1840 Shuster, G. N., ed. The English Ode from Milton to Keats. New York, Gloucester, Mass., P. Smith, 1964.

1841 Starkman, M. K., ed. Seventeenth Century English Poetry. New York, Knopf, 1967. 2 vols.

RESTORATION POETRY—CRITICISM

1842 Congleton, J. E. Theories of Pastoral Poetry in England, 1684-1798. Gainesville, University of Florida Press, 1952.

1843 Swedenberg, H. T. The Theory of the Epic in England, 1650-1800. Berkeley, University of California Press, 1944.

RESTORATION POETRY—INDIVIDUAL AUTHORS

John Milton (1608-1674)
WORKS

1844 L'Allegro, 1631
1845 Comus, 1634
1846 Lycidas, 1638
1847 Areopagitica, 1644
1848 Of Education, 1644

1849 Poems, 1645
1850 Paradise Lost, 1667, 1674
1851 The History of Britain, 1670
1852 Paradise Regained, 1671
1853 Samson Agonistes, 1671

BIBLIOGRAPHIES

1854 Huckabay, C. John Milton: An Annotated Bibliography, 1929-1968. Rev. ed. Pittsburgh, Pa., Duquesne University Press, 1969.

1855 Stevens, D. H. Reference Guide to Milton, from 1800 to the Present Day. Chicago, University of Chicago Press, 1930.

TEXTS

1856 Bush, D., ed. The Portable Milton. New York, Viking, 1949.

1857 _____ , ed. The Complete Poetical Works of John Milton. Boston, Houghton, 1965.

1858 Brooks, K., ed. Complete Poetry and Selected Prose. New York, Modern Library, 1942.

1859 Cross, T. P., ed. Milton's Minor Poems. Cambridge, Mass., Harvard University Press, 1936.

1860 Darbishire, H., ed. Poetical Works. Oxford, Oxford University Press, 1955. 2 vols.

1861 Fletcher, H. F., ed. The Complete Poetical Works of John Milton. Urbana, University of Illinois Press, 1943-1948. 4 vols.

1862 _____ , ed. John Milton's Complete Poetical Works Reproduced in Photographic Facsimile. Urbana, University of Illinois Press, 1945.

1863 Hanford, J. H., and J. C. Taafe, eds. A Milton Handbook. 5th ed. New York, Appleton, 1970.

1864 Hughes, M. Y., ed. The Complete Prose Works of John Milton. Vol. III: 1648-1649. New Haven, Conn., Yale University Press, 1962.

1865 _____ , ed. Complete Poems and Major Prose. New York, Odyssey, 1958.

1866 Patterson, F. E., ed. The Works of John Milton. New York, Columbia University Press, 1940. 18 vols.

1867 _____ , ed. Complete Poems. New York, Appleton, 1933.

1868 Sabine, G. H., ed. John Milton: Aeropagitica and Of Education with Autobiographical Passages from Other Prose Works. New York, St. Martin's, 1963.

1869 Showcross, J. T., ed. The Complete English Poetry of John Milton. Garden City, N. Y., Doubleday, 1963.

1870 Sirluck, E., ed. The Complete Works of John Milton. New Haven, Conn., Yale University Press, 1959.

1871 Visiak, E. H., ed. Complete Poetry and Selected Prose. New York, Random, 1938.

1872 Williams, C., ed. The English Poems. Oxford, World's Classics, 1941.

1873 Wolfe, D. M., ed. Complete Prose Works of John Milton. Vol. I: 1624-1642, Vol. IV, Parts 1 and 2: 1650-1655. New Haven, Conn., Yale University Press, 1966.

CRITICISM

1874 Allen, D. C. The Harmonious Vision: Studies in Milton's Poetry. Baltimore, Johns Hopkins, 1970.

1875 Babb, L. The Moral Cosmos of Paradise Lost. East Lansing, Michigan State University Press, 1971.

1876 Banks, T. H. Milton's Imagery. New York, AMS Press, 1969.

1877 Barker, A. E., ed. Milton: Modern Essays in Criticism. New York, Oxford University Press, 1965.

1878 Bush, D. Paradise Lost in Our Time. Ithaca, N. Y., Cornell University Press, 1945.

1879 _____ . John Milton: A Sketch of His Life and Writings. New York, Macmillan, 1964.

1880 Buxton, C. R. Prophets of Heaven and Hell. Cambridge, Cambridge University Press, 1945.

1881 Cope, J. I. The Metaphoric Structure of Paradise Lost. Baltimore, Johns Hopkins, 1962.

1882 Crump, G. M., ed. Twentieth Century Interpretations of Samson Agonistes: A Collection of Critical Essays. Englewood Cliffs, N. J., Prentice-Hall, 1968.

1883 Daniels, R. Milton, Mannerism, and Baroque. Toronto, Toronto University Press, 1963.

1884 Eastland, E. W. Milton's Ethics. Nashville, Tenn., Vanderbilt University Press, 1946.

1885 Empson, W. Milton's God. New York, New Directions, 1961.

1886 Fletcher, H. F. The Intellectual Development of John Milton. Vol. II: The Cambridge University Period, 1625-1632. Urbana, University of Illinois Press, 1961.

1887 French, J. M., ed. The Life Records of John Milton. Vol. I: 1608-1639. New Brunswick, Gordian, 1949-58. 5 vols.

1888 Frye, N. The Return of Eden: Five Essays on Milton's Epics. Toronto, University of Toronto Press, 1965.

1889 Frye, R. M. God, Man, and Satan: Patterns of Christian Thought and Life in Paradise Lost, Pilgrims Progress, and the Great Theologians. Princeton, Princeton University Press, 1960.

1890 Halkett, J. Milton and the Idea of Matrimony: A Study of the Divorce Tracts and Paradise Lost. New Haven, Conn., Yale University Press, 1970.

1891 Hamilton, G. R. Hero or Fool? A Study of Milton's Satan. London, Allen & Unwin, 1944.

1892 Hanford, J. H. John Milton: Poet and Humanist. Cleveland, World Publishing Company, 1966.

1893 Harding, D. P. Milton and the Renaissance Ovid. Urbana, University of Illinois Press, 1946.

1894 Harding, D. P. The Club of Hercules: Studies in the Classical Background of Paradise Lost. Urbana, University of Illinois Press, 1962.

1895 Hughes, M. Y. Ten Perspectives on Milton. New Haven, Conn., Yale University Press, 1965.

1896 _____ , ed. Variorum Commentary on the Poems of John Milton. Vol. I. New York, Columbia University Press, 1970.

1897 Hutchinson, F. E. Milton and the English Mind. New York, Collier, 1962.

1898 Kermode, F., ed. The Living Milton: Essays by Various Hands. London, Routledge & K. Paul, 1960.

1899 Kranidas, T., ed. New Essays on Paradise Lost. Berkeley, University of California Press, 1970.

1900 Krouse, F. M. Milton's Samson and the Christian Tradition. Princeton, Princeton University Press, 1949.

1901 Le Conte, E. S. A Milton Dictionary. New York, AMS Press, 1969.

1902 Lewis, C. S. A Preface to Paradise Lost. Oxford, Oxford University Press, 1942.

1903 Lockwood, L. E. Lexicon to the English Poetical Works of John Milton. New York, Macmillan, 1907; repr. New York, B. Franklin, 1969.

1904 Martz, L. L., ed. Milton: A Collection of Critical Essays. Englewood Cliffs, N. J., Prentice-Hall, 1966.

1905 Murray, P. Milton: The Modern Phase. A Study of Twentieth Century Criticism. London, Longmans, 1967.

1906 Nicolson, M. John Milton: A Reader's Guide to His Poetry. New York, Farrar, 1964.

1907 Parker, W. R. Milton: A Biography. Vol. I: The Life. Vol. II: Commentary, Notes, Index and Finding List. Oxford, Clarendon Press, 1968.

1908 Patrides, C. A. Milton and the Christian Tradition. Oxford, Clarendon Press, 1966.

1909 _____ . Milton's Lycidas: The Tradition and the Poem. New York, Holt, 1961.

1910 Peter, J. A Critique of Paradise Lost. New York, Archon, 1970.

1911 Pope, E. M. Paradise Regained: The Tradition and the Poem. New York, Russell & Russell, 1962.

1912 Ricks, C. B. Milton's Grand Style. Oxford, Clarendon Press, 1963.

1913 Samuel, I. Plato and Milton. Ithaca, N. Y., Cornell University Press, 1947.

1914 Steadman, J. M. Milton's Epic Characters: Image and Idol. Chapel Hill, University of North Carolina Press, 1968.

1915 Summers, J. H., ed. The Lyric and Dramatic Milton. New York, Columbia University Press, 1965.

1916 Thorpe, J. E., ed. Milton Criticism: Selections from Four Centuries. New York, Octagon, 1966.

1917 Tillyard, E. M. W. Studies in Milton. New York, Barnes & Noble, 1960.

1918 _____ . The Miltonic Setting. New York, Barnes & Noble, 1963.

1919 Wadlock, A. J. A. Paradise Lost and Its Critics. Cambridge, Cambridge University Press, 1961.

1920 Williamson, G. Milton and Others. 2d ed. Chicago, University of Chicago Press, 1970.

18TH CENTURY POETRY—TEXTS

1921 Bredvold, L. I., A. D. McKillop, and L. Whitney, eds. Eighteenth Century Poetry and Prose. New York, Ronald Press, 1956.

1922 Ellis, F. H., ed. Poems on Affairs of State: Augustan Satirical Verse, 1660-1714. Vol. 6: 1697-1704. New Haven, Conn., Yale University Press, 1970.

1923 Harrison, T. P., ed. The Pastoral Elegy. Austin, University of Texas Press, 1939.

1924 Lord, G. de F., ed. Poems on Affairs of State: Augustan Satirical Verse, 1660-1714. Vol. I: 1660-1678. New Haven, Conn., Yale University Press, 1963.

1925 Moore, C. A., ed. English Poetry of the Eighteenth Century. New York, Holt, 1935.

1926 Quintana, R., and A. Whitley, eds. English Poetry of the Mid and Late Eighteenth Century: An Historical Anthology. New York, Knopf, 1963.

1927 Smith, D. N., ed. The Oxford Book of Eighteenth Century Verse. Oxford, Oxford University Press, 1926.

1928 Spacks, P. M., ed. Eighteenth Century Poetry. Englewood Cliffs, N. J., Prentice-Hall, 1964.

1929 Sutherland, J. R., ed. Early Eighteenth Century Poetry. London, E. Arnold, 1965.

1930 Sypher, W., ed. Enlightened England. An Anthology of English Literature from Dryden to Blake. New York, Norton, 1962.

1931 Tillotson, G., P. Fussell, Jr., M. Waingrow, and B. Rogerson, eds. Eighteenth Century English Literature. New York, Harcourt, 1969.

18TH CENTURY POETRY—CRITICISM

1932 Arthos, J. The Language of Natural Description in Eighteenth Century Poetry. Ann Arbor, University of Michigan Press, 1949.

1933 Aubin, R. A. Topographical Poetry in XVIIIth Century England. New York, Modern Language Association of America, 1936.

1934 Bond, R. P. English Burlesque Poetry, 1700-1750. Cambridge, Mass., Harvard University Press, 1932.

1935 Brown, W. C. The Triumph of Form. A Study of the Later Masters of the Heroic Couplet. Chapel Hill, University of North Carolina Press, 1948.

1936 Deane, C. V. Aspects of Eighteenth Century Nature Poetry. New York, Barnes & Noble, 1968.

1937 Draper, J. W. The Funeral Elegy and the Rise of English Romanticism. New York, Octagon, 1967.

1938 Fitzgerald, M. M. First Follow Nature: Primitivism in English Poetry, 1725-1750. New York, King's Crown Press, 1947.

1939 Piper, W. B. The Heroic Couplet. Cleveland, Case Western Reserve, 1969.

1940 Sickels, E. M. The Gloomy Egoist: Moods and Themes of Melancholy from Gray to Keats. New York, Octagon, 1969.

1941 Spacks, P. A. The Insistance of Horror: Aspects of the Supernatural in Eighteenth Century Poetry. Cambridge, Mass., Harvard University Press, 1962.

1942 Spacks, P. M. The Poetry of Vision: Five Eighteenth Century Poets. Cambridge, Mass., Harvard University Press, 1967.

1943 Sutherland, J. R. A Preface to Eighteenth Century Poetry. Oxford, Clarendon Press, 1948.

1944 Tillotson, G. Augustan Poetic Diction. London, Athlone, 1964.

1945 Trickett, R. The Honest Muse: A Study in Augustan Verse. Oxford, Clarendon Press, 1967.

1946 Wasserman, E. R. Elizabethan Poetry in the Eighteenth Century. Urbana, University of Illinois Press, 1947.

18TH CENTURY POETRY—INDIVIDUAL AUTHORS

William Blake (1757-1827)

WORKS

1947 Songs of Innocence, 1789
1948 The Book of Thel, 1789
1949 The French Revolution, 1791
1950 The Marriage of Heaven and Hell, 1793
1951 Visions of the Daughters of Albion, 1793
1952 Songs of Innocence and Experience, 1794
1953 The Book of Urizen, 1794
1954 The Book of Los, 1795
1955 The Book of Ahania, 1795
1956 The Song of Los, 1795
1957 Milton, 1803
1958 Jerusalem, 1804
1959 The Ghost of Abel, 1822

BIBLIOGRAPHIES

1960 Bentley, G. E., Jr., and M. K. Nurmi. A Blake Bibliography: Annotated Lists of Works, Studies and Blakeana. Minneapolis, University of Minnesota Press, 1964.

1961 Jugaku, B. A Bibliographical Study of William Blake's Note-Book. 1953. Repr. New York, Haskell House, 1971.

1962 Keynes, G. L. A Bibliography of William Blake. New York, Grolier, 1921. Repr. New York, Kraus, 1969.

TEXTS

1963 Bateson, F. W., ed. Selected Poems. New York, Barnes & Noble, 1957.

1964 Bloom, H., and D. V. Erdman, eds. Complete Poetical Works. New York, Doubleday, 1965.

1965 Erdman, D. V., ed. The Poetry and Prose of William Blake. Garden City, N. Y., Doubleday, 1965.

1966 Frye, N., ed. Selected Poetry and Prose of William Blake. New York, Modern Library, 1953.

1967 Holloway, J., ed. Blake: The Lyric Poetry. London, E. Arnold, 1968.

1968 Kazin, A., ed. The Portable Blake. New York, Viking, 1946.

1969 Keynes, G. L., ed. The Letters of William Blake. London, Hart-Davies, 1968.

1970 _____ , ed. Complete Works: Variorum Edition. New York, Random, 1957.

1971 _____ , ed. The Complete Writings of William Blake with Variant Readings. Oxford, Standard Authors, 1966.

CRITICISM

1972 Adams, H. William Blake: A Reading of the Shorter Poems. Seattle, University of Washington Press, 1963.

1973 Altizer, T. J. The New Apocalypse: The Radical Christian Vision of William Blake. East Lansing, Michigan State University Press, 1967.

1974 Bentley, G. E., Jr. Blake Records. Oxford, Oxford University Press, 1969.

1975 Bloom, H. Blake's Apocalypse: A Study in Poetic Argument. New York, Doubleday, 1963.

1976 Davron, S. F. A Blake Dictionary: The Ideas and Symbols of William Blake. Providence, Brown University Press, 1965.

1977 Erdman, D. V. Blake: Prophet Against Empire. Princeton, Princeton University Press, 1954.

1978 _____ . A Concordance to the Writings of William Blake. Ithaca, N. Y., Cornell University Press, 1967.

1979 _____ , and J. E. Grant, eds. Blake's Visionary Forms Dramatic. Princeton, Princeton University Press, 1970.

1980 Fisher, P. F. The Valley of Vision: Blake as Prophet and Revolutionary. Ed. by N. Frye. Toronto, University of Toronto Press, 1961.

1981 Frye, N. Fearful Symmetry: A Study of William Blake. Princeton, Princeton University Press, 1947.

1982 _____ , ed. Blake: A Collection of Critical Essays. Englewood Cliffs, N. J., Prentice-Hall, 1966.

1983 Gilham, D. G. Blake Contrary States: The Songs of Innocence and Experience as Dramatic Poems. Cambridge, Cambridge University Press, 1966.

1984 Gleckner, R. F. The Piper and the Bard: A Study of William Blake. Detroit, Wayne University Press, 1959.

1985 Harper, G. M. The Neoplatonism of William Blake. Chapel Hill, University of North Carolina Press, 1961.

1986 Lister, R. William Blake: An Introduction to the Man and His Work. New York, Ungar, 1970.

1987 Ostriker, A. Vision and Verse in William Blake. Madison, University of Wisconsin Press, 1965.

1988 Paley, M. D., ed. Twentieth Century Interpretations of Songs of Innocence and of Experience: A Collection of Critical Essays. Englewood Cliffs, N. J., Prentice-Hall, 1969.

1989 Plowman, M. An Introduction to the Study of Blake. London, Frank Cass, 1967.

1990 Raine, K. Blake and Tradition. London, Routledge & K. Paul, 1968.

1991 Schorer, M. William Blake: The Politics of Vision. New York, Random, 1946.

1992 Singer, J. K. The Unholy Bible: A Psychological Interpretation of William Blake. London, Putnam, 1970.

Robert Burns (1759-1796)

WORKS

1993 Poems, Chiefly in the Scottish Dialect, 1786

BIBLIOGRAPHIES

1994 Egerer, J. W. A Bibliography of Robert Burns. Carbondale, Southern Illinois University Press, 1965.

1995 Gibson, J. The Bibliography of Robert Burns, with Biographical and Bibliographical Notes and Sketches of Burns Clubs, Monuments and Statues. Kilmarnock, McKie, 1881. Repr. New York, Kraus, 1969.

TEXTS

1996 Barke, J., ed. Poems and Songs. New York, Collins, 1955.

1997 Daiches, D. Robert Burns Commonplace Books. Carbondale, Southern Illinois University Press, 1966.

1998 Ferguson, J. de L., ed. Selected Letters of Robert Burns. Oxford, Clarendon Press, 1931.

1999 Fraser, G. S., ed. Selected Poems. New York, Barnes & Noble, 1960.

2000 Gray, A., ed. Poems and Songs. Edinburgh, Oliver & Boyd, 1945.

2001 Henley, W. E., ed. Complete Poetical Works. Boston, Houghton, 1968.

2002 Kinsley, J., ed. The Poems and Sonds of Robert Burns. Oxford, Clarendon Press, 1968.

2003 Robertson, J. L., ed. Poetical Works. Oxford, Standard Authors, 1904.

2004 Thornton, R. D., ed. Selected Poetry and Prose. Boston, Houghton, 1966.

2005 Weston, J. C., ed. Robert Burns: Selections. Indianapolis, Bobbs-Merrill, 1967.

CRITICISM

2006 Campbell, W. B. A Burns Companion. Aberdeen, Blair, 1953.

2007 Crawford, T. Burns: A Study of the Poems and Songs. Edinburgh, Oliver & Boyd, 1960.

2008 Daiches, D. Robert Burns. Rev. ed. New York, Macmillan, 1967.

2009 Ferguson, J. de L. Pride and Passion: Robert Burns. New York, Russell & Russell, 1964.

2010 Fitzhugh, R. T. Robert Burns, the Man and the Poet: A Round Unvarnished Account. Boston, Houghton, 1970.

2011 Hill, J. C. The Love Songs and Heroines of Robert Burns. London, Dent, 1961.

2012 Lindsay, J. M., ed. The Burns Encyclopaedia. London, Hutchinson, 1959.

2013 Reid, J. B. A Complete Word and Phrase Concordance to the Poems and Songs of Robert Burns. Glasgow, Kerr, 1889. Repr. New York, B. Franklin, 1969.

2014 Snyder, F. B. Burns: His Personality, his Reputation, and his Art. Toronto, University of Toronto Press, 1936.

William Cowper (1731-1800)

WORKS

2015 Olney Hymns, 1779   2016 The Task, 1785

BIBLIOGRAPHIES

2017 Russell, N. A Bibliography of William Cowper to 1837. Oxford, Bibliographical Society, 1963.

TEXTS

2018 Jeffares, A. N., ed. Selected Poems and Letters. Oxford, Oxford University Press, 1963.

2019 Milford, H. S., ed. Poetical Works. 4th ed. Oxford, Standard Authors, 1934.

2020 Spiller, B., ed. Cowper: Poetry and Prose. London, Hart & Davis, 1968.

2021 Van Doren, M., ed. Selected Letters. New York, Farrar, 1951.

CRITICISM

2022 Golden, M. In Search of Stability: The Poetry of William Cowper. New York, Bookman Associates, 1960.

2023 Hartley, L. C. Cowper Humanitarian. Chapel Hill, University of North Carolina Press, 1938.

2024 Neve, J. A Concordance to the Poetical Works of William Cowper. 1887. Repr. New York, Haskell House, 1969.

Thomas Gray (1716-1771)

WORKS

2025 Elegy Written In a Country Churchyard, 1751

2026 Poems, 1753

2027 Installation Ode, 1769

BIBLIOGRAPHIES

2028 Northup, C. S. A Bibliography of Thomas Gray. New Haven, Conn., Yale University Press, 1916. Repr. New York, Russell & Russell, 1970.

2029 Starr, H. W. A Bibliography of Thomas Gray, 1917-1951; with Material Supplementary to C. S. Northup's Bibliography of Thomas Gray. Philadelphia, University of Pennsylvania Press, 1953. Repr. New York, Kraus, 1969.

TEXTS

2030 Beresford, J., ed. Letters. Oxford, World's Classics, 1925.

2031 Gosse, E., ed. Works in Verse and Prose. New York, AMS Press, 1844. 4 vols.

2032 Johnston, A., ed. Selected Poems of Thomas Gray and William Collins. London, E. Arnold, 1967.

2033 Krutch, J. W., ed. Selected Letters of Thomas Gray. New York, Farrar, 1952.

2034 Starr, H. W., and J. R. Hendrickson, eds. The Complete Poems of Thomas Gray, English, Latin, and Greek. Oxford, Clarendon Press, 1966.

CRITICISM

2035 Cook, A. S. A Concordance to the English Poems of Thomas Gray. London, P. Smith, 1968.

2036 Golden, M. Thomas Gray. New York, Twayne, 1964.

2037 Jones, W. Powell. Thomas Gray, Scholar. New York, Russell & Russell, 1937.

2038 Ketton-Cremer, R. W. Thomas Gray: A Biography. London, Cambridge University Press, 1958..

2039 Starr, H. W. Gray as a Literary Critic. Philadelphia, Ph.D. Thesis, University of Pennsylvania, 1941.

2040 _____ . Twentieth Century Interpretations of Gray's Elegy: A Collection of Critical Essays. Englewood Cliffs, N. J., Prentice-Hall, 1968.

Alexander Pope (1688-1744)

WORKS

2041 An Essay on Criticism, 1711
2042 Windsor Forest, 1713
2043 The Rape of the Lock, 1714
2044 Iliad, trans., 1720
2045 Odyssey, trans., 1726
2046 The Dunciad, 1728, 1743
2047 An Essay on Man, 1734

BIBLIOGRAPHIES

2048 Griffith, R. H. Alexander Pope: A Bibliography. Austin, University of Texas Press, 1922-1927.

2049 Guerinot, J. V. Pamphlet Attacks on Alexander Pope, 1711-1744: A Descriptive Bibliography. New York, New York University Press, 1969.

2050 Tobin, J. E. Pope: A List of Critical Studies, 1895-1944. New York, Cosmopolitan Science and Art Service Co., 1945.

TEXTS

2051 Audra, E., and A. Williams, eds. Pastoral Poetry and an Essay on Criticism. London, Methuen, 1961.

2052 Bateson, F. W., ed. Epistles to Several Persons. London, Methuen, 1961.

2053 Boynton, H. W., ed. Complete Poetical Works. Boston, Houghton, 1968.

2054 Butt, J., ed. The Poems of Alexander Pope. New Haven, Conn., Yale University Press, 1963.

2055 Davis, H., ed. Poetical Works. Oxford, Authors, 1967.

2056 Erskine-Hill, H. N., ed. Horatian Satires and Epistles. London, Oxford University Press, 1964.

2057 Goldgar, B. A., ed. Literary Criticism of Alexander Pope. Lincoln, University of Nebraska Press, 1965.

2058 Sherburn, G., ed. The Correspondence. Oxford, University of Oxford Press, 1956. 5 vols.

2059 _____ , ed. The Best of Pope. New York, Ronald, 1940.

CRITICISM

2060 Abbott, E. Concordance to the Works of Alexander Pope. 1875. Repr. New York, Kraus, 1968.

2061 Aden, J. M. Something Like Horace: Studies in the Art and Allusions of Pope's Horatian Satires. Nashville, Tenn., Vanderbilt University Press, 1969.

2062 Boyce, B. The Character-Sketches in Pope's Poetry. Durham, N. C., Duke University Press, 1962.

2063 Brower, R. A. Alexander Pope: The Poetry of Allusion. London, Oxford University Press, 1968.

2064 Dixon, P., ed. The World of Pope's Satires: An Introduction to the Epistles and Imitation of Horace. New York, Methuen, 1969.

2065 Dobrée, B. Alexander Pope. Oxford, Oxford University Press, 1963.

2066 Edwards, T. R., Jr. The Dark Estate: A Reading of Pope. Berkeley, University of California Press, 1963.

2067 Harte, W. An Essay on Satire, Particularly on the Dunciad. Los Angeles, W. A. Clark Memorial Library, 1968.

2068 Knight, D. M. Pope and the Heroic Tradition: A Critical Study of His Iliad. New Haven, Conn., Yale University Press, 1951.

2069 Mack, M., ed. Essential Articles for the Study of Alexander Pope. Hamden, Conn., Archon, 1968.

2070 _____ . The Garden and the City: Retirement and Politics in the Later Poetry of Pope, 1731-1743. Toronto, University of Toronto Press, 1969.

2071 McDonald, W. L. Pope and His Critics: A Study in Eighteenth Century Personalities. London, Dent, 1951.

2072 O'Neill, J. Critics on Pope: Readings in Literary Criticism. Coral Gables, Fla., University of Miami Press, 1969.

2073 Rogers, R. W. The Major Satires of Pope. Urbana, University of Illinois Press, 1955.

2074 Rousseau, G. S., ed. Twentieth Century Interpretations of The Rape of the Lock. Englewood Cliffs, N. J., Prentice-Hall, 1969.

2075 Sherburn, G. The Early Career of Alexander Pope. Oxford, Clarendon Press, 1968.

2076 Tillotson, G. On the Poetry of Pope. Oxford, Oxford University Press, 1938.

2077 _____ . The Moral Poetry of Pope. New Castle-on-Tyne, Literary & Philosophical Society of N.C.U.T., 1946.

2078 White, D. H. Pope and the Context of Controversy: The Manipulation of Ideas in An Essay on Man. Chicago, University of Chicago Press, 1970.

2079 Williams, A. L. Pope's Dunicad: A Study of Its Meaning. Baton Rouge, Louisiana State University Press, 1955.

2080 Wimsatt, W. K., Jr. The Portraits of Alexander Pope. New Haven, Conn., Yale University Press, 1965.

James Thomson (1700-1748)

WORKS

2081 The Seasons:
    Winter, 1726
    Summer, 1727
    Spring, 1728
    Autumn, 1730

2082 Liberty, 1736
2083 Agamemnon, 1738
2084 Edward and Eleanora, 1744
2085 Castle of Indolence, 1748
2086 Coriolanus, 1749

TEXTS

2087 Poems and Plays. London, Smith, 1941.

2088 The Poetical Works of James Thomson. Ed. Rev. D. C. Tovey. London, Bell, 1897. 2 vols.

2089 Robertson, J. L., ed. Complete Poetical Works. Oxford, Oxford University Press, 1908.

CRITICISM

2090 Cohen, R. The Art of Discrimination: Thomson's The Seasons and the Language of Criticism. Berkeley, University of California Press, 1964.

2091 _____ . The Unfolding of The Seasons: A Study of James Thomson's Poem. Baltimore, Johns Hopkins, 1970.

2092 Grant, D. James Thomson: Poet of The Seasons. London, Cressett, 1951.

2093 Spacks, P. M. The Varied God: A Critical Study of Thomson's The Seasons. Berkeley, University of California Press, 1959.

PROSE FICTION 1660-1800—BIBLIOGRAPHIES

2094 Bell, I. F., and D. Baird. The English Novel: 1578-1956. A Checklist of Twentieth Century Criticism. Denver, Swallow, 1959.

2095 Bonheim, H. The English Novel Before Richardson: A Checklist of Texts and Criticism to 1970. Metuchen, Scarecrow, 1971.

2096 Cordasco, F. The Eighteenth Century Novel: A Handlist of General Histories and Articles of the Last Twenty-Five Years with a Notice of Bibliographical Guides. Brooklyn, B. Franklin, 1950.

2097 McBurney, W. H., and C. M. Taylor. English Prose Fiction 1700-1800. Urbana, University of Illinois Press, 1965.

PROSE FICTION 1660-1800—TEXTS

2098 Bredvold, L. I., A. D. McKillop, and L. Whitney, eds. Eighteenth Century Poetry and Prose. New York, Ronald Press, 1956.

2099 Mish, C. C., ed. English Prose Fiction 1661-1700. Charlotesville, University of Virginia Press, 1953.

2100 _____ , ed. The Anchor Anthology of Short Fiction of the Seventeenth Century. Garden City, N. Y., Doubleday, 1963.

2101 _____ , ed. Restoration Prose Fiction, 1666-1700: An Anthology of Representative Pieces. Lincoln, University of Nebraska Press, 1970.

2102 Paterson, S., ed. The Counterfeit Laty Unveiled and Other Criminal Fiction of Seventeenth Century England: A Selection. New York, Anchor, 1961.

2103 Spector, R. D., ed. Seven Masterpieces of Gothic Horror. New York, Bantam, 1963.

2104 Steeves, H. R., ed. Three Eighteenth Century Romances: The Castle of Otrando, Vathek, The Romance of the Forest. New York, Scribner's, 1931.

2105 Tillotson, G., P. Fussell, Jr., M. Waingrow, and B. Rogerson, eds. Eighteenth Century English Literature. New York, Harcourt, 1969.

2106 Würzbach, N., ed. The Novel in Letters: Epistolary Fiction in the Early English Novel, 1678-1740. Miami, University of Miami Press, 1969.

PROSE FICTION 1660-1800—CRITICISM

2107 Barnett, G. L., ed. Eighteenth Century British Novelists on the Novel. New York, Appleton, 1968.

2108 Black, F. G. The Epistolary Novel in the Late Eighteenth Century: A Descriptive and Bibliographical Study. Eugene, University of Oregon Press, 1940.

2109 Block, A. The English Novel, 1740-1850: A Catalogue. New York, Oceana, 1962.

2110 Donovan, R. A. The Shaping Vision: Imagination in the English Novel from Defoe to Dickens. Ithaca, N. Y., Cornell University Press, 1966.

2111 Forster, E. M. Aspects of the Novel. New York, Harcourt, 1947.

2112 Foster, J. R. History of the Pre-Romantic Novel in England. New York, Kraus, 1966.

2113 Hamilton, K. G. The Two Harmonies: Poetry and Prose in the Seventeenth Century. Oxford, Clarendon Press, 1963.

2114 Kettle, A. Introduction to the English Novel. New York, Harper, 1960. 2 vols.

2115 McKillop, A. D. The Early Masters of English Fiction. Lawrence, University of Kansas Press, 1956.

2116 Paulson, R. Satire and the Novel in Eighteenth Century England. New Haven, Conn., Yale University Press, 1967.

2117 Sherbo, A. Studies in the Eighteenth Century English Novel. East Lansing, Michigan State University Press, 1970.

2118 Spearman, D. The Novel and Society. London, Routledge & K. Paul, 1966.

2119 Spector, R. D., ed. Essays on the Eighteenth Century Novel. Bloomington, Indiana University Press, 1965.

2120 Steeves, H. R. Before Jane Austen: The Shaping of the English Novel in the Eighteenth Century. New York, Holt, 1965.

2121 Sutherland, J. R. English Literature of the Late Seventeenth Century. London, Oxford University Press, 1969.

2122 Tompkins, J. M. S. The Popular Novel in England, 1770-1800. Lincoln, University of Nebraska Press, 1961.

PROSE FICTION 1660-1800—INDIVIDUAL AUTHORS

John Bunyan (1628-1688)

WORKS

2123 The Pilgrim's Progress, 1678

2124 The Life and Death of Mr. Badman, 1680

2125 The Holy War, 1682

2126 The Pilgrim's Progress, 2d Part, 1684

BIBLIOGRAPHIES

2127 Harrison, F. M. A Bibliography of the Works of John Bunyan. London, Bibliographical Society, 1932.

TEXTS

2128 Adams, A. K., ed. The Pilgrim's Progress. New York, Dodd, 1968.

2129 Harrison, G. B., ed. The Pilgrim's Progress. New York, Dutton, 1941.

2130 Kepler, T. S., ed. The Spiritual Riches of John Bunyan: Selected Prose. Cleveland, World Publishing Company, 1952.

2131 Sharrock, R., ed. The Pilgrim's Progress. Baltimore, Penguin, 1965.

2132 Talon, H. A., ed. God's Knotty Log: Selected Writings of John Bunyan. Cleveland, World Publishing Company, 1961.

2133 Thorpe, J. E., ed. The Pilgrim's Progress, Boston, Houghton, 1969.

2134 Wharey, J. B., ed. The Pilgrim's Progress, From This World To That Which Is To Come. Oxford, Oxford University Press, 1960.

CRITICISM

2135 Frye, R. M. God, Man and Satan: Patterns of Christian Thought and Life in Paradise Lost, Pilgrim's Progress and the Great Theologians. Princeton, Princeton University Press, 1960.

2136 Macauley, T. B., ed. Essays on The Pilgrim's Progress. Cambridge, Cambridge University Press, 1962.

2137 Sharrock, R. John Bunyan. London, Macmillan, 1968.

2138 Talon, H. A. John Bunyan: The Man and His Works. Trans. by Barbara Well. London, British Book Center, 1955.

2139 Tindall, W. Y. John Bunyan, Mechanic Preacher. New York, Russell & Russell, 1964.

2140 Winslow, O. E. John Bunyan. New York, Macmillan, 1961.

Daniel Defoe (1660-1731)

WORKS

2141 Robinson Crusoe, 1719

2142 The Life of Captain Singleton, 1720

2143 Annus Mirabilis, 1722

2144 Moll Flanders, 1722

2145 A Journal of the Plague Years, 1722

2146 Colonel Jack, 1722

2147 Roxana, 1724

2148 History of the Pirates, 1724-28

TEXTS

2149 Boulton, J. T., ed. Daniel Defoe. New York, Schocken, 1965.

2150 Healey, G. H., ed. The Meditations of Daniel Defoe, Now First Printed. Cummington, Mass., Cummington Press, 1946.

2151 _____ , ed. Letters. Oxford, Clarendon Press, 1955.

2152 Novak, M. E., ed. Of Captain Mission and His Crew. Los Angeles, W. A. Clark Memorial Library, 1961.

2153 Novels and Miscellaneous Works of Daniel De Foe. London, G. Bell, 1878-81. 7 vols.

2154 Novels and Selected Writings. New York, Houghton, 1928. 14 vols.

2155 Shugrue, M., ed. Selected Poetry and Prose of Daniel Defoe. New York, Holt, 1968.

CRITICISM

2156 Baine, R. M. Defoe and the Supernatural. Chicago, Chicago University Press, 1969.

2157 Ellis, F. H., ed. Twentieth Century Interpretations of Robinson Crusoe. Englewood Cliffs, N. J., Prentice-Hall, 1969.

2158 Freeman, W. The Incredible Defoe. London, Jenkins, 1950.

2159 Hunter, J. P. The Reluctant Pilgrim. Defoe's Emblematic Method and Quest for Form in Robinson Crusoe. Baltimore, Johns Hopkins, 1966.

2160 Moore, J. R. Daniel Defoe: Citizen of the Modern World. Chicago, University of Chicago Press, 1958.

2161 Novak, M. E. Defoe and the Nature of Man. London, Oxford University Press, 1963.

2162 Ross, J. F. Swift and Defoe: A Study in Relationship. Berkeley, University of California Press, 1941.

2163 Secord, A. W. Studies in the Narrative Method of Defoe. Urbana, University of Illinois Press, 1924.

2164 Shinagel, M. Daniel Defoe and Middle Class Gentility. Cambridge, Mass., Harvard University Press, 1968.

2165 Starr, G. A. Defoe and Spiritual Autobiography. Princeton, Princeton University Press, 1965.

2166 Watt, I. The Rise of the Novel: Studies in Defoe, Richardson and Fielding. Berkeley, University of California Press, 1957.

Henry Fielding (1707-1754)

WORKS

2167 An Apology for the Life of Mrs. Shamela Andrews, 1741

2168 The History of the Adventures of Joseph Andrews, and of His Friend Mr. Abraham Adams, 1742

2169 The History of Tom Jones, a Foundling, 1747

2170 Amelia, 1751

BIBLIOGRAPHIES

2171 Cordasco, F. Fielding: A List of Critical Studies, 1895-1946. Brooklyn, B. Franklin, 1948.

TEXTS

2172 Henley, W. E., et al., eds. Complete Works. 16 vols. Repr. 1903 ed. New York, Barnes & Noble, 1967.

2173 Williams, J., ed. The Criticism of Henry Fielding. New York, Barnes & Noble, 1970.

CRITICISM

2174 Alter, R. Fielding and the Nature of the Novel. Cambridge, Mass., Harvard University Press, 1968.

2175 Batterstin, M. C. The Moral Basis of Fielding's Art: A Study of Joseph Andrews. Middletown, Conn., Wesleyan University Press, 1959.

2176 _____ . Twentieth Century Interpretations of Tom Jones. Englewood Cliffs, N. J., Prentice-Hall, 1968.

2177 Bissell, F. O. Fielding's Theory of the Novel. Ithaca, N. Y., Cornell University Press, 1933.

2178 Cross, W. L. The History of Henry Fielding. New Haven, Conn., Yale University Press, 1918.

2179 Golden, M. Fielding's Moral Philosophy. Amherst, University of Massachusetts Press, 1966.

2180 Hatfield, G. W. Henry Fielding and the Language of Irony. Chicago, University of Chicago Press, 1968.

2181 Irwin, W. R. The Making of Jonathan Wild: A Study in the Literary Method of Henry Fielding. Hamden, Conn., Archon, 1966.

2182 Johnson, M. Fielding's Art of Fiction: Eleven Essays on Shamela, Joseph Andrews, Tom Jones and Amelia. Philadelphia, University of Pennsylvania Press, 1962.

2183 Levine, G. R. Henry Fielding and the Dry Mock: A Study of the Techniques of Irony in his Early Works. The Hague, Mouton, 1967.

2184 Miller, H. K. Essays on Fielding's Miscellanies: A Commentary on Volume One. Princeton, Princeton University Press, 1961.

2185 Paulson, R., ed. Fielding: A Collection of Critical Essays. Englewood Cliffs, N. J., Prentice-Hall, 1962.

2186 _____ , and T. Lockwood, eds. Henry Fielding: The Critical Heritage. New York, Barnes & Noble, 1969.

2187 Rawson, C. J. Henry Fielding. London, Routledge & K. Paul, 1968.

2188 Woods, C. B., ed. The Author's Farce. Lincoln, University of Nebraska Press, 1966.

2189 Wright, A. H. Henry Fielding: Mask and Feast. Berkeley, University of California Press, 1965.

Samuel Richardson (1689-1761)

WORKS

2190 Pamela, 1740
2191 Clarissa, 1748

2192 The History of Sir Charles Grandison, 1754

BIBLIOGRAPHIES

2193 Cordasco, F., ed. Samuel Richardson: A List of Critical Studies, 1896-1946. Brooklyn, B. Franklin, 1948.

2194 Sale, W. M. Samuel Richardson: A Bibliographical Record of his Literary Career with Historical Notes. Hamden, Conn., Archon, 1969.

TEXTS

2195 Barbauld, A. L., ed. The Correspondence of Samuel Richardson. 6 vols. New York, AMS Press, 1968.

2196 Carroll, J. J., ed. Selected Letters of Samuel Richardson. Oxford, Clarendon Press, 1964.

2197 The History of Sir Charles Grandison. 7 vols. New York, Croscup & Sterling, 1902.

2198 Pamela. New York, Croscup & Sterling, 1901.

2199 Sherburn, G., ed. Clarissa or The History of a Young Lady. Boston, Houghton, 1962.

CRITICISM

2200 Bullen, T. S. Time and Space in the Novels of Samuel Richardson. Logan, Utah State University Press, 1965.

2201 Carroll, J. J., ed. Samuel Richardson: A Collection of Critical Essays. Englewood Cliffs, N. J., Prentice-Hall, 1969.

2202 Cowler, P., ed. Twentieth Century Interpretations of Pamela. Englewood Cliffs, N. J., Prentice-Hall, 1969.

2203 Dobson, A. Samuel Richardson. Detroit, Gale, 1968.

2204 Downs, B. W. Richardson. New York, Barnes & Noble, 1970.

2205 Golden, M. Richardson's Characters. Ann Arbor, University of Michigan Press, 1963.

2206 Kearney, J. W. Samuel Richardson. London, Routledge & K. Paul, 1968.

2207 Koningberg, I. Samuel Richardson and the Dramatic Novel. Lexington, University of Kentucky Press, 1968.

2208 Kreissman, B. Pamela-Shamela: A Study of the Criticisms, Parodies and Adaptations of Richardson's Pamela. Lincoln, University of Nebraska Press, 1960.

2209 Krutch, J. W. Five Masters: A Study in the Mutations of the Novel. Bloomington, University of Indiana Press, 1959.

2210 McKillop, A. D., ed. Critical Remarks on Sir Charles Grandison, Clarissa and Pamela. Ann Arbor, University of Michigan Pub. No. 21, 1950.

2211 _____ . Richardson: Printer and Novelist. Chapel Hill, University of North Carolina Press, 1936.

Tobias George Smollett (1721-1771)

WORKS

2212 The Adventures of Roderick Random, 1748

2213 The Adventures of Peregrine Pickle, 1751

2214 The Adventures of Ferdinand Count Fathom, 1753

2215 The Reprisal, 1757

2216 The History and Adventures of an Atom, 1769

2217 The Expedition of Humphrey Clinker, 1771

BIBLIOGRAPHIES

2218 Cordasco, F. Smollett Criticism, 1770-1924: An Enumerative Bibliography. New York, B. Franklin, 1948.

2219 _____ . Smollett Criticism, 1925-1945. New York, B. Franklin, 1948.

TEXTS

2220 The Expedition of Humphrey Clinker. New York, Modern Library, 1929.

2221 Knapp, L. M., ed. The Expedition of Humphrey Clinker. Oxford, Oxford University Press, 1966.

2222 Novels. Boston, Houghton, 1926. 11 vols.

CRITICISM

2223 Boege, F. W. Smollett's Reputation as a Novelist. Princeton, Princeton University Press, 1947.

2224 Brander, L. Smollett. New York, Longmans, Green, 1951.

2225 Giddings, R. The Tradition of Smollett. London, Methuen, 1967.

2226 Goldberg, M. A. Smollett and the Scottish School: Studies in Eighteenth Century Thought. Albuquerque, University of New Mexico Press, 1959.

2227 Jones, Claude Edward. Smollett Studies. New York, Phaeton, 1971.

2228 Kahrl, G. M. Tobias Smollett, Traveller-Novelist. New York, Octagon, 1968.

2229 Knapp, L. M. Smollett: Doctor of Men and Manners. Princeton, Princeton University Press, 1949.

2230 Martz, L. L. The Later Career of Tobias Smollett. New Haven, Conn., Yale University Press, 1942.

Laurence Sterne (1713-1768)

WORKS

2231 The Case of Elijah, 1747
2232 Tristram Shandy, 1759
2233 A Sentimental Journey through France and Italy, 1768

BIBLIOGRAPHIES

2234 Cordasco, F. Laurence Sterne: A List of Critical Studies, 1896-1946. New York, B. Franklin, 1948.

2235 Hartley, L. Laurence Sterne in the Twentieth Century: An Essay and a Bibliography of Sternean Studies, 1900-1965. Chapel Hill, University of North Carolina Press, 1966.

TEXTS

2236 Cross, W. L., ed. Works. New York, AMS Press, 1970. 12 vols.

2237 Grant, D., ed. Memoirs; The Life and Opinions of Tristram Shandy; A Sentimental Journey; Selected Sermons and Letters. Cambridge, Mass., Harvard University Press, 1950.

CRITICISM

2238 Cash, A. H. Sterne's Comedy of Moral Sentiments: The Ethical Dimensions of the Journey. Pittsburgh, Duquesne University Press, 1966.

2239 Dilworth, E. N. The Unsentimental Journey of Laurence Sterne. New York, Octagon, 1969.

2240 Hartley, L. This is Lorence: A Narrative of the Reverend Lawrence Sterne. Chapel Hill, University of North Carolina Press, 1943.

2241 New, M. Laurence Sterne as Satirist: A Reading of "Tristram Shandy." Gainesville, Florida, University of Florida Press, 1969.

2242 Stedmond, J. M. The Comic Art of Laurence Sterne: Convention and Innovation in Tristram Shandy and A Sentimental Journey. Toronto, Toronto University Press, 1967.

2243 Traugott, J., ed. Laurence Sterne: A Collection of Critical Essays. Englewood Cliffs, Prentice-Hall, 1968.

2244 Watkins, W. B. C. Perilous Balance: The Tragic Genius of Swift, Johnson, and Sterne. Princeton, Princeton University Press, 1939.

2245 Yoseloff, T. A Fellow of Infinite Jest. Englewood Cliffs, N. J., Prentice-Hall, 1945.

Jonathan Swift (1667-1745)

WORKS

2246 A Tale of a Tub, 1696, 1699   2248 Gullivers Travells, 1721-25
2247 Journal to Stella, 1713   2249 A Modest Proposal, 1729

BIBLIOGRAPHIES

2250 Landa, L. A., and J. E. Tobin, eds. Swift: A List of Critical Studies Published from 1895 to 1945, with Remarks on Same Swift Manuscripts in the U.S. By H. Davis. New York, Cosmopolitan Science and Art Service Company, 1945.

2251 Scouten, A. H., ed. A Bibliography of the Writings of Jonathan Swift. Philadelphia, University of Pennsylvania Press, 1963.

2252 Stathis, J. J., comp. A Bibliography of Swift Studies, 1945-1965. Nashville, Tenn., Vanderbilt University Press, 1967.

TEXTS

2253 Collected Poems. Cambridge, Mass., Harvard University Press, 1958.

2254 Davis, H., ed. The Prose Works of Jonathan Swift. Oxford, B. Blackwell, 1939-59.

2255 _____ , ed. Poetical Works. London, Oxford University Press, 1967.

2256 Hayward, J., ed. Selected Prose Writings of Swift. New York, Random, 1949.

2257 Landa, L. A., ed. Gulliver's Travels and Other Writings. Boston, Houghton, 1960.

2258 Reeves, J., ed. Selected Poems. New York, Barnes & Noble, 1967.

2259 Rosenheim, E. W., ed. Selected Prose and Poetry. New York, Holt, 1959.

2260 Ross, J. F., ed. Gulliver's Travels. London, E. Arnold, 1968.

2261 Williams, H., ed. Journal to Stella. Oxford, Oxford University Press, 1948. 2 vols.

2262 _____ , ed. The Poems of Jonathan Swift. Oxford, Clarendon Press, 1937.

2263 _____ , ed. The Correspondence of Jonathan Swift. Oxford, Clarendon, 1963. 5 vols.

2264 Van Doren, C., ed. The Portable Swift. New York, Viking, 1948.

CRITICISM

2265 Brady, F., ed. Twentieth Century Interpretations of Gulliver's Travels: A Collection of Critical Essays. Englewood Cliffs, N. J., Prentice-Hall, 1968.

2266 Bullitt, J. M. Jonathan Swift and the Anatomy of Satire: A Study of Satiric Technique. Cambridge, Mass., Harvard University Press, 1953.

2267 Case, A. E. Four Essays on Gulliver's Travels. Princeton, Princeton University Press, 1945.

2268 Clark, J. R. Form and Frenzy in Swift's Tale of a Tub. Ithaca, N. Y., Cornell University Press, 1970.

2269 Davis, H. The Satire of Swift. Oxford, Oxford University Press, 1964.

2270 Dennis, N. Jonathan Swift: A Short Character. New York, Macmillan, 1964.

2271 Eddy, W. A. Gulliver's Travels: A Critical Study. New York, Russell & Russell, 1963.

2272 Ehrenpreis, I. Swift: The Man, His Works and His Age. Cambridge, Mass., Harvard University Press, 1967. 3 vols.

2273 Ewald, W. B. The Masks of Swift. Oxford, B. Blackwell, 1954.

2274 Goldgar, B. A. The Curse of Party: Swift's Relation with Addison and Steele. Lincoln, University of Nebraska Press, 1961.

2275 Johnson, M. The Son of Wit: Swift as a Poet. Syracuse, University of Syracuse Press, 1950.

2276 Murry, J. M. Swift: A Critical Biography. New York, Farrar, 1967.

2277 Price, M. Swift's Rhetorical Art. New Haven, Conn., Yale University Press, 1953.

2278 Quintana, R. The Mind and Art of Swift. London, P. Smith, 1936.

2279 _____ . Swift: An Introduction. London, Oxford University Press, 1962.

2280 Rosenheim, E. W., Jr. Swift and the Satirist's Art. Chicago, University of Chicago Press, 1963.

2281 Ross, J. F. Swift and Defoe: A Study in Relationship. Berkeley, University of California Press, 1941.

2282 Tuveson, E. L., ed. Swift: A Collection of Critical Essays. Englewood Cliffs, N. J., Prentice-Hall, 1964.

2283 Vickers, B., ed. The World of Jonathan Swift: Essays for the Tercentenary. London, B. Blackwell, 1968.

2284 Voigt, M. Swift and the Twentieth Century. Detroit, Wayne University Press, 1964.

2285 Williams, K. Swift and the Age of Compromise. Lawrence, Kansas University Press, 1959.

Horace Walpole, Earl of Oxford (1717-1797)

WORKS

2286 The Castle of Otranto, 1765   2288 The Mysterious Mother, 1768
2287 Historic Doubt on the Life
and Reign of King Richard
the Third, 1768

BIBLIOGRAPHIES

2289 Hagen, A. T., ed. A Bibliography of the Strawberry Hill Press. New Haven, Conn., Yale University Press, 1942.

2290 _____ , ed. A Bibliography of Horace Walpole. New Haven, Conn., Yale University Press, 1948.

TEXTS

2291 Lewis, W. S., ed. The Castle of Otranto: A Gothic Story. London, Oxford University Press, 1964.

2292 _____ , ed. The Yale Edition of Walpole's Correspondence. New Haven, Conn., Yale University Press, 1937-1955. 21 vols.

2293 _____ , and R. S. Brown, Jr., eds. Horace Walpole's Correspondence with George Montagu. New Haven, Conn., Yale University Press, 1941.

CRITICISM

2294 Hagen, A. T. A Catalogue of Horace Walpole's Library. New Haven, Conn., Yale University Press, 1948.

2295 Mehrotra, K. K. Horace Walpole and the English Novel: A Study of the Influence of the Castle of Otranto, 1764-1820. London, Russell & Russell, 1970.

2296 Smith, W. H., ed. Horace Walpole: Writer, Politician, and Connoisseur. Essays on the 250th Anniversary of Walpole's Birth. New Haven, Conn., Yale University Press, 1967.

PROSE NON-FICTION—TEXTS

2297 Adams, H. H., and B. Hathaway, eds. Dramatic Essays of the Neo-classic Age. New York, Blom, 1965.

2298 Chapman, G. W., ed. Literary Criticism in England, 1660-1800. New York, Knopf, 1966.

2299 Durham, W. H., ed. Critical Essays of the Eighteenth Century, 1700-1725. New York, Russell & Russell, 1961.

2300 Elledge, S., ed. Eighteenth Century Critical Essays. Ithaca, Cornell University Press, 1961. 2 vols.

2301 Hynes, S., ed. Literary Criticism. Restoration and Eighteenth Century. New York, Appleton, 1963.

2302 Sackett, S. J., ed. English Literary Criticism, 1726-1750. Fort Hays, Kan., Fort Hays State College, 1962.

2303 Spacks, Patricia Ann, ed. Late Augustan Prose. Englewood Cliffs, N. J., Prentice-Hall, 1970.

PROSE NON-FICTION—CRITICISM

2304 Bate, W. J., ed. From Classic to Romantic. New York, Harper, 1961.

2305 Foerster, D. M. Homer in English Criticism: The Historical Approach in the Eighteenth Century. New Haven, Conn., Yale University Press, 1947.

2306 French, M. The English Essay of the Restoration. Urbana, University of Illinois Press, 1934.

2307 Marks, E. R. The Poetics of Reason: English Neoclassical Criticism. New York, Random, 1968.

2308 Monk, S. H. The Sublime: A Study of Critical Theories in Eighteenth Century England. Ann Arbor, University of Michigan Press, 1960.

2309 Stauffer, D. A. The Art of Biography in Eighteenth Century England. Princeton, Princeton University Press, 1941. 2 vols.

2310 Tave, S. M. The Amiable Humorist: A Study in the Comic Theory and Criticism of the Eighteenth and Early Nineteenth Centuries. Chicago, University of Chicago Press, 1960.

PROSE NON-FICTION—INDIVIDUAL AUTHORS

Joseph Addison (1672-1719)

WORKS

2311 Letters from Italy, 1704
2312 The Campaign, 1705
2313 The Tender Husband, 1705
2314 Rosamond, 1707
2315 Spectator Articles, 1711-12
2316 Cato, 1713
2317 The Drummer, 1716

TEXTS

2318 Graham, W. J., ed. The Letters of Joseph Addison. Oxford, Clarendon Press, 1941.

2319 Green, J. R., ed. The Essays of Joseph Addison. New York, St. Martin's, 1968.

2320 Guthkelch, A. C., ed. Works. London, G. Bell & Sons, 1914. 2 vols.

CRITICISM

2321 Elioseff, L. A. The Cultural Milieu of Addison's Literary Criticism. Austin, University of Texas Press, 1963.

2322 Humphreys, A. R. Steele, Addison, and their Periodical Essays. London, Longmans, Green, 1959.

2323 Smithers, P. The Life of Joseph Addison. Oxford, Clarendon Press, 1968.

Edmund Burke (1729-1797)

WORKS

2324 A Philosophical Enquiry Into the Origin of our Ideas of the Sublime and Beautiful, 1757
2325 Annual Register, 1759
2326 Reflections on the Revolution in France, 1790
2327 Appeal from the New and the Old Whigs, 1791

BIBLIOGRAPHIES

2328 Cordasco, F., ed. Burke: A Handlist of Critical Notices and Studies. New York, B. Franklin, 1950.

2329 Todd, W. B. A Bibliography of Edmund Burke. London, Hart-Davis, 1964.

TEXTS

2330 Bredvold, L. I., and R. G. Ross, eds. The Philosophy of Edmund Burke: A Selection from his Speeches and Writings. Ann Arbor, University of Michigan Press, 1960.

2331 Copeland, T. W., ed. Letters. Cambridge, Cambridge University Press, 1958.

2332 Guttridge, G. H., ed. The Correspondence of Edmund Burke. Chicago, Chicago University Press, 1961.

2333 Marshall, P. J., and J. H. Woods, eds. The Correspondence of Edmund Burke. Chicago, Chicago University Press, 1968.

2334 Stanlis, P. J., ed. Edmund Burke: Selected Writings and Speeches. Garden City, N. Y., Doubleday, 1963.

2335 Woods, J. A., ed. The Correspondence of Edmund Burke. Cambridge, Cambridge University Press, 1963.

CRITICISM

2336 Canavan, F. P. The Political Reason of Edmund Burke. Durham, N. C., Duke University Press, 1960.

2337 Chapman, G. W. Edmund Burke: The Practial Imagination. Cambridge, Mass., Harvard University Press, 1967.

2338 Cobban, A. Edmund Burke and the Revolt Against the Eighteenth Century: A Study of the Political and Social Thinking of Burke, Worksworth, Coleridge, and Southey. New York, Barnes & Noble, 1960.

2339 Copeland, T. W. An Eminent Friend, Edmund Burke: Six Essays. New Haven, Conn., Yale University Press, 1949.

2340 Kirk, R. Edmund Burke: A Genius Reconsidered. New Rochelle, N. Y., Arlington House, 1967.

2341 Moore, T. M. The Background of Burke's Theory of the Sublime, 1660-1759. Ithaca, N. Y., Cornell University Press, 1933.

Edward Gibbon (1737-1784)

WORKS

2342 Essays, 1764

2343 The History of the Decline and Fall of the Roman Empire, 1779

2344 Memoirs of My Life and Writings, 1796

BIBLIOGRAPHIES

2345 Cordasco, F., ed. Gibbon: A Handlist of Critical Notices and Studies. New York, B. Franklin, 1950.

2346 Norton, J. E., ed. Bibliography of the Works of Gibbon. Oxford, Oxford University Press, 1940. Rev. ed. New York, B. Franklin, 1970.

TEXTS

2347 Daunders, D. A., ed. The Portable Gibbon. New York, Viking, 1952.

2348 Norton, J. E., ed. Letters. London, Cassell, 1956. 3 vols.

CRITICISM

2349 Beer, G. de. Gibbon and His World. New York, Viking, 1968.

Thomas Hobbes (1588-1679)

WORKS

2350 Leviathan, 1651

2351 The History of Civil Wars of England, 1679

TEXTS

2352 Brown, K. C., ed. Hobbes Studies. Cambridge, Mass., Harvard University Press, 1965.

2353 Lamprecht, S. P., ed. De Cive or The Citizen. New York, Appleton, 1949.

2354 Oakeshott, M., ed. Leviathan. Oxford, B. Blackwell, 1946.

2355 Peters, R. S., ed. Leviathan. New York, Collier, 1962.

2356 Waller, A. R., ed. Leviathan. Cambridge, Cambridge University Press, 1935.

CRITICISM

2357 Baumrin, B. H., ed. Leviathan: Interpretation and Criticism. Belmont, Calif., Wadsworth Publishing Company, 1969.

2358 Hood, F. C. The Divine Politics of Thomas Hobbes: An Interpretation of Leviathan. Oxford, Clarendon Press, 1964.

2359 Jessop, T. E. Thomas Hobbes. London, Longmans, Green, 1960.

2360 MacIver, R. M. Leviathan and the People. Baton Rouge, La., La Salle University Press, 1939.

2361 McNeilly, F. S. The Anatomy of Leviathan. London, Macmillan, 1968.

David Hume (1711-1776)

WORKS

2362 A Treatise of Human Nature, 1739

2363 Philosophical Essays, Concerning Human Understanding, 1748

2364 An Enquiry Concerning Human Understanding, 1758

2365 History of England, 1763

BIBLIOGRAPHIES

2366 Jessop, T. E., ed. A Bibliography of Hume and of Scottish Philosophy from Hutcheson to Lord Balfour. New York, Russell & Russell, 1966.

TEXTS

2367 Essays Literary, Moral and Political by David Hume. London, Ward, No date.

2368 Greig, J. W. T., ed. The Letters of David Hume. Oxford, Clarendon Press, 1932.

2369 Hendel, C. W., ed. Selections. New York, Scribner's, 1927.

2370 Lenz, J. W., ed. Of the Standard Taste and Other Essays. Indianapolis, Bobbs-Merrill, 1965.

CRITICISM

2371 Letwin, S. R. The Pursuit of Certainty: David Hume, Jeremy Bentham, John Stuart Mill, Beatrice Webb. Cambridge, Cambridge University Press, 1965.

2372 Maund, C. Hume's Theory of Knowledge. London, Macmillan, 1937.

2373 Price, H. H. Hume's Theory of the External World. Oxford, Clarendon Press, 1940.

2374 Price, J. V. The Ironic Hume. Austin, University of Texas Press, 1965.

2375 Smith, N. K. The Philosophy of David Hume: A Critical Study of Its Origins and Central Doctrines. New York, St. Martin's, 1966.

Samuel Johnson (1709-1784)

WORKS

2376 London, 1738
2377 The Vanity of Human
       Wishes, 1749
2378 The Rambler, 1750-56
2379 A Dictionary of the
       English Language, 1755

2380 Rasselas, 1759
2381 The Idler, 1761
2382 The Plays of William Shake-
       speare, 1765
2383 Prefaces, 1779-81

BIBLIOGRAPHIES

2384 Clifford, J. L., et al., ed. Johnsonian Studies, 1887-1950: A Survey
       and Bibliography. Minneapolis, University of Minnesota Press, 1969.

2385 Wahba, M., ed. Johnsonian Studies, Including a Bibliography of
       Johnsonian Studies, 1950-1960, Compiled by J. L. Clifford and
       D. J. Greene. London, Oxford University Press, 1962.

TEXTS

2386 Bate, W. J., J. M. Bullitt, and L. F. Powell, eds. Samuel Johnson:
       The Idler and the Adventurer. The Yale Edition of the Works of
       Samuel Johnson. Vol. II. New Haven, Conn., Yale University Press,
       1963.

2387 Chapman, R. W., ed. The Letters of Johnson with Mrs. Thrale's
       Genuine Letters to Him. Oxford, Clarendon Press, 1952. 3 vols.

2388 _____ , ed. Selections: Prose and Verse. Oxford, Oxford
       University Press, 1955.

2389 Davies, R. T., ed. Samuel Johnson: Selected Writings. London,
       Faber & Faber, 1965.

2390 Hardy, J. P., ed. The Political Writings of Dr. Johnson: A Selection.
       London, Routledge & K. Paul, 1968.

2391 Hill, G. B., ed. Johnsonian Miscellanies. New York, Barnes & Noble,
       1966. 2 vols.

2392 _____ , ed. Lives of the English Poets. New York, Octagon,
       1967. 3 vols.

2393 Kronenberger, L., ed. The Portable Johnson and Boswell. New
       York, Viking, 1947.

CRITICISM

2394 Alkon, P. K. Samuel Johnson and Moral Discipline. Evanston, Ill.,
       Northwestern University Press, 1967.

2395 Bate, W. J. The Achievement of Johnson. New York, Oxford University Press, 1955.

2396 Chapin, C. F. The Religious Thought of Samuel Johnson. Ann Arbor, Michigan University Press, 1968.

2397 Clifford, J. L. The Young Samuel Johnson. New York, Oxford University Press, 1961.

2398 Greene, D. J. Samuel Johnson. New York, Twayne, 1970.

2399 _____ . The Politics of Samuel Johnson. New Haven, Conn., Yale University Press, 1960.

2400 Hagstrum, J. H. Johnson's Literary Criticism. Chicago, Chicago University Press, 1967.

2401 Marshall, D. Dr. Johnson's London. London, Wiley, 1968.

2402 Osgood, C. G. Poetry as a Means of Grace: Dante, Spenser, Milton, and Johnson. Princeton, Princeton University Press, 1941.

2403 Voitle, R. Samuel Johnson, The Moralist. Cambridge, Mass., Harvard University Press, 1961.

2404 Watkins, W. B. C. Johnson and English Poetry Before 1660. Princeton, Princeton University Press, 1936.

2405 _____ . Perilous Balance: The Tragic Genius of Swift, Johnson, and Sterne. Princeton, Princeton University Press, 1939.

2406 Wimsatt, W. K., Jr. The Prose Style of Samuel Johnson. New Haven, Conn., Yale University Press, 1941.

John Locke (1632-1704)

WORKS

2407 An Essay Concerning Human Understanding, 1671, 1687, 1689

2408 Some Thoughts Concerning Education, 1693

TEXTS

2409 Axtell, J. L., ed. The Educational Writings of John Locke. Cambridge, Cambridge University Press, 1968.

2410 Essay Concerning Human Understanding. Ed. by A. C. Fraser. New York, Dover, 1959. 2 vols.

2411 Garforth, F. W., ed. Some Thoughts Concerning Education. London, Heinemann, 1964.

2412 Philosophical Works. Freeport, N. Y., Books for Libraries Press, 1969. 2 vols.

2413 Sherman, C. L., ed. Treatise of Civil Government and A Letter Concerning Toleration. New York, Appleton, 1965.

CRITICISM

2414 Aaron, R. I. John Locke. 2d ed. Oxford, Clarendon, 1955.

2415 Cox, R. H. Locke on War and Peace. Oxford, Clarendon Press, 1960.

2416 Dewhurst, K. John Locke, Physician and Philosopher: A Medical Biography. London, Wellcome Historical Medical Library, 1963.

2417 Kendall, W. John Locke and the Doctrine of Majority Rule. Urbana, University of Illinois Press, 1941.

2418 Tuveson, E. L. The Imagination as a Means of Grace. Berkeley, University of California Press, 1960.

Samuel Pepys (1633-1703)

WORKS

2419 The Diary, 1659-99

TEXTS

2420 Heath, H. T., ed. Letters of Pepys and His Family Circle. Oxford, Clarendon Press, 1955.

2421 Latham, R., et al., eds. The Diary of Samuel Pepys: A New and Complete Transcription. Berkeley, University of California Press, 1970.

CRITICISM

2422 Emden, C. S. Pepys Himself. London, Oxford University Press, 1963.

2423 Taylor, I. E. Samuel Pepys. New York, Twayne, 1968.

Richard Steele (1672-1729)

WORKS

2424 The Funeral, 1702
2425 The Lying Lover, 1704
2426 The Tender Husband, 1705
2427 The Tatler, 1710-11

2428 The Spectator, 1711-12
2429 The Guardian, 1713
2430 Town Talk, 1716
2431 The Conscious Lovers, 1723

TEXTS

2432 Blanchard, R., ed. The Englishman. Oxford, Oxford University Press, 1955.

2433 _____ , ed. Tracts and Pamphlets. New York, Octagon, 1966.

2434 _____ , ed. The Occasional Verses of Richard Steele. Oxford, Clarendon Press, 1952.

2435 _____ , ed. The Correspondence of Richard Steele. London, Oxford University Press, 1970.

2436 _____ , ed. Richard Steele's Periodical Journalism, 1714-16. Oxford, Oxford University Press, 1959.

2437 Bond, D. F., ed. The Spectator. Oxford, Oxford University Press, 1966. 5 vols.

2438 Gibbs, L., ed. The Tatler. New York, Dutton, 1968.

2439 Loftis, J., ed. Richard Steele's The Theatre, 1720. Oxford, Clarendon Press, 1962.

CRITICISM

2440 Goldgar, B. A. The Curse of Party: Swift's Relations with Addison and Steele. Lincoln, University of Nebraska Press, 1961.

2441 Humphreys, A. R. Steele, Addison, and Their Periodical Essays. London, Longmans, Green, 1959.

2442 Loftis, J. Steele and Drury Lane. Berkeley, University of California Press, 1952.

2443 Winton, C. Captain Steele: The Early Career of Richard Steele. Baltimore, Johns Hopkins, 1964.

NINETEENTH CENTURY

19TH CENTURY—GENERAL WORKS

2444 Ball, P. M. The Central Self: A Study in Romantic and Victorian Imagination. London, Athlone, 1968.

2445 Buck, P. M., Jr. The World's Great Age: The Story of a Century's Search for a Philosophy of Life. New York, Macmillan, 1936.

2446 Chew, S. C. A Literary History of England. Vol. 4. The Nineteenth Century and After, 1789-1839. 2d ed. New York, Appleton, 1968.

2447 Davis, S. H., et al., ed. Nineteenth Century Studies. Ithaca, N. Y., Cornell University Press, 1940.

2448 Day, M. S. History of English Literature; 1837 to the Present. Garden City, N. Y., Doubleday, 1964.

2449 Dodds, J. W. The Age of Paradox. A Biography of England, 1841-1851. New York, Rinehart, 1952.

2450 Hicks, G. Figures of Transition: A Study of British Literature at the End of the Nineteenth Century. New York, Macmillan, 1939.

2451 Kirk, R. The Conservative Mind from Burke to Santayana. Chicago, Regnery, 1964.

2452 Kunitz, S. J., and H. Haycraft. British Authors of the Nineteenth Century. New York, H. W. Wilson, 1936.

2453 Le Roy, G. C. Perplexed Prophets. Six Nineteenth Century British Authors. Philadelphia, University of Pennsylvania Press, 1953.

2454 Mead, G. H. Movements of Thought in the Nineteenth Century. Chicago, Chicago University Press, 1967.

2455 Miles, J. Pathetic Fallacy in the Nineteenth Century. Berkeley, University of California Press, 1942.

2456 Neill, T. P. Makers of the Modern Mind. Milwaukee, Bruce Publishing Company, 1958.

2457 Peckham, M. Beyond the Tragic Vision: The Quest for Identity in the Nineteenth Century. New York, G. Braziller, 1962.

2458 Routh, H. V. Towards the Twentieth Century: Essays in the Spiritual History of the Nineteenth. New York, Macmillan, 1937.

2459 Williams, R. Culture and Society, 1780-1950. New York, Harper, 1966.

19TH CENTURY DRAMA—TEXTS

2460 Ashley, L. R. N., ed. Nineteenth Century British Drama: An Anthology of Representative Plays. London, Scott, Foresman, 1967.

2461 Bailey, J. O., ed. British Plays of the Nineteenth Century. New York, Odyssey, 1966.

2462 Booth, M. R., ed. English Plays of the Nineteenth Century. Oxford, Clarendon Press, 1969. 2 vols.

2463 Corrigan, R. W. Masterpieces of British Drama: The Nineteenth Century. New York, Dell, 1967.

2464 Rowell, G., ed. Nineteenth Century Plays. Oxford, Oxford University Press, 1953.

2465 _____ , ed. Late Victorian Plays. Oxford, Oxford University Press, 1968.

19TH CENTURY DRAMA—CRITICISM

2466 Block, A. The Changing World in Plays and Theatre. Boston, Little, Brown, 1939.

2467 Booth, M. R. English Melodrama. London, Eyre & Spottiswoode, 1965.

2468 Disher, M. W. Blood and Thunder: Mid-Victorian Melodrama and Its Origins. London, F. Muller, 1949.

2469 Hudson, L. The English Stage, 1850-1950. London, Harrap, 1951.

2470 James, D. G. The Romantic Comedy. Oxford, Oxford University Press, 1949.

2471 Nicoll, A. A History of the Late Nineteenth Century Drama, 1850-1900. Cambridge, Cambridge University Press, 1946. 2 vols.

2472 Reynolds, E. Early Victorian Drama: 1830-1870. New York, Blom, 1965.

2473 Sawyer, N. W. The Comedy of Manners from Sheridan to Maugham. Philadelphia, University of Pennsylvania Press, 1931.

2474 Taylor, J. R. The Rise and Fall of the Well-Made Play. London, Methuen, 1967.

2475 Watson, E. B. Sheridan to Robertson: A Study of the Nineteenth Century London Stage. New York, Blom, 1963.

19TH CENTURY DRAMA—INDIVIDUAL AUTHORS

Sir William Schwenck Gilbert (1836-1911)

WORKS

2476 Bab Ballads, 1869

2477 The Palace of Truth, 1871

2478 Pygmalion and Galathea, 1873

2479 Sweethearts, 1874

2480 Tom Cobb, 1875

2481 Broken Hearts, 1875

2482 The Mikado, 1885

2483 Ruddigore, 1887

2484 The Gondoliers, 1889

2485 Fallen Fairies, 1909

TEXTS

2486 The Complete Plays of Gilbert and Sullivan. New York, Modern Library, 1936.

2487 Fabel, W., and M. Hyatt, eds. Gilbert and Sullivan Song Book. New York, Random, 1955.

2488 Green, M., ed. Martyn Green's Treasury of Gilbert and Sullivan. New York, Simon & Schuster, 1961.

2489 Lyrics from Gilbert and Sullivan Operas. New York, Collins, 1968.

2490 The Savoy Operas, 1875-96. London, St. Martin's, 1953.

2491 Stedman, J. W., ed. Gilbert Before Sullivan. Six Comic Plays by W. S. Gilbert. Chicago, Chicago University Press, 1968.

CRITICISM

2492 Allen, R. William Schwenck Gilbert: An Anniversary Survey and Exhibition Checklist. Charlottesville, University of Virginia Press, 1964.

2493 Darlington, W. A. The World of Gilbert and Sullivan. New York, Crowell, 1950.

2494 Moore, F. L., comp. Crowell's Handbook of Gilbert and Sullivan. London, Crowell, 1962.

Oscar Fingall O'Flahertie Wills Wilde (1854-1900)

WORKS

2495 A House of Pomegranates, 1891

2496 The Picture of Dorian Gray, 1891

2497 Lady Windermere's Fan, 1893

2498 Salome, 1893

2499 The Importance of Being Ernest, 1899

BIBLIOGRAPHIES

2500 Mason, S. Bibliography of Oscar Wilde. London, B. Rota, 1967.

TEXTS

2501 Aldington, R., ed. The Portable Oscar Wilde. New York, Viking, 1946.

2502 Ellman, R., ed. The Artist As Critic: Critical Writings of Oscar Wilde. New York, Random, 1969.

2503 _____ , ed. Selected Writings of Oscar Wilde. Oxford, World's Classics, 1968.

2504 Guthrie, T., ed. Complete Plays. New York, Norton, 1959.

2505 Hart-Davis, R., ed. The Letters of Oscar Wilde. London, Hart-Davis, 1962.

2506 Hewetson, C., comp. Wit and Wisdom of Oscar Wilde. New York, Philosophical Lib., 1967.

2507 Pearson, H., ed. Plays, Prose Writings and Poems. New York, Dutton, 1955.

2508 Redman, A., ed. The Wit and Humor of Oscar Wilde. London, P. Smith, 1959.

2509 _____ , ed. The Epigrams of Oscar Wilde. London, A. Redman, 1962.

2510 Weintraub, S., ed. The Literary Criticism of Oscar Wilde. Lincoln, University of Nebraska Press, 1969.

CRITICISM

2511 Beckson, K. E., ed. Oscar Wilde: The Critical Heritage. New York, Barnes & Noble, 1970.

2512 Bentley, E. R. The Playwright as Thinker: A Study of Drama in Modern Times. New York, Harcourt, 1967.

2513 Cowan, R. E., and W. A. Clark. The Library of W. A. Clark: Wilde and Wildeana. San Francisco, J. H. Nash, 1922.

2514 Ellman, R., ed. Oscar Wilde: A Collection of Critical Essays. Englewood Cliffs, N. J., Prentice-Hall, 1969.

2515 Harris, F. Oscar Wilde: His Life and Confessions. East Lansing, Michigan State University Press, 1959. 2 vols.

2516 Holland, V. Oscar Wilde: A Pictorial Biography. London, Thaimes & Hudson, 1961.

2517 Hyde, M. H. Oscar Wilde: The Aftermath. London, Methuen, 1963.

2518 Perry, H. T. E. Masters of Dramatic Comedy and Their Social Themes. Cambridge, Mass., Harvard University Press, 1939.

19TH CENTURY POETRY—TEXTS

2519 Auden, W. H., ed. Nineteenth Century British Minor Poets. New York, Dell, 1966.

2520 Hayward, J., ed. The Oxford Book of Nineteenth Century Verse. Oxford, Oxford University Press, 1964.

2521 Milford, H. S., ed. The Oxford Book of Regency Verse, 1798-1837. Oxford, Oxford University Press, 1928.

19TH CENTURY POETRY—CRITICISM

2522 Benziger, J. Images of Eternity: Studies in the Poetry of Religious Vision from Wordsworth to T. S. Eliot. Carbondale, Southern Illinois University Press, 1962.

2523 Davies, H. S. The Poets and Their Critics. Vol. II: Blake to Browning. London, Hutchinson, 1962.

2524 Hanley, E. A. Stoicism in Major English Poets of the Nineteenth Century. New York, Haskell House, 1964.

2525 Warren, A. H. English Poetic Theory, 1825-65. Princeton, Princeton University Press, 1950.

ROMANTIC PERIOD

2526 Abrams, M. H. The Mirror and the Lamp: Romantic Theory and the Critical Tradition. New York, Oxford University Press, 1953.

2527 Addison, A. Romanticism and the Gothic Revival. Philadelphia, P. Smith, 1938.

2528 Barzun, J. Romanticism and the Modern Ego. Boston, Little, Brown, 1944.

2529 Bernbaum, E., ed. Anthology of Romanticism. New York, Ronald Press, 1948. 5 vols.

2530 _____ , ed. A Guide Through the Romantic Movement. New York, Ronald Press, 1949.

2531 Bowra, C. M. The Romantic Imagination. Oxford, Galaxy Books, 1961.

2532 Fairchild, H. N. The Romantic Quest. New York, Russell & Russell, 1965.

2533 Frye, N. A Study of English Romanticism. New York, Random, 1968.

2534 Harris, R. W. Romanticism and the Social Order, 1780-1830. New York, Barnes & Noble, 1969.

2535 James, D. G. The Romantic Comedy: An Essay on English Romanticism. Oxford, P. Smith, 1963.

2536 Kermode, F. The Romantic Image. New York, Random, 1964.

2537 Kroeber, K. Romantic Narrative Art. Madison, University of Wisconsin Press, 1960.

2538 Levin, H. The Broken Column: A Study in Romantic Hellenism. Cambridge, Mass., Harvard University Press, 1931.

ROMANTIC POETRY

BIBLIOGRAPHIES

2539 Bernbaum, E., et al., eds. The English Romantic Poets: A Review of Research. New York, Modern Language Association of America, 1956.

2540 Green, D. B., and E. G. Wilson. Keats, Shelley, Byron, Hunt, and Their Circle: A Bibliography, 1950-1962. Lincoln, University of Nebraska Press, 1964.

2541 Houtchens, C. W., and L. H., eds. The English Romantic Poets and Essayists: A Review of Research and Criticism. New York, Modern Language Association of America, 1964.

TEXTS

2542 Bloom, H., ed. English Romantic Poetry: An Anthology. New York, Doubleday, 1961.

2543 Campbell, O. J., J. F. A. Pyre, and B. Weaver, eds. Poetry and Criticism of the Romantic Movement. New York, Appleton, 1960.

2544 Creeger, G. R., and J. W. Reed, Jr., eds. Selected Prose and Poetry of the Romantic Period. New York, Holt, 1964.

2545 Marshall, W. H., ed. The Major English Romantic Poets: An Anthology. New York, Washington Square Press, 1963.

2546 Milford, H. S., ed. The Oxford Book of English Verse of the Romantic Period, 1798-1837. Oxford, Oxford University Press, 1935.

2547 Wright, D., ed. The Penguin Book of English Romantic Verse. Baltimore, Penguin, 1968.

CRITICISM

2548 Abrams, M. H., ed. English Romantic Poets: Essays in Criticism. Oxford, Galaxy Books, 1960.

2549 Beach, J. W. A Romantic View of Poetry. Minneapolis, University of Minnesota Press, 1944.

2550 Bloom, H. The Visionary Company: A Reading of English Romantic Poetry. Rev. ed. Ithaca, N. Y., Cornell University Press, 1971.

2551 Brinton, C. The Political Ideas of the English Romantics. Ann Arbor, University of Michigan Press, 1966.

2552 Bush, D. Mythology and the Romantic Tradition in English Poetry. New York, Norton, 1963.

2553 Elwin, M. The First Romantics. London, Macdonald, 1947.

2554 Ford, B., et al., eds. From Blake to Byron. Baltimore, Penguin, 1969.

2555 Hough, G. The Last Romantics. London, Methuen, 1961.

2556 Kumar, S. K., ed. British Romantic Poets: Recent Revaluations. New York, New York University Press, 1966.

2557 Logan, J. V., J. E. Jordan, and N. Frye, eds. Some British Romantics: A Collection of Critical Essays. Columbus, Ohio State University Press, 1966.

2558 Piper, H. W. The Active Universe: Pantheism and the Concept of Imagination in the English Romantic Poets. London, University of London Press, 1962.

2559 Sherwood, M. Undercurrents of Influence in English Romantic Poetry. Cambridge, Mass., Harvard University Press, 1934.

2560 Wilkie, B. Romantic Poets and Epic Tradition. Madison, University of Wisconsin Press, 1965.

2561 Winwar, F. The Romantic Rebels, Boston, Little, Brown, 1935.

2562 Woodring, C. Politics in English Romantic Poetry. Cambridge, Mass., Harvard University Press, 1970.

George Gordon Byron, Baron Byron (1788-1824)

WORKS

2563 Hours of Idleness, 1807

2564 Childe Harold's Pilgrim-age, 1812

2565 The Bride of Abydos, 1813

2566 The Giaour, 1813

2567 Manfred, 1817

2568 Don Juan, 1819

2569 Cain, 1821

2570 Vision of Judgment, 1821

BIBLIOGRAPHIES

2571 Wise, T. J. A Bibliography of the Writings in Prose and Verse of George Noel, Baron Byron. London, Dawson, 1964.

TEXTS

2572 Auden, W. H., ed. Selected Poetry and Prose. New York, New American Library, 1966.

2573 Barzun, J., ed. The Selected Letters of Lord Byron. New York, Farrar, 1953.

2574 Bostetter, E. E. George Gordon: Selected Poetry and Letters. New York, Holt, 1951.

2575 Chew, S. C., ed. Childe Harold's Pilgrimage and Other Romantic Poems. New York, Odyssey, 1936.

2576 Coleridge, E. H., and R. E. Prothero, eds. Works. 13 vols. 1898-1904. Rev. ed. New York, Octagon, 1966.

2577 Marchand, L. A., ed. Selected Poetry. New York, Modern Library, 1968.

2578 More, P. E., ed. Complete Poetical Works. Boston, Houghton, 1968.

2579 Quennell, P., ed. Selections from Poetry, Letters and Journals. New York, Random, 1950.

2580 _____ , ed. Byron, a Self Portrait: Letters and Diaries, 1798-1824. New York, Humanities Press, 1950. 2 vols.

2581 Skelton, R., ed. Selected Poems. London, Heinemann, 1964.

CRITICISM

2582 Bostetter, E. E., ed. Twentieth Century Interpretations of Don
      Juan. Englewood Cliffs, N. J., Prentice-Hall, 1969.

2583 Cline, C. L. Byron, Shelley and Their Pisan Circle. Cambridge,
      Mass., Harvard University Press, 1952.

2584 Connely, W. Byron as Satirist. Nottingham, Nottingham University
      Press, 1936.

2585 Cooke, M. G. The Blind Man Traces the Circle: On the Patterns and
      Philosophy of Byron's Poetry. Princeton, Princeton University Press,
      1969.

2586 Dobrée, B. Byron's Dramas. Nottingham, Nottingham University
      Press, 1962.

2587 Ellege, W. P. Byron and the Dynamics of Metaphor. Nashville,
      Tenn., Vanderbilt University Press, 1968.

2588 Faulkner, C. W. Byron's Poetical Verse Satire. Urbana, University
      of Illinois Press, 1947.

2589 Gleckner, R. F. Byron and the Ruins of Paradise. Baltimore, Johns
      Hopkins, 1968.

2590 Gray, D. The Life and Work of Byron. Nottingham, Nottingham
      University Press, 1946.

2591 James, D. G. Byron and Shelley. Nottingham, Nottingham Univer-
      sity Press, 1951.

2592 Joseph, M. K. Byron the Poet. London, V. Gollancz, 1964.

2593 Lovell, E. J., Jr. Byron: The Record of a Quest. Studies in a Poet's
      Concept and Treatment of Nature. Austin, University of Texas
      Press, 1949.

2594 McGann, J. J. Fiery Dust. Byron's Poetic Development. Chicago,
      Chicago University Press, 1968.

2595 Marchand, L. A. Byron's Poetry: A Critical Introduction. Boston,
      Houghton, 1965.

2596 _____ . Byron: A Portrait. New York, Knopf, 1970.

2597 Martin, L. C. Byron's Lyrics. Nottingham, Nottingham University
      Press, 1948.

2598 Mayne, E. C. Byron. 2d ed. New York, Barnes & Noble, 1969.

2599 Moore, D. Langley. The Late Lord Byron. Philadelphia, Lippincott,
      1961.

2600 Parker, D. Byron and His World. New York, Viking, 1967.

2601 Quennell, P., ed. Byronic Thoughts. London, J. Murray, 1960.

2602 Rainwater, F. Lord Byron: A Study of the Development of His Philosophy with Special Emphasis upon the Dramas. Nashville, Tenn., Vanderbilt University Press, 1949.

2603 Steffan, T. G., comp. Lord Byron's Cain: Twelve Essays and a Text with Variants and Annotations. Austin, University of Texas Press, 1969.

2604 Thorslev, P. L., Jr. The Byronic Hero: Types and Prototypes. Minneapolis, University of Minnesota Press, 1962.

2605 Trueblood, P. G. The Flowering of Byron's Genius: Studies in Byron's Don Juan. New York, Russell & Russell, 1962.

2606 _____ . Lord Byron. New York, Twayne, 1969.

2607 West, P., ed. Byron: A Collection of Critical Essays. Englewood Cliffs, N. J., Prentice-Hall, 1963.

2608 Wilson, Knight G. Byron: Christian Virtues. New York, Barnes & Noble, 1967.

2609 _____ . Byron's Dramatic Prose. Nottingham, Nottingham University Press, 1953.

Samuel Taylor Coleridge (1772-1834)

WORKS

2610 Poems on Various Subjects, 1796

2611 Poems, 1797

2612 Christabel, 1798

2613 Lyrical Ballads, 1798

2614 Biographia Literaria, 1817

BIBLIOGRAPHIES

2615 Kennedy, R. W., and M. N. Barton, eds. Samuel Taylor Coleridge: A Selected Bibliography of the Best Available Editions of the Writings of Biographies and Criticism of Him and of References Showing His Relations with Contemporaries for Student and Teachers. Baltimore, Enoch Pratt Free Library, 1935. Repr. New York, Kraus, 1969.

2616 Wise, T. J. A Bibliography of the Writings and Verse of Samuel Taylor Coleridge. London, Bibliographical Society, 1913.

TEXTS

2617 Coleridge, E. H., ed. Complete Poetical Works. Oxford, Oxford University Press, 1912. 2 vols.

2618 Foakes, R. A., ed. Coleridge on Shakespeare; the Text of the Lectures of 1811-12. Charlottesville, Folger Shakespeare Library, University of Virginia Press, 1971.

2619 Griggs, E. L., ed. Unpublished Letters of S. T. Coleridge. New Haven, Conn., Yale University Press, 1933. 2 vols.

2620 _____ , ed. The Best of Coleridge. New York, T. Nelson, 1934.

2621 _____ , ed. Collected Letters of Samuel Taylor Coleridge. Vols. I and II. Oxford, Oxford University Press, 1956. 6 vols.

2622 Patton, L., and P. Mann, eds. Collected Works of Samuel Taylor Coleridge. Vol. I: Lectures 1795 on Politics and Religion. Princeton, Princeton University Press, 1971.

2623 Potter, S., ed. Selected Poetry and Prose. London, Nonesuch Press, 1962.

2624 Raysor, T. M., ed. Shakespearean Criticism. New York, Dutton, 1960. 2 vols.

2625 Richards, I. A., ed. The Portable Coleridge. New York, Viking, 1950.

2626 Schneider, E., ed. Samuel Taylor Coleridge: Selected Poetry and Prose. New York, Modern Library, 1951.

2627 Showcross, J. T., ed. Biographia Literaria. Oxford, Oxford University Press, 1907. 2 vols.

2628 Watson, G., ed. Biographia Literaria. New York, Dutton, 1956.

CRITICISM

2629 Adair, P. M. The Waking Dream: A Study of Coleridge's Poetry. London, E. Arnold, 1967.

2630 Barth, J. R. Coleridge and Christian Doctrine. Cambridge, Mass., Harvard University Press, 1969.

2631 Bate, W. J. Coleridge. New York, Macmillan, 1968.

2632 Beer, J. B. Coleridge, the Visionary. London, Collier, 1964.

2633 Boulger, J. D. Coleridge as Religious Thinker. New Haven, Conn., Yale University Press, 1961.

2634 Coburn, K., ed. Coleridge: A Collection of Critical Essays. Englewood Cliffs, N. J., Prentice-Hall, 1967.

2635 Colmer, J. Coleridge, Critic of Society. Oxford, Oxford University Press, 1959.

2636 Fields, B. Reality's Dark Dream: Dejection in Coleridge. Kent, Ohio, Kent State University Press, 1968.

2637 Fogle, R. H. The Idea of Coleridge's Criticism. Berkeley, University of California Press, 1962.

2638 Gerard, A. S. English Romantic Poetry: Ethos, Structure, and Symbol in Coleridge, Wordsworth, Shelley, and Keats. Los Angeles, University of California Press, 1968.

2639 Hanson, L. The Life of Samuel Taylor Coleridge: The Early Years. New York, Russell & Russell, 1962.

2640 Haven, R. Patterns of Consciousness: An Essay on Coleridge. Amherst, University of Massachusetts Press, 1969.

2641 Kennedy, W. L. The English Heritage of Coleridge of Bristol, 1798: The Basis in Eighteenth Century English Thought for His Distinction Between Imagination and Fancy. New Haven, Conn., Yale University Press, 1947.

2642 Knight, G. W. The Starlit Dome: On the Poetry of Wordsworth, Coleridge, Shelley, and Keats. New York, Barnes & Noble, 1960.

2643 Lawrence, B. Coleridge and Wordsworth in Somerset. Newton Abbot, Devon, David & Charles, 1970.

2644 Logan, E., ed. A Concordance to the Poetry of Samuel Taylor Coleridge. New York, Macmillan, 1968.

2645 McFarland, T. Coleridge and the Pantheist Tradition. Oxford, Clarendon Press, 1969.

2646 Richards, I. A. Coleridge on Imagination. Bloomington, Indiana University Press, 1934.

2647 Schneider, E. Coleridge, Opium, and Kubla Khan. New York, Octagon, 1966.

2648 Suther, M. The Dark Night of Samuel Taylor Coleridge. New York, Columbia University Press, 1960.

John Keats (1795-1821)

WORKS

2649 Poems, 1817
2650 Endymion, 1818
2651 Hyperion, 1819
2652 Odes, 1819

2653 Lamia, Isabella, The Eve of St. Agnes, and Other Poems, 1820

BIBLIOGRAPHIES

2654 MacGillivray, J. R., ed. Keats: A Bibliography and Reference Guide. Toronto, University of Toronto Press, 1949.

TEXTS

2655 Briggs, H. E., ed. Complete Poetry and Selected Prose. New York, Modern Library, 1951.

2656 Carmichael, K. K., ed. A Critical Edition of the Early Poems of John Keats with a Philosophical Supplement. Nashville, Tenn., Vanderbilt University Press, 1944.

2657 Fogle, R. H., ed. John Keats: Selected Poetry and Letters. New York, Rinehart, 1951.

2658 Forman, H. B., ed. Complete Works. Glasgow, Gowars & Gray, 1900-1901. 5 vols.

2659 _____ , ed. The Poetical Works and Other Writings. Rev. by M. B. Forman. London, Phaeton, 1970.

2660 Forman, M. B., ed. The Letters. 4th ed. Oxford, Oxford University Press, 1960.

2661 Rollins, H. E., ed. The Keats Circle: Letters and Papers, 1816-78. Cambridge, Mass., Harvard University Press, 1948. 2 vols.

2662 Scudder, H. E., ed. Complete Poetical Works. Boston, Houghton, 1968.

2663 Thorpe, C. DeWitt, ed. Complete Poems and Selected Letters. New York, Odyssey, 1935.

CRITICISM

2664 Bate, W. J. John Keats: The Growth of a Genius. Cambridge, Mass., Harvard University Press, 1963.

2665 _____ . Negative Capability: The Intuitive Approach in Keats. Cambridge, Mass., Harvard University Press, 1939.

2666 _____ , ed. Keats: A Collection of Critical Essays. Englewood Cliffs, N. J., Prentice-Hall, 1960.

2667 Blackstone, B. The Consecrated Urn: An Interpretation of Keats in Terms of Growth and Form. London, Longmans, 1966.

2668 Bush, D. John Keats: His Life and Writings. New York, Macmillan, 1966.

2669 Colvin, S. John Keats: His Life and Poetry, His Friends, Critics, and After-Fame. New York, Octagon, 1970.

2670 D'Avanzo, M. L. Keats's Metaphors for the Poetic Imagination. Durham, N. C., Duke University Press, 1967.

2671 Evert, W. H. Aesthetic and Myth in the Poetry of Keats. Princeton, Princeton University Press, 1965.

2672 Fogle, R. H. The Imagery of Keats and Shelley: A Comparative Study. Chapel Hill, University of North Carolina Press, 1949.

2673 Ford, G. H. Keats and the Victorians: A Study of His Influence and Rise to Fame, 1821-1895. Hamden, Conn., Shoe String Press, 1962.

2674 Ford, N. E. The Prefigurative Imagination of Keats. Palo Alto, Stanford University Press, 1951.

2675 Gerard, A. S. English Romantic Poetry: Ethos, Structure, and Symbol in Coleridge, Wordsworth, Shelley, and Keats. Los Angeles, University of California Press, 1968.

2676 Gittings, R. The Odes of Keats and Their Earliest Known Manuscripts. Kent, Ohio, Kent State University Press, 1970.

2677 Hewlett, D. Adonais: A Life of Keats. 2d ed. New York, Hurst & Blackett, 1949.

2678 _____ . A Life of John Keats. 3d Rev. ed. New York, Barnes & Noble, 1970.

2679 Jack, I. Keats and the Mirror of Art. Oxford, Clarendon Press, 1967.

2680 Jones, H. J. F. John Keats's Dream of Truth. New York, Barnes & Noble, 1969.

2681 Kauvar, G. B. The Other Poetry of Keats. Rutherford, N. J., Fairleigh Dickinson, 1970.

2682 Knight, G. W. The Starlit Dome: On the Poetry of Wordsworth, Coleridge, Shelley, and Keats. New York, Barnes & Noble, 1960.

2683 Muir, K., ed. John Keats: A Reassessment. Liverpool, University of Liverpool Press, 1959.

2684 Murry, J. M. The Mystery of Keats. New York, Farrar, 1962.

2685 _____ . Keats and Shakespeare. Oxford, Oxford University Press, 1925.

2686 O'Neill, J., ed. Critics on Keats. Coral Gables, Fla., University of Miami Press, 1969.

2687 Perkins, D. The Quest for Permanence: The Symbolism of Wordsworth, Shelley, and Keats. Cambridge, Mass., Harvard University Press, 1959.

2688 Ridley, M. R. Keats's Craftsmanship: A Study in Poetic Development. Lincoln, University of Nebraska Press, 1963.

2689 Stillinger, J., ed. Twentieth Century Interpretations of Keats's Odes. Englewood Cliffs, N. J., Prentice-Hall, 1968.

2690 Talbot, N. The Major Poems of John Keats. Sydney, University of Sydney Press, 1968.

2691 Weller, E. V. Autobiography of John Keats, Compiled from His Letters and Essays. Stanford, Stanford University Press, 1934.

2692 Wilson, K. M. The Nightingale and the Hawk: A Psychological Study of Keats' Ode. London, Allen & Unwin, 1964.

Percy Bysshe Shelley (1792-1822)

WORKS

2693 Queen Mab, 1812

2694 Cenci, 1819

2695 Oedipus Tyrannus, 1820

2696 Prometheus Unbound, 1820

2697 Adonais, 1821

2698 Defence of Poetry, 1821

2699 Epipsychidion, 1821

2700 Hellas, 1822

TEXTS

2701 Barnard, E., ed. Selected Poems, Essays, and Letters. New York, Odyssey, 1944.

2702 Cameron, K. N., ed. Shelley and His Circle, 1773-1822. Cambridge, Mass., Harvard University Press, 1970. 2 vols.

2703 _____ , ed. Selected Poetry and Prose. New York, Holt, 1951.

2704 _____ , ed. The Esdaile Notebook: A Volume of Early Poems by Percy Bysshe Shelley. New York, Knopf, 1964.

2705 Glover, A. S. B. Selected Poetry, Prose and Letters. New York, Random, 1968.

2706 Hutchinson, T. The Complete Poetical Works. Oxford, Standard Authors, 1934.

2707 Ingpen, R., and W. E. Peck, eds. The Complete Works. New York, Gordian, 1965.

2708 Zillman, L. J., ed. Shelley's Prometheus Unbound, A Variorum Edition. Seattle, University of Washington Press, 1959.

CRITICISM

2709 Baker, C. Shelley's Major Poetry: The Fabric of a Vision. Princeton, Princeton University Press, 1966.

2710 Barrell, J. Shelley and the Thought of His Time: A Study in the History of Ideas. New Haven, Conn., Yale University Press, 1947.

2711 Cameron, K. N. The Young Shelley: Genesis of a Radical. New York, Collier, 1962.

2712 Curran, Stuart. Shelley's Cenci: Scorpions Ringed with Fire. Princeton, Princeton University Press, 1970.

2713 Evans, B. Gothic Drama from Walpole to Shelley. Berkeley, University of California Press, 1947.

2714 Fuller, J. O. Shelley: A Biography. London, Cape, 1968.

2715 Gerard, A. S. English Romantic Poetry: Ethos, Structure and Symbol in Coleridge, Wordsworth, Shelley and Keats. Los Angeles, University of California Press, 1968.

2716 Notopoulos, J. A. The Platonism of Shelley: A Study of Platonism and the Poetic Mind. Durham, N. C., Duke University Press, 1949.

2717 O'Malley, G. Shelley and Synesthesia. Evanston, Ill, Northwestern University Press, 1964.

2718 Perkins, D. The Quest for Permanence: The Symbolism of Wordsworth, Shelley and Keats. Cambridge, Mass., Harvard University Press, 1959.

2719 Pottle, F. A. Shelley and Browning: A Myth and Some Facts. Hamden, Conn, Archon, 1965.

2720 Pulos, C. E. The Deep Truth: A Study of Shelley's Skepticism. Lincoln, University of Nebraska Press, 1962.

2721 Reiter, S. A Study of Shelley's Poetry. Albuquerque, University of New Mexico Press, 1967.

2722 Ridenour, G. M., ed. Shelley: A Collection of Critical Essays. Englewood Cliffs, N. J., Prentice-Hall, 1965.

2723 Rieger, J. The Mutiny Within: The Heresies of Percy Bysshe Shelley. New York, Braziller, 1968.

2724 Rogers, N. Shelley at Work: A Critical Inquiry. Oxford, Clarendon Press, 1967.

2725 Rush, P. The Young Shelley. New York, Roy, 1961.

2726 Stovall, F. Desire and Restraint in Shelley. Durham, N. C., Duke University Press, 1931.

2727 Wasserman, E. R. Shelley's Prometheus Unbound: A Critical Reading. Baltimore, Johns Hopkins, 1965.

2728 White, N. I. Portrait of Shelley. New York, Knopf, 1945. 2 vols.

2729 _____ , F. L. Jones, and K. N. Cameron. An Examination of
the Shelley Legend. Philadelphia, University of Pennsylvania Press,
1951.

2730 Wise, T. J. A Shelley Library: A Catalogue of Printed Books, Manu-
scripts and Autographed Letters by Percy Bysshe Shelley, Harriet
Shelley and Mary Wollstonecraft Shelley. 1924. Repr. New York,
Haskell House, 1971.

2731 Woodman, R. G. The Apocalyptic Vision in the Poetry of Shelley.
Toronto, University of Toronto Press, 1964.

William Wordsworth (1770-1850)

WORKS

2732 An Evening Walk, 1793	2736 The Prelude, 1805-06
2733 Descriptive Sketches, 1793	2737 The Excursion, 1814
2734 Lyrical Ballads, 1798, 1800	2738 Sonnets, 1838
2735 The Recluse, 1800	

BIBLIOGRAPHIES

2739 Henley, E. F. Wordsworthian Criticism, 1945-1959: An Annotated
Bibliography. New York, New York Public Library, 1965.

2740 Logan, J. V. Wordsworthian Criticism: A Guide and Bibliography.
Columbus, Ohio State University Press, 1947.

TEXTS

2741 Batho, E., ed. A Wordsworth Selection. London, Athlone Press,
1962.

2742 Beatty, A., ed. Representative Poems. New York, Odyssey, 1968.

2743 Brett, R. L., and A. R. Jones, eds. Lyrical Ballads, Wordsworth and
Coleridge. Edinburgh, Constable, 1963.

2744 Davies, H., comp. A Wordsworth Anthology. New York, Collins,
1965.

2745 George, A. J., ed. Complete Poetical Works. Boston, Houghton,
1961.

2746 Housman, L., ed. A Wordsworth Anthology. New York, Scribner's,
1946.

2747 Meyer, G. W., ed. Wordsworth: Selected Poems. New York, Appleton, 1950.

2748 Owen, W. J. B., ed. Wordsworth and Coleridge, Lyrical Ballads, 1798. London, Oxford University Press, 1967.

2749 Selincourt, de E., and H. Darbishire, eds. The Poetical Works. Oxford, Oxford University Press, 1940-1949. 5 vols.

2750 Stillinger, J., ed. Selected Poems and Prefaces. Boston, Houghton, 1968.

2751 Van Doren, M., ed. Selected Poetry. New York, Modern Library, 1950.

CRITICISM

2752 Abercombie, L. The Art of Wordsworth. Repr. Hamden, Conn., Archon, 1965.

2753 Blanshard, F. M. B. Portraits of Wordsworth. Ithaca, N. Y., Cornell University Press, 1959.

2754 Cooper, L. A Concordance to the Poems of William Wordsworth. New York, Russell & Russell, 1968.

2755 Danby, J. F. The Simple Wordsworth: Studies in the Poems, 1797-1807. London, Routledge & K. Paul, 1960.

2756 Durrant, G. Wordsworth and the Great System: A Study of Wordsworth's Poetic Universe. Cambridge, University of Cambridge Press, 1970.

2757 Ferry, D. The Limits of Morality: An Essay on Wordsworth's Major Poems. Middletown, Wesleyan University Press, 1959.

2758 Gerard, A. S. English Romantic Poetry: Ethos, Structure and Symbol in Coleridge, Wordsworth, Shelley, and Keats. Los Angeles, University of California Press, 1968.

2759 Griggs, E. L., ed. Wordsworth and Coleridge: Studies in Honor of G. M. Harper. New York, Russell & Russell, 1962.

2760 Hamilton, C. C. Wordsworth's Decline in Poetic Power: Prophet into High Priest. New York, Exposition Press, 1963.

2761 Havens, R. D. The Mind of a Poet: A Study of Wordsworth's Thought with Practical Reference to the Prelude. Baltimore, Johns Hopkins, 1941.

2762 Heath, W. Wordsworth and Coleridge, A Study of Their Literary Relations in 1801-1802. Oxford, Oxford University Press, 1971.

2763 Jones, H. J. F. The Egotistical Sublime: A History of Wordsworth's Imagination. London, Chatto & Windus, 1954.

2764 Knight, G. W. The Starlit Dome: On the Poetry of Wordsworth, Coleridge, Shelley, and Keats. New York, Barnes & Noble, 1960.

2765 Lacey, N. Wordsworth's View of Nature. Cambridge, Cambridge University Press, 1948.

2766 McLean, K. Agrarian Age: A Background for Wordsworth. New Haven, Conn., Yale University Press, 1950.

2767 Marsh, F. Wordsworth's Imagery: A Study in Poetic Vision. New Haven, Conn., Yale University Press, 1952.

2768 Meyer, G. W. Wordsworth's Formative Years. Ann Arbor, Michigan University Press, 1943.

2769 Miles, J. Wordsworth and the Vocabulary of Emotion. Berkeley, University of California Press, 1942.

2770 Moorman, M. C. Wordsworth: A Biography. Vol. I, 1770-1803. Oxford, Oxford University Press, 1965.

2771 _____ . William Wordsworth: A Biography, the Later Years, 1803-1850. Oxford, Clarendon Press, 1965.

2772 Perkins, D. The Quest for Permanence: The Symbolism of Wordsworth, Shelley, and Keats. Cambridge, Mass., Harvard University Press, 1959.

2773 _____ . Wordsworth and the Poetry of Sincerity. Cambridge, Mass., Harvard University Press, 1964.

2774 Potts, A. F. The Elegiac Mode: Poetic Form in Wordsworth and Other Elegists. Ithaca, N. Y., Cornell University Press, 1967.

2775 Prickett, S. Coleridge and Wordsworth: The Poetry of Growth. Cambridge, Cambridge University Press, 1970.

2776 Rader, M. Wordsworth: A Philosophical Approach. Oxford, Clarendon Press, 1967.

2777 Stallknecht, N. R. Strange Seas of Thought: Studies in William Wordsworth's Philosophy of Man and Nature. Durham, N. C., Duke University Press, 1945.

2778 Thomson, A. W., comp. and ed. Wordsworth's Mind and Art: Essays Old and New. New York, Barnes & Noble, 1970.

VICTORIAN AGE
VICTORIAN LITERATURE
BIBLIOGRAPHIES

2779 Ehrsam, T. G., and R. H. Deily, eds. Bibliographies of Twelve Victorian Authors. New York, Octagon, 1968.

2780 Slack, R. C. Bibliographies of Studies in Victorian Literature for the Ten Years 1955-1965. Urbana, University of Illinois Press, 1967.

2781 Templeman, W. D. Bibliographies of Studies in Victorian Literature for the Thirteen Years 1932-1944. Urbana, University of Illinois Press, 1945.

2782 Wright, A. H. Bibliographies of Studies in Victorian Literature for the Ten Years 1945-1954. Urbana, University of Illinois Press, 1956.

TEXTS

2783 Buckley, J. H., ed. Victorian Poets and Prose Writers. New York, Appleton, 1966.

2784 Cooke, J. D., and L. Stevenson, eds. English Literature of the Victorian Period. New York, Appleton, 1949.

2785 Houghton, W. E., and G. R. Stange, eds. Victorian Poetry and Poetics. 2d ed. New York, Houghton Mifflin, 1968.

2786 Johnson, E. D. H., ed. The World of the Victorians: An Anthology of Poetry and Prose. New York, Scribner's 1964.

2787 Parrott, T. M., and R. B. Martin, eds. Companion to Victorian Literature. New York, Scribner's, 1955.

CRITICISM

2788 Baker, J. E., ed. The Reinterpretation of Victorian Literature. Princeton, Princeton University Press, 1950.

2789 Buckley, J. H. The Victorian Temper: A Study in Literary Culture. Cambridge, Mass., Harvard University Press, 1951.

2790 Chesterton, G. K. The Victorian Age in Literature. Notre Dame, Ind., University of Notre Dame Press, 1963.

2791 Evans, J. The Victorians. London, Cambridge University Press, 1966.

2792 Himmelfarb, G. Victorian Minds. New York, Knopf, 1968.

2793 Houghton, W. E. Victorian Frame of Mind, 1830-1870. 2d ed. New Haven, Conn., Yale University Press, 1971.

2794 Marchand, L. A. The Athenaeum, A Mirror of Victorian Culture. Chapel Hill, University of North Carolina Press, 1941.

2795 Reader, W. J. Life in Victorian England. London, Batsford, 1964.

2796 Schilling, B. N. Human Dignity and the Great Victorians. New York, Pub. for Grinnell College by Columbia University Press, 1946.

2797 Wright, A. H., ed. Victorian Literature: Modern Essays in Criticism. New York, Oxford University Press, 1961.

VICTORIAN POETRY
BIBLIOGRAPHIES

2798 Faverty, F. E., ed. The Victorian Poets: A Guide to Research. 2d ed. Cambridge, Mass., Harvard University Press, 1968.

TEXTS

2799 Auden, W. H., ed. Nineteenth Century Minor Poets. London, Faber, 1966.

2800 Beck, E. L., and R. H. Snow, eds. Victorian and Later English Poets. New York, American Book Company, 1949.

2801 Brett, R. L., ed. Poems of Faith and Doubt: The Victorian Age. London, E. Arnold, 1965.

2802 Buckley, J. H., ed. Victorian Poets and Prose Writers. New York, Appleton, 1966.

2803 Evans, B. I., ed. English Poetry in the Later Nineteenth Century. London, Methuen, 1933.

2804 Houghton, W. E., and G. R. Stange, eds. Victorian Poetry and Poetics. 2d ed. New York, Houghton Mifflin, 1968.

2805 McBeth, G., ed. The Penguin Book of Victorian Verse: A Critical Anthology. Harmondsworth, Penguin, 1969.

2806 Marshall, W. H. The Major Victorian Poets: An Anthology. New York, Washington Square Press, 1966.

2807 Quiller-Couch, A., ed. The Oxford Book of Victorian Verse. Oxford, Oxford University Press, 1913.

2808 Wright, D., ed. Seven Victorian Poets. London, Heinemann, 1964.

CRITICISM

2809 Armstrong, I., ed. The Major Victorian Poets: Reconsiderations. London, Routledge & K. Paul, 1969.

2810 Brown, E. K., and J. O. Bailey. Victorian Poetry. New York, Ronald, 1962.

2811 Colville, D. Victorian Poetry and the Romantic Religion. New York, State University of New York, 1970.

Robert Browning (1812-1889)

WORKS

2812 Incondita, 1824

2813 Paracelsus, 1835

2814 Bells and Pomegranates, 1841

2815 Pipa Passes, 1841

2816 Men and Women, 1855

2817 The Ring and the Book, 1868-69

2818 Dramatic Idyls, 1879— and 1880

BIBLIOGRAPHIES

2819 Broughton, L. N., C. S. Northup, and R. Pearsall, eds. Robert Browning: A Bibliography, 1830-1950. Ithaca, N. Y., Cornell University Press, 1953.

TEXTS

2820 Berkey, J., and M. Peckham, eds. The Complete Works of Robert Browning. Athens, Ohio University Press, 1969.

2821 De Vane, W. C., ed. Selected Poems of Robert Browning. New York, Appleton, 1949.

2822 Hood, T. L., ed. Letters of Robert Browning, Collected by Thomas J. Wise. New Haven, Conn., Yale University Press, 1933.

2823 King, R. A., ed. The Complete Works of Robert Browning. Athens, Ohio University Press, 1969.

2824 Nowell-Smith, S., ed. Poetry and Prose. Cambridge, Mass., Harvard University Press, 1950.

2825 Porter, C., and H. A. Clarke, eds. Works. New York, E. R. Dumont, 1900. 12 vols.

2826 Ricks, C. B., comp. The Brownings: Letters and Poetry. New York, Doubleday, 1970.

2827 Scudder, H. E., ed. Complete Poetical and Dramatic Works. Boston, Houghton, 1947.

CRITICISM

2828 Blackburn, T. Robert Browning: A Study of His Poetry. London, Eyre & Spottiswoode, 1967.

2829 Broughton, L. N., and B. S. Stelter. Concordance to the Poems of Robert Browning. Repr. New York, Haskell House, 1969.

2830 Burrows, L. Browning the Poet: An Introductory Study. Nedlands Perth, University of Western Australia Press, 1969.

2831 Collins, T. J. Robert Browning's Moral-Aesthetic Theory, 1833-1855. Lincoln, University of Nebraska Press, 1967.

2832 Crowell, N. B. The Triple Soul: Browning's Theory of Knowledge. Albuquerque, University of New Mexico Press, 1963.

2833 _____ . The Convex Glass: The Mind of Robert Browning. Albuquerque, University of New Mexico Press, 1968.

2834 Davies, H. S. Browning and the Modern Novel. Hull, Hull University Press, 1962.

2835 Drew, P., ed. Robert Browning: A Collection of Critical Essays. Boston, Houghton, 1966.

2836 Fuson, B. W. Browning and His English Predecessors in the Dramatic Monologue. Iowa City, State University of Iowa Press, 1948.

2837 Honan, P. Browning's Characters: A Study in Poetic Technique. New Haven, Conn., Yale University Press, 1961.

2838 Johnson, E. D. H. The Alien Vision of Victorian Poetry: Sources of the Poetic Imagination in Tennyson, Browning and Arnold. Princeton, Princeton University Press, 1952.

2839 Kenmare, D. An End to Darkness: A New Approach to Robert Browning and His Work. London, P. Owen, 1962.

2840 King, R. A., Jr. The Focusing Artifice: The Poetry of Robert Browning. Athens, Ohio University Press, 1969.

2841 Miller, B. Robert Browning: A Portrait. New York, Hillary House, 1952.

2842 Pottle, F. A. Shelley and Browning: A Myth and Some Facts. Hamden, Conn., Archon, 1965.

2843 Raymond, W. O. The Infinite Moment and Other Essays in Browning. 2d ed. Toronto, University of Toronto Press, 1965.

2844 Smith, C. W. Browning's Star Imagery: The Study of a Detail in Poetic Design. Princeton, Princeton University Press, 1941.

2845 Tracy, C. Browning's Mind and Art. New York, Barnes & Noble, 1970.

2846 Ward, M. Robert Browning and His World, I: The Private Face, 1812-1861. New York, Cassell, 1967.

Gerard Manley Hopkins (1844-1889)

WORKS

2847 A Vision of the Mermaids, 1862

2848 Poems, Prose, Journals, n.d.

BIBLIOGRAPHIES

2849 Cohen, E. Works and Criticism of Gerard Manley Hopkins: A Comprehensive Bibliography. Washington, Catholic University Press, 1969.

TEXTS

2850 Devlin, C., ed. The Sermons and Devotional Writings. London, Oxford University Press, 1959.

2851 Gardner, W. H., ed. Poems and Prose. 1918. London, P. Smith, 1948.

2852 _____ , and N. H. Mackenzie, eds. Poems. 4th ed. Oxford, Oxford University Press, 1947.

2853 Hopkins Reader. ed. J. Pick. New York, Oxford University Press, 1953.

2854 House, H., ed. The Journals and Papers of Gerard Manley Hopkins. London, Oxford University Press, 1959.

2855 Reeves, J., ed. Selected Poems. New York, Barnes & Noble, 1953.

CRITICISM

2856 Bender, T. K. Gerard Manley Hopkins: The Classical Background and Critical Reception of His Work. Baltimore, Johns Hopkins, 1966.

2857 Borrello, A., ed. A Concordance of the Poetry in English of Gerard Manley Hopkins. Metuchen, N. J., Scarecrow, 1969.

2858 Boyle, R. S. J. Metaphor in Hopkins. Chapel Hill, University of North Carolina Press, 1961.

2859 Dilligan, R. J., and T. K. Bender. A Concordance to the English Poetry of Gerard Manley Hopkins. Madison, University of Wisconsin Press, 1970.

2860 Downes, D. Gerard Manley Hopkins: A Study of His Ignatian Spirit. New York, Twayne, 1959.

2861 Hartman, G. H., ed. Hopkins: A Collection of Critical Essays. Englewood Cliffs, N. J., Prentice-Hall, 1966.

2862 Hartman, G. H. The Unmeditated Vision. New York, Harcourt, 1966.

2863 McChesney, D. A Hopkins Commentary: An Explanatory Commentary on the Main Poems, 1876-89. New York, University of New York Press, 1970.

2864 Mariani, P. L. A Commentary on the Complete Poems of Gerard Manley Hopkins. Ithaca, Cornell University Press, 1970.

2865 Pick, J. Gerard Manley Hopkins, Priest and Poet. New York, Oxford University Press, 1942.

2866 Seelhammer, R. Hopkins Collected at Gozaga. Chicago, Loyola University Press, 1970.

Alfred Edward Housman (1859-1936)

WORKS

2867 Manilius, 1903
2868 Juvenal, 1905
2869 Last Poems, 1922
2870 Lucan, 1926

2871 The Name and Nature of Poetry, 1933
2872 More Poems, 1936

BIBLIOGRAPHIES

2873 Ehrsam, T. G. A Bibliography of Alfred Edward Housman. Boston, Faxon, 1941.

TEXTS

2874 Carter, J., ed. Alfred Edward Housman: Selected Prose. Cambridge, Cambridge University Press, 1961.

2875 Davenport, B., ed. Collected Poems. New York, Holt, 1959.

2876 Haber, T. B., ed. The Manuscript Poems. Minneapolis, University of Minnesota Press, 1955.

2877 _____ , ed. Complete Poems. Centennial Edition. New York, Holt, 1959.

CRITICISM

2878 Hyder, C. K., ed. A Concordance to the Poems of Housman. London, P. Smith, 1940.

2879 Marlow, N. Alfred Edward Housman: Scholar and Poet. Minneapolis, University of Minnesota Press, 1957.

2880 Robinson, O. Angry Dust: The Poetry of Housman. Boston, Humphries, 1950.

2881 Skutsch, O. Alfred Edward Housman, 1859-1936. London, University of London Press, 1960.

Rudyard Kipling (1865-1936)

WORKS

2882 Life's Handicap, 1891

2883 Barrack-Room Ballads, 1892

2884 Many Inventions, 1893

2885 Jungle Books, 1894, 1895

2886 The Day's Work, 1898

2887 From Sea to Sea, 1899

2888 Traffics and Discoveries, 1904

2889 Puck of Pook's Hill, 1906

2890 Actions and Reactions, 1909

2891 Rewards and Fairies, 1910

2892 Debits and Credits, 1926

2893 Limits and Renewals, 1932

2894 Something of Myself, 1936

BIBLIOGRAPHIES

2895 Livingston, F. V. Bibliography of the Works of Rudyard Kipling. London, B. Franklin, 1927-1939. 2 vols.

2896 Stewart, J. McG., ed. Rudyard Kipling: A Bibliographical Catalogue. Ed. by A. W. Yeats. Toronto, Dalhouise University Press, 1959.

TEXTS

2897 Beecroft, J., ed. Kipling: A Selection of His Stories and Poems. New York, Doubleday, 1956.

2898 The Best of Kipling. Garden City, N. Y., Doubleday, 1968.

2899 Collected Verse of Rudyard Kipling. New York, Doubleday, 1910.

2900 Eliot, T. S., ed. A Choice of Kipling's Verse. New York, Doubleday, 1956.

2901 Jarrell, R. The Best Short Stories of Rudyard Kipling. New York, Doubleday, 1961.

2902 Selected Prose and Poetry. New York, Garden City Publishing Company, 1937.

2903 Selected Stories from Kipling. Ed. W. L. Phelps. Garden City, N. Y., Doubleday, 1921.

CRITICISM

2904 Bodelsen, C. A. Aspects of Kipling's Art. New York, Barnes & Noble, 1964.

2905 Carrington, C. Kipling: A Life. London, Macmillan, 1955.

2906 Dobrée, B. Rudyard Kipling: Realist and Fabulist. London, Oxford University Press, 1967.

2907 Gilbert, E. L., ed. Kipling and the Critics. New York, New York University Press, 1965.

2908 Rutherford, A. Kipling's Mind and Art: Selected Critical Essays. Edinburgh, Oliver & Boyd, 1964.

2909 Tompkins, J. M. S. The Art of Rudyard Kipling. London, P. Smith, 1965.

2910 Young, A., and J. H. McGivering. A Kipling Dictionary. London, St. Martin's, 1968.

Dante Gabriel Rossetti (1828-1882)

WORKS

2911 The Blessed Damozel, 1850
2912 Poems, 1870
2913 Ballads and Sonnets, 1881
2914 The House of Life, 1928

TEXTS

2915 Baum, P. F., ed. Rossetti's Letters to Fanny Cornworth. Baltimore, Johns Hopkins, 1940.

2916 Doughty, O., ed. Poems. New York, Longmans, Green, 1957.

2917 Rossetti, W. M., ed. Works. Boston, Little, Brown, 1901.

CRITICISM

2918 Doughty, O. Dante Gabriel Rossetti: A Victorian Romantic. London, Oxford University Press, 1969.

2919 Fleming, G. H. Rossetti and the Pre-Raphaelite Brotherhood. London, Hart-Davis, 1967.

2920 Pedrick, G. Life with Rossetti, or No Peacocks Allowed. London, Macdonald, 1964.

Algernon Charles Swinburne (1837-1909)

WORKS

2921 Atalanda, In Calydon, 1865
2922 Chastelard, 1865
2923 Poems and Ballads, 1866, 1878
2924 Songs Before Sunrise, 1871
2925 Erechtheus, 1876
2926 Love's Cross-Currents, 1877
2927 Mary Stuart, 1881
2928 Tristram of Lyonesse, 1882
2929 Lesbia Brandon, 1952

BIBLIOGRAPHIES

2930 Wise, T. J. A Bibliography of the Writings in Prose and Verse of Algernon Charles Swinburne. London, Dawsons, Pall Mall, 1966.

TEXTS

2931 Gosse, E., and T. J. Wise, eds. Complete Works. New York, Russell & Russell, 1965. 20 vols.

2932 Lang, C. Y., ed. The Swinburne Letters. New Haven, Conn., Yale University Press, 1962.

2933 Rosenberg, J. D., ed. Selected Poetry and Prose. New York, Modern Library, 1968.

2934 Wilson, E., ed. The Novels: Love's Cross-Currents, Lesbia. New York, Brandon, 1962.

CRITICISM

2935 Fuller, J. O. Swinburne: A Critical Biography. London, Chatto & Windus, 1968.

2936 Hyder, C. K. Swinburne's Literary Career and Fame. New York, Russell & Russell, 1963.

2937 Peters, R. L. The Crowns of Apollo: Swinburne's Principles of Literature and Art. A Study in Victorian Criticism and Aesthetics. Detroit, Wayne State University Press, 1965.

Alfred, Baron Tennyson (1809-1892)

WORKS

2938 Poems, Chiefly Lyrical, 1830
2939 The Lady of Shalott, 1832
2940 The Lotus Eaters, 1832
2941 Morte D'Arthur, 1833
2942 The Silent Voices, 1833
2943 Ulysses, 1833
2944 In Memoriam, 1850
2945 Maud and Other Poems, 1852

2946 Idylls of the King, 1859, 1869, 1889
2947 The May Queen, 1861
2948 The Holy Grail, and Other Poems, 1869
2949 Tiresias and Other Poems, 1885
2950 Saint Agnes Eve, 1911

BIBLIOGRAPHIES

2951 Tennyson, C., and C. Fall. Alfred Tennyson: An Annotated Bibliography. Athens, University of Georgia Press, 1967.

2952 Wise, T. J. A Bibliography of the Writings of Alfred, Lord Tennyson. London, Dawsons, Pall Mall, 1967.

TEXTS

2953 Auden, W. H., ed. Selections from the Poems. London, Phoenix, 1946.

2954 Blunden, E. C., ed. Selected Poems. London, Heinemann, 1960.

2955 Chew, S. C., ed. Representative Poems. New York, Odyssey, 1941.

2956 DeVane, W. L., and M. P., eds. Selections. New York, Barnes & Noble, 1960.

2957 Ricks, C. B., ed. The Poems of Tennyson. New York, Longmans, 1968.

2958 Rolphe, W. J., ed. Complete Poetical Works. Boston, Houghton, 1947.

CRITICISM

2959 Baker, A. E. Tennyson Dictionary: The Characters and Place-Names Contained in the Poetical and Dramatic Works of the Poet Alphabetically Arranged and Described. New York, Haskell House, 1969.

2960 _____ . A Concordance to the Poetical and Dramatic Works of Alfred, Lord Tennyson. New York, Barnes & Noble, 1966.

2961 Brashear, W. R. The Living Will: A Study of Tennyson and Nineteenth Century Subjectivism. The Hague, Mouton, 1969.

2962 Brightwell, D. B. A Concordance to the Entire Works of Alfred Tennyson. 1869. Repr. New York, Haskell House, 1970.

2963 Buckley, J. H. Tennyson: The Growth of a Poet. Boston, Houghton, 1965.

2964 Dixon, W. M. A Primer of Tennyson with a Critical Essay. 1896. Repr. New York, Haskell House, 1970.

2965 Eisden, J. O. Tennyson in America: His Reputation and Influence from 1827 to 1858. Athens, University of Georgia Press, 1943.

2966 Johnson, E. D. H. The Alien Vision of the Poetic Imagination in Tennyson, Browning and Arnold. Princeton, Princeton University Press, 1952.

2967 Killham, J., ed. Critical Essays on the Poetry of Tennyson. New York, Barnes & Noble, 1960.

2968 Kissane, J. D. Alfred Tennyson. New York, Twayne, 1970.

2969 Marshall, G. O., Jr. A Tennyson Handbook. New York, Twayne, 1963.

2970 Rader, R. W. Tennyson's Maud: The Biographical Genesis. Berkeley, University of California Press, 1963.

2971 Richardson, J. The Pre-Eminent Victorian: A Study of Tennyson. London, J. Cape, 1962.

2972 Ryals, C. de L. Theme and Symbol in Tennyson's Poems to 1850. Philadelphia, University of Pennsylvania Press, 1964.

2973 Smith, E. E. The Two Voices: A Tennyson Study. Lincoln, University of Nebraska Press, 1964.

Francis Thompson (1859-1907)

WORKS

2974 Poems, 1893, 1897

2975 Sister Songs, 1895

2976 New Poems, 1897

2977 Health and Holiness, 1905

2978 Life of Saint Ignatius Loyola, 1909

2979 Life of Blessed John Baptist De Le Galle, 1911

TEXTS

2980 Complete Poetical Works of Franics Thompson. New York, Modern Library, 1913.

2981 Connolly, T. L., ed. Poems. New York, Appleton, 1941.

2982 _____ , ed. Account of Books and Manuscripts of Thompson. Boston, Boston College, 1937.

2983 _____ , ed. Literary Criticism by Thompson. New York, Dutton, 1948.

2984 Meynell, W., ed. Poems. Oxford, Standard Authors, 1937.

CRITICISM

2985 Butter, P. Francis Thompson. London, Longmans, Green, 1961.

2986 Thomson, P. Van K. Francis Thompson: A Critical Biography. New York, Nelson, 1961.

2987 Walsh, J. Strange Harp, Strange Symphony: The Life of Francis Thompson. New York, Hawthorn Books, 1967.

2988 Weyand, N. T. Francis Thompson: His Theory of Poetry. Ann Arbor, University of Michigan Press, 1940.

19TH CENTURY PROSE FICTION—BIBLIOGRAPHIES

2989 Bleiler, E. F. The Checklist of Fantastic Literature: A Bibliography of Fantasy, Weird, and Science Fiction Books in English. Chicago, Shastor Publishers, 1948.

2990 Ehrsam, T. G., and R. H. Deily, eds. Bibliographies of Twelve Victorian Authors. New York, Octagon, 1968.

2991 Queen, E. The Detective Short Story: A Bibliography. Boston, Little, Brown, 1943.

2992 Ray, G. N. Bibliographical Resources for the Study of Nineteenth Century English Fiction. Los Angeles, School of Library Service, University of California, 1964.

2993 Stevenson, L., ed. Victorian Fiction: A Guide to Research. Cambridge, Mass., Harvard University Press, 1964.

19TH CENTURY PROSE FICTION—TEXTS

2994 Booth, B. A., ed. A Cabinet of Gems: Short Stories from the English Annuals. Berkeley, University of California Press, 1938.

2995 Harrold, C. F., and W. D. Templeman, eds. English Prose of the Victorian Era. New York, Oxford University Press, 1938.

2996 Johnson, E. D. H., ed. The World of the Victorians: An Anthology of Poetry and Prose. New York, Scribner's, 1964.

19TH CENTURY PROSE FICTION—CRITICISM

2997 Bruner, D. K. Family Life in Early Victorian Prose Fiction. Urbana, University of Illinois Press, 1941.

2998 Cecil, D. Victorian Novelists. Chicago, Chicago University Press, 1958.

2999 Chesterson, G. K. The Victorian Age in Literature. Notre Dame, Ind., University of Notre Dame Press, 1963.

3000 Colby, R. A. Fiction with a Purpose: Major and Minor Nineteenth Century Novels. Bloomington, Indiana University Press, 1967.

3001 Colby, V. The Singular Anomaly. Women Novelists of the Nineteenth Century. New York, University of New York Press, 1970.

3002 Daiches, D. The Novel and the Modern World. Chicago, Chicago University Press, 1960.

3003 Ellman, R., ed. Edwardians and Victorians. New York, Columbia University Press, 1960.

3004 Ford, B., et al., eds. From Dickens to Hardy. Baltimore, Penguin, 1969.

3005 Frierson, W. C. The English Novel in Transition, 1885-1940. Norman, University of Oklahoma Press, 1942.

3006 Gibson, B. H. The History, from 1800 to 1832, of English Criticism and of Prose Fiction. Urbana, University of Illinois Press, 1931.

3007 Graham, K. English Criticism of the Novel, 1865-1900. Oxford, Oxford University Press, 1965.

3008 Howard, D. F., J. Lucas, and J. Goode. Tradition and Tolerance in Nineteenth Century Fiction. New York, Barnes & Noble, 1967.

3009 Karl, F. R. An Age of Fiction. The Nineteenth Century British Novel. New York, Farrar, 1965.

3010 Kunitz, S. J., and H. Haycraft. British Authors of the Nineteenth Century. New York, Wilson, 1936.

3011 Laver, J. Manners and Morals in the Age of Optimism, 1848-1914. New York, Harper, 1967.

3012 Marshall, W. H. The World of the Victorian Novel. South Brunswick, N. J., A. S. Barnes, 1967.

3013 Miller, J. H. The Form of Victorian Fiction: Thackeray, Dickens, Trollope, George Eliot, Meredith, and Hardy. Notre Dame, Ind., University of Notre Dame Press, 1968.

3014 Russell, F. T. Satire in the Victorian Novel. New York, Russell & Russell, 1964.

19TH CENTURY PROSE FICTION—INDIVIDUAL AUTHORS

Jane Austen (1775-1817)

WORKS

3015 Sense and Sensibility, 1795   3018 Mansfield Park, 1811
3016 Pride and Prejudice, 1796-97   3019 Emma, 1815
3017 Northanger Abbey, 1798-99   3020 Persuasion, 1815

BIBLIOGRAPHIES

3021 Chapman, R. W. Jane Austen: A Critical Bibliography. Oxford, Clarendon Press, 1969.

TEXTS

3022 Chapman, R. W., ed. The Novels of Jane Austen. Oxford, Oxford University Press, 1923-1954. 6 vols.

3023 _____ , ed. Letters. 2d ed. Oxford, Oxford University Press, 1952.

3024 Southam, B. C., ed. Jane Austen: Volume the Second. Oxford, Clarendon Press, 1963.

3025 _____ , ed. Jane Austen's Literary Manuscripts. Oxford, Clarendon Press, 1964.

CRITICISM

3026 Apperson, G. L. A Jane Austen Dictionary. London, C. Palmer, 1932. Repr. New York, Haskell House, 1969.

3027 Babb, H. S. Jane Austen's Novels: The Fabric of Dialogue. Columbus, Ohio State University Press, 1962.

3028 Bradbrook, F. W. Jane Austen: Emma. London, E. Arnold, 1961.

3029 Brown, I. Jane Austen and Her World. London, Butterworth, 1966.

3030 Chapman, R. W. Jane Austen: Facts and Problems. Oxford, Oxford University Press, 1948.

3031 Craik, W. A. Jane Austen: The Six Novels. London, Methuen, 1968.

3032 Fleishman, A. A Reading of Mansfield Park: An Essay in Critical Synthesis. Minneapolis, University of Minnesota Press, 1967.

3033 Lascelles, M. Jane Austen and Her Art. Oxford, Clarendon Press, 1963.

3034 Laski, M. Jane Austen and Her World. New York, Viking, 1969.

3035 Liddell, R. The Novels of Jane Austen. London, Longmans, 1963.

3036 Litz, A. W. Jane Austen: A Study of Her Artistic Development. New York, Oxford University Press, 1965.

3037 Lodge, D., ed. Jane Austen: Emma. A Casebook. New York, Macmillan, 1968.

3038 Moler, K. L. Jane Austen's Art of Allusion. Lincoln, University of Nebraska Press, 1968.

3039 Mudrick, M. Jane Austen: Irony as Defense and Discovery. Berkeley, University of California Press, 1968.

3040 Southam, B. C., ed. Jane Austen: A Critical Heritage. London, Routledge & K. Paul, 1968.

3041 Ten Harmsel, H. Jane Austen: A Study of Fictional Conventions. The Hague, Mouton, 1964.

3042 Watt, I., ed. Jane Austen: A Collection of Critical Essays. Englewood Cliffs, N. J., Prentice-Hall, 1963.

3043 Wright, A. H. Jane Austen's Novels: A Study in Structure. Oxford, Oxford University Press, 1953.

The Brontës — Charlotte Brontë (1816-1855)
Emily Jane Brontë (1818-1848)

WORKS

3044 Jane Eyre, 1846

3045 Poems by Currer, Ellis, and Acton Bell, 1846

3046 The Professor, 1847

3047 Wuthering Heights, 1847

BIBLIOGRAPHIES

3048 Wise, T. J. A Bibliography of the Writings in Prose and Verse of the Brontë Family. Repr. London, Dawsons, 1965.

TEXTS

3049 Complete Works of Charlotte Brontë and Her Sisters. San Francisco, Wheeler, 1848. 6 vols.

3050 Crehan, T., ed. Wuthering Heights. London, London University Press, 1962.

3051 Hatfield, C. W., ed. The Complete Poems of Emily Brontë. New York, Columbia University Press, 1941.

3052 Jack, J., and M. Smith, eds. Charlotte Brontë. Jane Eyre. Oxford, Clarendon Press, 1969.

3053 Spark, M., ed. The Letters of the Brontës. Norman, University of Oklahoma Press, 1954.

CRITICISM

3054 Bentley, P. The Brontës and Their World. New York, Viking, 1969.

3055 Craik, W. A. The Brontë Novels. London, Methuen, 1968.

3056 Everitt, A., comp. Wuthering Heights: An Anthology of Criticism. London, Frank Cass, 1967.

3057 Ewbank, I. S. Their Proper Sphere: A Study of the Brontë Sisters as Early Victorian Novelists. Cambridge, Mass., Harvard University Press, 1966.

3058 Gaskell, E. C. Life of Charlotte Brontë. Oxford, World's Classics, 1857.

3059 Gerin, W. Charlotte Brontë: The Evaluation of Genius. Oxford, Clarendon Press, 1967.

3060 Hewisch, J. Emily Brontë: A Critical and Biographical Study. London, St. Martin's, 1969.

3061 Knies, E. A. The Art of Charlotte Brontë. Athens, Ohio University Press, 1970.

3062 Martin, H. T. Petticoat Rebels: A Study of the Novels of Social Protest of George Eliot, Elizabeth Gaskell and Charlotte Brontë. New York, Helios, 1968.

3063 Maurat, C. The Brontës' Secret. Trans. by M. Meldrum. New York, Barnes & Noble, 1970.

3064 O'Neill, J. Critics on Charlotte and Emily Brontë. Coral Gables, University of Miami Press, 1969.

3065 Pollard, A. Charlotte Brontë. London, Routledge & K. Paul, 1968.

3066 Spark, M., and D. Stanford. Emily Brontë: Her Life and Work. New York, Coward, 1960.

3067 Stevenson, W. H. Emily and Anne Brontë. London, Routledge & K. Paul, 1968.

3068 Visick, M. The Genesis of Wuthering Heights. 2d ed. Oxford, Oxford University Press, 1965.

3069 Vogler, T. A., ed. Twentieth Century Interpretations of Wuthering Heights: A Collection of Critical Essays. Englewood Cliffs, N. J., Prentice-Hall, 1968.

3070 Wroot, H. E. The Persons and Places of the Brontë Novels. Bradford, Brontë Society, 1906.

Samuel Butler (1835-1902)
WORKS

3071 Erewhon, 1872
3072 Evolution, Old and New, 1879
3073 Unconscious Memory, 1890
3074 The Way of All Flesh, 1903
3075 God the Known and God the Unknown, 1909
3076 The Humour of Homer, and Other Essays, 1913

BIBLIOGRAPHIES

3077 Harkness, S. B., ed. The Career of Samuel Butler: A Bibliography. London, B. Franklin, 1955.

TEXTS

3078 Howard, D. F., ed. Ernest Pontifex or the Way to All Flesh. Boston, Houghton, 1964.

3079 _____ , ed. The Correspondence of Samuel Butler with His Sister May. Berkeley, University of California Press, 1962.

3080 Jones, H. F., and A. T. Bartholomew, eds. Works. 20 vols. London, Cape, 1923-1926. Repr. New York, AMS Press, 1968.

3081 Silver, A., ed. The Family Letters of Samuel Butler, 1841-1886.
Stanford, Stanford University Press, 1962.

Lewis Carroll (1832-1898)

WORKS

3082 Alice's Adventures in
Wonderland, 1865
3083 Through the Looking-Glass,
1872

3084 Sylvia and Bruno, 1889,
1893

TEXTS

3085 The Complete Works of Lewis Carroll. New York, Modern Library,
1937.

3086 Green, R. L., ed. The Diaries. London, Gassell, 1954. 2 vols.

CRITICISM

3087 Green, R. L. The Story of Lewis Carroll. London, Methuen, 1962.

3088 Hudson, D. Lewis Carroll. London, British Book Center, 1955.

3089 Lennon, F. B. Victoria Through the Looking-Glass: The Life of
Lewis Carroll. New York, Collier, 1962.

3090 Weaver, W. Alice in Many Tongues: The Translations of Alice in
Wonderland. Madison, University of Wisconsin Press, 1964.

3091 Williams, S., and F. Madan. The Lewis Carroll Handbook. Oxford,
Oxford University Press, 1962.

Charles Dickens (1812-1870)

WORKS

3092 The Pickwick Papers,
1836-37
3093 Oliver Twist, 1838
3094 Nicholas Nickleby,
1838-39
3095 The Old Curiosity Shop,
1841

3096 A Christmas Carol, 1843
3097 David Copperfield, 1849-50
3098 Bleak House, 1852-53
3099 Hard Times, 1854
3100 A Tale of Two Cities, 1859
3101 Great Expectations, 1860-61
3102 Our Mutual Friend, 1864-65

BIBLIOGRAPHIES

3103 Halton, T., and A. H. Cleaver. A Bibliography of the Periodical
Works of Charles Dickens. London, Chapman & Hall, 1933.

3104 Kitton, F. G., comp. Dickensiana: A Bibliography of the Literature Relating to Charles Dickens and His Writings. 1886. Repr. New York, Haskell House, 1971.

3105 _____ , ed. The Minor Writings of Charles Dickens: A Bibliography and Sketch. 1900. Repr. New York, Haskell House, 1970.

3106 Miller, W. The Dickens Student and Collector: A List of Writings Relating to Dickens and His Work, 1836-1945. Cambridge, Mass., Harvard University Press, 1946.

TEXTS

3107 Dupée, F. W., ed. The Selected Letters of Charles Dickens. New York, Farrar, 1960.

3108 House, M., and G. Storey, eds. The Letters of Charles Dickens. Vol. I: 1820-1839. Oxford, Clarendon Press, 1965.

3109 The New Oxford Illustrated Edition. Oxford, Oxford University Press, 1947-1958. 21 vols.

CRITICISM

3110 Barlow, R. B., ed. Dickens Studies Annual, Vol. I. Carbondale, Southern Illinois University Press, 1970– .

3111 Blount, T. Dickens: The Early Novels. London, Longmans, Green, 1968.

3112 Brown, I. Dickens in His Time. London, Nelson, 1963.

3113 Burton, H. M. Dickens and His Works. London, Methuen, 1968.

3114 Butt, J., and K. Tillotson. Dickens at Work. London, Methuen, 1968.

3115 Cockshut, A. O. J. The Imagination of Charles Dickens. London, Collins, 1961.

3116 Collins, P. Dickens and Crime. London, St. Martin's, 1962.

3117 _____ . Dickens and Education. London, St. Martin's, 1963.

3118 _____ , ed. Dickens: The Critical Heritage. New York, Barnes & Noble, 1971.

3119 Dabney, R. H. Love and Poverty in the Novels of Dickens. London, Chatto & Windus, 1967.

3120 Donovan, F. R. Dickens and Youth. New York, Dodd, 1968.

3121 Dyson, A. E. Dickens: Modern Judgments. New York, Macmillan, 1968.

3122 Engel, M. The Maturity of Dickens. Cambridge, Mass., Harvard University Press, 1959.

3123 Fido, M. Charles Dickens. London, Routledge & K. Paul, 1968.

3124 Fielding, K. J. Charles Dickens: A Critical Introduction. Boston, Houghton, 1965.

3125 Ford, B., et al. From Dickens to Hardy. Rev. ed. Baltimore, Penguin, 1969.

3126 Ford, G. H. Dickens and His Readers: Aspects of Novel Criticism Since 1836. Princeton, Princeton University Press, 1955.

3127 _____ , and L. Lane, eds. Dickens Critics. Ithaca, N. Y., Cornell University Press, 1955.

3128 Forster, J. The Life of Charles Dickens. London, Dent, 1966. 2 vols.

3129 Fyfe, T. H., comp. Who's Who in Dickens: A Complete Dickens Repertory in Dickens' Own Words. 1913. Repr. New York, Haskell House, 1971.

3130 Gissing, G. Critical Studies of the Works of Charles Dickens. New York, Russell & Russell, 1924.

3131 Gray, P. E., ed. Twentieth Century Interpretations of Hard Times: A Collection of Critical Essays. Englewood Cliffs, N. J., Prentice-Hall, 1969.

3132 Hardwick, M., and M. The Charles Dickens Companion. London, Murray, 1965.

3133 Hardy, B. The Moral Art of Dickens. Oxofrd, Oxford University Press, 1970.

3134 _____ . Dickens: The Later Novels. New York, Longmans, Green, 1968.

3135 Hayward, A. L. The Dickens Encyclopedia: An Alphabetical Dictionary of the Reference to Every Character and Place Mentioned in the Works of Fiction with Explanatory Notes on Obscure Allusions and Phrases. Hamden, Conn., Archon, 1969.

3136 Hilbert, C. The Making of Charles Dickens. New York, Harper, 1967.

3137 House, H. The Dickens World. Oxford, Oxford University Press, 1941.

3138 Johnson, E. Charles Dickens: His Tragedy and Triumph. Boston, Little, Brown, 1965. 2 vols.

3139 _____ . Charles Dickens: An Introduction to His Novels. New York, Random, 1969.

3140 Korg, J., ed. Twentieth Century Interpretations of Bleak House. Englewood Cliffs, N. J., Prentice-Hall, 1968.

3141 Leacock, S. Charles Dickens, His Life and Work. Garden City, N. Y., Doubleday, 1934.

3142 Monod, S. Dickens the Novelist. Norman, Oklahoma University Press, 1968.

3143 Pierce, G. A. Dickens Dictionary. New York, Kraus, 1914.

3144 Price, M., ed. Dickens: A Collection of Critical Essays. Englewood Cliffs, N. J., Prentice-Hall, 1967.

3145 Priestley, J. B. Charles Dickens: A Pictorial Biography. London, Thames & Hudson, 1961.

3146 Slater, M., ed. Dickens 1970; Centenary Essays by W. Allen and Others. New York, Stein & Day, 1970.

3147 Sucksmith, H. P. The Narrative Art of Charles Dickens: The Rhetoric of Sympathy and Irony in His Novels. Oxford, Oxford University Press, 1970.

3148 Szladits, L. L. Charles Dickens: An Anthology from Materials in the Berg Collection of English and American Literature, in Commemoration of the Centennial of Dickens' Death. New York, New York Public Library & Arno, 1970.

3149 Tomlin, E. W. F. Charles Dickens, 1812-1870; A Centennial Volume. New York, Simon & Schuster, 1970.

3150 Williams, M. The Dickens Concordance: Being a Compendium of Names and Characters and Principal Places Mentioned in All the Works of Charles Dickens. 1907. Repr. New York, Haskell House, 1970.

3151 Wilson, A. The World of Charles Dickens. New York, Viking, 1970.

George Eliot (1819-1880)
WORKS

3152 Adam Bede, 1859
3153 The Mill on the Floss, 1860
3154 Silas Marner, 1861
3155 Felix Holt the Radical, 1866
3156 Middlemarch, 1871-72
3157 Daniel Deronda, 1876

TEXTS

3158 The Best-Known Novels of George Eliot. New York, Modern Library, 1968.

3159 Haight, G. S., ed. The Letters. New Haven, Conn., Yale University Press, 1954-1956. 7 vols.

3160 Pinney, T., ed. Essays of George Eliot. New York, Columbia University Press, 1963.

CRITICISM

3161 Beaty, J. Middlemarch from Notebook to Novel: A Study of George Eliot's Creative Method. Urbana, University of Illinois Press, 1960.

3162 Bennett, J. George Eliot: Her Mind and Her Art. Cambridge, Cambridge University Press, 1962.

3163 Cooper, L. U. George Eliot. London, British Book Center, 1951.

3164 Daiches, D. George Eliot: Middlemarch. London, E. Arnold, 1963.

3165 Haight, G. S. A Century of George Eliot Criticism. London, Methuen, 1966.

3166 _____ . George Eliot: A Biography. New York, Oxford University Press, 1968.

3167 Hardy, B. The Novels of George Eliot: A Study in Form. London, Oxford University Press, 1959.

3168 _____ , ed. Middlemarch: Critical Approaches to the Novel. New York, Oxford University Press, 1967.

3169 Harvey, W. J. The Art of George Eliot. London, Chatto & Windus, 1961.

3170 Holmstrom, J., and L. Lerner, eds. George Eliot and Her Readers: A Selection of Contemporary Reviews. New York, Barnes & Noble, 1966.

3171 Knoepflmacher, V. C. George Eliot's Early Novels; the Limits of Realism. Berkeley, University of California Press, 1968.

3172 Martin, H. T. Petticoat Rebels: A Study of the Novels of Social Protest of George Eliot, Elizabeth Gaskell, and Charlotte Brontë. New York, Helios, 1968.

3173 Paris, B. J. Experiment in Life: George Eliot's Quest for Values. Detroit, Wayne State University Press, 1965.

3174 Sprague, R. George Eliot: A Biography. Philadelphia, Chilton, 1968.

3175 Stump, R. Movement and Vision in George Eliot's Novels. Seattle, University of Washington Press, 1959.

3176 Thale, J. The Novels of George Eliot. New York, Columbia University Press, 1959.

Thomas Hardy (1840-1928)

WORKS

3177 Far from the Madding Crowd, 1874

3178 The Return of the Native, 1878

3179 The Major of Caterbridge, 1886

3180 Wessex Tales, 1888

3181 Tess of the D'Urbervilles, 1891

3182 Jude the Obscure, 1896

BIBLIOGRAPHIES

3183 Purdy, R. L., ed. Thomas Hardy: A Bibliographical Study. London, Oxford University Press, 1954.

3184 Weber, C. J. The First Hundred Years of Thomas Hardy, 1840-1940: A Centenary Bibliography of Hardiana. New York, Russell & Russell, 1965.

TEXTS

3185 Elledge, S., ed. Tess of the D'Urbervilles: An Authoritative Text, Hardy and the Novel, Criticism. New York, Norton, 1965.

3186 Orel, H., ed. Personal Writings: Prefaces, Literary Opinions, Reminiscences. Lawrence, University of Kansas Press, 1966.

3187 Ransom, J. C., ed. Selected Poems. New York, Macmillan, 1961.

3188 Wain, J., ed. Selected Shorter Poems. London, Macmillan, 1966.

3189 Weber, C. J., ed. The Letters of Hardy. Waterville, Maine, Colby College Press, 1954.

3190 Works. 19 vols. London, St. Martin's, 1968.

CRITICISM

3191 Abercombie, L. Thomas Hardy: A Critical Study. New York, Russell & Russell, 1912.

3192 Bailey, J. O. The Poetry of Thomas Hardy: A Handbook and Commentary. Chapel Hill, University of North Carolina Press, 1970.

3193 Bowra, C. M. The Lyrical Poetry of Hardy. Nottingham, Nottingham University Press, 1947.

3194 Brown, D. Thomas Hardy: The Major of Casterbridge. London, E. Arnold, 1962.

3195 Carpenter, R. C. Thomas Hardy. New York, Twayne, 1964.

3196 Cox, R. G., ed. Thomas Hardy: The Critical Heritage. New York, Barnes & Noble, 1970.

3197 Guerard, A. J., ed. Hardy: A Collection of Critical Essays. Englewood Cliffs, N. J., Prentice-Hall, 1963.

3198 _____ . Hardy: The Novels and Stories. Cambridge, Mass., Harvard University Press, 1949.

3199 _____ . Thomas Hardy: A Critical Study. New York, New Directions, 1964.

3200 Hardy, E. Some Recollections by Emma Hardy, with Notes by Evelyn Hardy. Together with some Relevant Poems by Thomas Hardy, with Notes by Robert Gittings. London, Oxford University Press, 1961.

3201 Hardy, F. E. The Life of Thomas Hardy, 1840-1928. Hamden, Conn., Archon, 1970.

3202 Hawkins, D. Thomas Hardy the Novelist. New York, Taplinger, 1966.

3203 Hynes, S. The Patterns of Hardy's Poetry. Chapel Hill, University of North Carolina Press, 1961.

3204 LaValley, A. J., ed. Twentieth Century Interpretations of Tess of the D'Urbervilles. Englewood Cliffs, N. J., Prentice-Hall, 1969.

3205 Miller, J. H. Thomas Hardy: Distance and Desire. Cambridge, Mass., Harvard University Press, 1970.

3206 Orel, H. Thomas Hardy's Epic Drama: A Study of the Dynasts. Lawrence, University of Kansas Press, 1963.

3207 Pinion, F. B. A Hardy Companion: A Guide to the Works of Thomas Hardy and their Background. New York, Macmillan, 1968.

3208 Rutland, W. R. Thomas Hardy. New York, Russell & Russell, 1962.

3209 Sankey, B. The Major Novels of Thomas Hardy. Denver, Swallow, 1965.

3210 Saxelby, F. O. A Thomas Hardy Dictionary. New York, Humanities Press, 1968.

3211 Weber, C. J. Hardy of Wessex: His Life and Literary Career. New
York, Columbia University Press, 1940.

3212 _____ , and C. C. Weber. Thomas Hardy's Correspondence
at Max Gate: A Descriptive Check List. Maine, Colby College, 1968.

3213 Webster, H. C. On a Darkling Plain: The Art and Thought of
Thomas Hardy. Hamden, Conn., Shoe String Press, 1947.

3214 Wright, W. F. The Shaping of the Dynasts: A Study of Thomas
Hardy. Lincoln, University of Nebraska Press, 1967.

George Meredith (1828-1909)

WORKS

3215 The Ordeal of Richard
Feverel, 1859

3216 Rhonda Fleming, 1865

3217 The Egoist, 1879

3218 The Tragic Comedians, 1880

3219 Poems and Lyrics of the Joy
of Earth, 1883

3220 Diana of the Crossways, 1885

3221 Ballads and Poems of Tragic
Life, 1887

3222 One of Our Conquerors, 1891

BIBLIOGRAPHIES

3223 Forman, M. B. A Bibliography of the Writings in Prose and Verse of
George Meredith. London, Bibliographical Society, 1922. Repr.
New York, Haskell House, 1971.

3224 _____ . Meredithiana: Being a Supplement to the Bibliography of Meredith. 1924. Repr. New York, Haskell House, 1971.

TEXTS

3225 Hough, G., ed. Selected Poems. Oxford, Oxford University Press,
1962.

3226 Works of George Meredith. New York, Russell & Russell, 1965.
29 vols.

CRITICISM

3227 Bartlett, P. George Meredith. New York, Longmans, Green, 1963.

3228 Beach, J. W. The Comic Spirit in George Meredith. New York,
Russell & Russell, 1963.

3229 Beer, G. Meredith: A Change of Masks; A Study of the Novels.
New York, Oxford University Press, 1970.

3230 Kelvin, N. A Troubled Eden: Nature and Society in the Works of
George Meredith. Stanford, Stanford University Press, 1961.

3231 Peel, R. The Creed of a Victorian Pagan. Cambridge, Mass., Harvard University Press, 1931.

3232 Stevenson, L. The Ordeal of George Meredith. New York, Russell & Russell, 1953.

3233 Trevelyan, G. M. The Poetry and Philosophy of George Meredith. New York, Russell & Russell, 1966.

3234 Wright, W. F. Art and Substance in George Meredith: A Study in Narrative. Lincoln, University of Nebraska Press, 1963.

Sir Walter Scott (1771-1832)

WORKS

3235 The Minstrelsy of the Scottish Border, 1802-03

3236 Sir Tristrem, 1804

3237 The Lay of the Last Minstrel, 1805

3238 Ballads and Lyrical Pieces, 1806

3239 The Lady of the Lake, 1810

3240 Waverly, 1814

3241 The Antiquary, 1816

3242 Tales of My Landlord, 1816-19

3243 Rob Roy, 1818

3244 The Heart of the Midlothian, 1818

3245 Ivanhoe, 1819

3246 The Bride of the Lammermoor, 1819

3247 The Abbot, 1820

3248 The Monastery, 1820

3249 Kenilworth, 1821

3250 The Pirate, 1822

3251 Tales of the Crusaders, 1825

3252 Woodstock, 1826

BIBLIOGRAPHIES

3253 Corson, J. C., ed. A Bibliography of Sir Walter Scott: A Classified and Annotated List of Books and Articles Relating to His Life and Works, 1797-1940. Edinburgh, Oliver & Boyd, 1943. Repr. New York, B. Franklin, 1969.

3254 Ruff, W., ed. A Bibliography of the Poetical Works of Sir Walter Scott, 1796-1832. Edinburgh, Edinburgh Bibliographical Society, 1938.

TEXTS

3255 Carpenter, G., ed. The Lady of the Lake. New York, Longmans, Green, 1903.

3256 Complete Poetical and Dramatic Works. New York, J. Alden, 1884. 4 vols.

3257 Complete Poetical Works of Sir Walter Scott. Boston, Houghton, 1900.

3258 Grierson, H. J. C., ed. Letters. London, Constable, 1932-1937.
      12 vols.

3259 The Heart of the Midlothian. Boston, Estes & Lauriat, 1893.

3260 Ivanhoe. New York, Heritage, 1950.

3261 Kenilworth. New York, Heritage, 1966.

3262 The Monastery. Boston, Ticknor & Fields, 1893.

3263 The Pirate. Boston, Ticknor & Fields, 1893.

3264 Rob Roy. London, Dent, 1908.

3265 Tait, J. G., ed. Journal. Edingurgh, Oliver & Boyd, 1939-46. 3 vols.

3266 Tales of the Crusaders. New York, Dodd, 1943.

3267 Waverly. Philadelphia, Lippincott, 1887.

3268 Woodstock. Boston, Ticknor & Fields, 1858.

CRITICISM

3269 Clark, A. M. Sir Walter Scott: The Formative Years. New York,
      Barnes & Noble, 1970.

3270 Cockshut, A. O. J. The Achievement of Walter Scott. New York,
      University of New York Press, 1969.

3271 Davie, D. The Heyday of Sir Walter Scott. London, Routledge &
      K. Paul, 1961.

3272 Devlin, D. D., ed. Walter Scott: Modern Judgements. New York,
      Macmillan, 1968.

3273 Hayden, J. O., ed. Scott: The Critical Heritage. New York, Barnes
      & Noble, 1970.

3274 Hillhouse, J. T. The Waverly Novels and Their Critics. New York,
      Octagon, 1967.

3275 Husband, M. F. A. A Dictionary of Character in the Waverly
      Novels of Scott. New York, Humanities Press, 1962.

3276 Jack, I. Sir Walter Scott. London, British Book Center, 1959.

3277 Jeffares, A. N., ed. Scott's Mind and Art, by Thomas Crawford.
      New York, Barnes & Noble, 1970.

3278 Lauber, J. Sir Walter Scott. New York, Twayne, 1966.

3279 Parsons, C. O. Witchcraft and Demonology in Scott's Fiction:
      With Chapters on the Supernatural in Scottish Literature. Edin-
      burgh, Oliver & Boyd, 1964.

3280 Williams, J. Sir Walter Scott on Novelists and Fiction. London, Routledge & K. Paul, 1968.

Robert Louis Stevenson (1850-1894)

WORKS

3281 Treasure Island, 1883

3282 Kidnapped, 1886

3283 Strange Case of Dr. Jekyll and Mr. Hyde, 1886

3284 The Black Arrow, 1888

BIBLIOGRAPHIES

3285 Prideaux, W. F. A Bibliography of the Works of Robert Louis Stevenson. London, Hollings, 1917.

TEXTS

3286 Commings, S., ed. Selected Writings. New York, Modern Library, 1947.

3287 Great Short Stories. New York, Washington Square, 1961.

3288 Neider, C., ed. Complete Short Stories of Robert Louis Stevenson. Garden City, Doubleday, 1969.

3289 Ricklefs, R., ed. The Mind of Robert Louis Stevenson: Selected Essays, Letters and Prayers. New York, T. Yoseloff, 1963.

3290 Smith, J. A., ed. Collected Poems. Philadelphia, Dufour, 1954.

CRITICISM

3291 Caldwell, E. N. Last Witness for Robert Louis Stevenson. Norman, University of Oklahoma Press, 1960.

3292 Daiches, D. Robert Louis Stevenson. New York, New Directions, 1947.

3293 Kiely, R. Robert Louis Stevenson and the Fiction of Adventure. Cambridge, Mass., Harvard University Press, 1964.

3294 Swinnerton, F. Robert Louis Stevenson: A Critical Study. New York, Kennikat, 1915.

William Makepeace Thackeray (1811-1863)

WORKS

3295 Vanity Fair, 1848

3296 The History of Pendennis, 1849-50

3297 The Newcomes, 1854-55

3298 The Virginians, 1858-59

BIBLIOGRAPHIES

3299 Flamm, D. Thackeray's Critics: An Annotated Bibliography of British and American Criticism, 1836-1901. Chapel Hill, University of North Carolina Press, 1967.

3300 Van Duzer, H. S. Thackeray Bibliography. New York, Kennikat, 1968.

TEXTS

3301 Ray, G. N., ed. The Letters and Private Papers of William Makepeace Thackeray. Cambridge, Mass., Harvard University Press, 1945-1946. 4 vols.

3302 The Works of William Makepeace Thackeray. London, Smith, Elder, 1869. 24 vols.

3303 The Works of William Makepeace Thackeray. New York, Harper, 1910-1911. 26 vols.

3304 Works. Philadelphia, Lippincott, 1901. 26 vols.

CRITICISM

3305 Dodds, J. W. Thackeray: A Critical Portrait. New York, Russell & Russell, 1963.

3306 Elwin, M. Thackeray: A Personality. New York, Russell & Russell, 1966.

3307 Ennis, L. Thackeray, the Sentimental Cynic. Evanston, Ill., Northwestern University Press, 1951.

3308 Mudge, I. G., and M. E. Sears. A Thackeray Dictionary. New York, Humanities Press, 1962.

3309 Sundell, M. G., ed. Twentieth Century Interpretations of Vanity Fair: A Collection of Critical Essays. Englewood Cliffs, N. J., Prentice-Hall, 1969.

3310 Tillotson, G. Thackeray the Novelist. New York, Barnes & Noble, 1964.

3311 Welsh, A., ed. Thackeray: A Collection of Critical Essays. Englewood Cliffs, N. J., Prentice-Hall, 1968.

Anthony Trollope (1815-1882)

WORKS

3312 The Warden, 1855
3313 Barchester Towers, 1857
3314 Doctor Thorne, 1858
3315 Orley Farm, 1861-62
3316 The Small House at Arlington, 1864
3317 Can You Forgive Her, 1864-65

3318 He Knew He Was Right, 1868-69
3319 The Eustace Diamonds, 1873
3320 The Way We Live Now, 1874-75
3321 The Duke's Children, 1880
3322 Mr. Scarborough's Family, 1883

BIBLIOGRAPHIES

3323 Sadleir, M. Trollope: A Bibliography. London, Constable, 1928.

TEXTS

3324 Booth, B. A., ed. The Letters of Anthony Trollope. Oxford, Oxford University Press, 1951.

3325 Dunn, E. C., and M. E. Dodd, eds. The Trollope Reader. New York, Oxford University Press, 1947.

3326 Sadleir, M., and F. Page, eds. The Oxford Illustrated Trollope. Oxford, Oxford University Press, 1948-1954. 15 vols.

3327 The Writings of Anthony Trollope. Philadelphia, Gebbie, 1900. 30 vols.

CRITICISM

3328 Cockshut, A. O. J. Anthony Trollope. London, Methuen, 1968.

3329 Edwards, P. D. Anthony Trollope. London, Routledge & K. Paul, 1968.

3330 Gerould, W. G., and J. T. Gerould, eds. Guide to Trollope. Princeton, Princeton University Press, 1948.

3331 Pollard, A. Trollope's Political Novels. Hull, Hull University Press, 1968.

3332 Sadleir, M. Trollope: A Contemporary. Oxford, Oxford University Press, 1961.

19TH CENTURY PROSE NON-FICTION—GENERAL WORKS

3333 Foakes, R. A. Romantic Criticism, 1800-1850. London, E. Arnold, 1968.

3334 Hoffman, D. G., and S. Hynes, eds. English Literary Criticism: Romantic and Victorian. New York, Appleton, 1963.

3335 Jones, E. D., ed. English Critical Essays: Nineteenth Century. Oxford, Oxford University Press, 1968.

3336 Kauvar, G. B., and G. C. Sorensen, eds. The Victorian Mind: An Anthology. New York, Putnam, 1969.

3337 Tillotson, G. Criticism in the Nineteenth Century. Hamden, Conn., Archon, 1967.

19TH CENTURY PROSE NON-FICTION—INDIVIDUAL AUTHORS

Matthew Arnold (1822-1888)

WORKS

3338 Cromwell, 1843
3339 Empedocles on Etna and Other Poems, 1852
3340 Merope, 1858
3341 On Translating Homer, 1861
3342 Essays in Criticism, 1865
3343 New Poems, 1867
3344 On the Study of Celtic Literature, 1867
3345 Culture and Anarchy, 1869
3346 Literature and Dogma, 1873
3347 God and the Bible, 1875
3348 The English Poets, 1880

BIBLIOGRAPHIES

3349 Ehrsam, T. G., and R. H. Deily, eds. Bibliographies of Twelve Victorian Authors. New York, Octagon, 1968.

3350 Smart, T. B. The Bibliography of Matthew Arnold. London, Davy, 1892. Repr. New York, 1968.

TEXTS

3351 Allott, K., ed. Poems. New York, Barnes & Noble, 1960.

3352 Brown, E. K., ed. Matthew Arnold: Selected Poems. New York, Appleton, 1951.

3353 Bryson, J., ed. Poetry and Prose. Cambridge, Mass., Harvard University Press, 1954.

3354 Buckler, W. E., ed. Passages from the Prose Writing of Matthew Arnold Selected by the Author. New York, New York University Press, 1963.

3355 Littlewood, S. R., ed. Essays in Criticism: Second Series. New York, St. Martin's, 1968.

3356 Mulhauser, F. L., ed. Matthew Arnold: Selected Poetry and Prose. New York, Holt, 1953.

3357 Neiman, F., ed. Essays, Letters and Reviews by Matthew Arnold. Cambridge, Mass., Harvard University Press, 1960.

3358 Super, R. H., ed. The Complete Prose Works of Matthew Arnold. Ann Arbor, University of Michigan Press, 1960-1968. 3 vols.

3359 Tinker, C. B., and H. F. Lowry, eds. Poetical Works. Oxford, Standard Authors, 1950.

3360 Trilling, L., ed. The Portable Matthew Arnold. New York, Viking, 1949.

CRITICISM

3361 Anderson, W. D. Matthew Arnold and the Classical Tradition. Ann Arbor, University of Michigan Press, 1965.

3362 Brown, E. K. Matthew Arnold: A Study in Conflict. Chicago, E. K. Brown, 1948.

3363 Chambers, E. K. Matthew Arnold: A Study. New York, Russell & Russell, 1964.

3364 Culler, A. D. Imaginative Reason: The Poetry of Matthew Arnold. New Haven, Conn., Yale University Press, 1960.

3365 Duffin, H. C. Arnold the Poet. London, Bowes & Bowes, 1962.

3366 Gottfried, L. Matthew Arnold and the Romantics. Lincoln, University of Nebraska Press, 1963.

3367 James, D. G. Matthew Arnold and the Decline of English Romanticism. Oxford, Clarendon Press, 1961.

3368 Johnson, E. D. H. The Alien Vision of Victorian Poetry: Sources of the Poetic Imagination in Tennyson, Browning and Arnold. Princeton, Princeton University Press, 1952.

3369 Johnson, W. S. The Voice of Matthew Arnold: An Essay in Criticism. New Haven, Conn., Yale University Press, 1961.

3370 Lippincott, B. E. Victorian Critics of Democracy: Carlyle, Ruskin, Arnold, Maine, Lecky. Minneapolis, University of Minnesota Press, 1938.

3371 Lowry, H. F. Matthew Arnold and the Modern Spirit. Princeton, Princeton University Press, 1941.

3372 Madden, W. A. Matthew Arnold. A Study of the Aesthetic Temperament in Victorian England. Bloomington, Indiana University Press, 1967.

3373 Parrish, S. M. A Concordance to the Poems by Matthew Arnold. Ithaca, N. Y., Cornell University Press, 1959.

3374 Roper, A. Arnold's Poetic Landscapes. Baltimore, Johns Hopkins, 1969.

3375 Stange, G. R. Matthew Arnold: The Poet as Humanist. Princeton, Princeton University Press, 1967.

3376 Super, R. H. The Time-Spirit of Matthew Arnold. Ann Arbor, University of Michigan Press, 1970.

3377 Walcott, Fred G. The Origins of Culture and Anarchy: Matthew Arnold and Popular Education in England. New York, University of Toronto Press, 1970.

Thomas Carlyle (1795-1881)
WORKS

3378 Sartor Resartus, 1830
3379 The French Revolution, 1834
3380 On Heroes and Hero Worship, 1841
3381 The Heroic in History, 1841
3382 Past and Present, 1843
3383 The History of Friedrich II of Prussia, 1858-65
3384 Reminiscences, 1881

BIBLIOGRAPHIES

3385 The Bibliography of Carlyle: A Bibliographical List Arranged in Chronological Order of the Published Writings in Prose and Verse of Thomas Carlyle. 1881. Repr. New York, Haskell House, 1970.

3386 Dyer, I. W. A Bibliography of Thomas Carlyle's Writings. Portland, Maine, Southworth Press, 1928.

TEXTS

3387 Sanders, C. R., et al., eds. The Collected Letters of Thomas and Jane Welsh Carlyle. Durham, N. C., Duke University Press, 1970.

3388 Symons, J., ed. Selected Works, Reminiscences and Letters. Cambridge, Mass., Harvard University Press, 1957.

3389 Tennyson, G. B., ed. A Carlyle Reader. New York, Modern Library, 1969.

CRITICISM

3390 Bentley, E. R. A Century of Hero-Worship: A Study of the Idea of Heroism in Carlyle and Nietzsche. 2d ed. Boston, Beacon Press, 1957.

3391 LaValley, A. J. Carlyle and the Idea of the Modern: Studies in Carlyle's Prophetic Literature and Its Relation to Blake, Nietzsche, Marx and Others. New Haven, Conn., Yale University Press, 1968.

3392 Lehman, B. H. Carlyle's Theory of the Hero. New York, AMS Press, 1968.

3393 Tennyson, G. B. Sartor Called Resartus: The Genesis, Structure, and Style of Thomas Carlyle's First Major Work. Princeton, Princeton University Press, 1965.

Thomas De Quincey (1785-1859)
WORKS

3394 Confessions of an English Opium Eater, 1821, 1822, 1856

TEXTS

3395 Dobrée, B., ed. Thomas De Quincey. New York, Schocken, 1965.

3396 Masson, D., ed. Collected Writings. New York, AMS Press, 1968. 14 vols.

CRITICISM

3397 Davies, H. S. Thomas De Quincey. London, Longmans, Green, 1964.

3398 Goldman, A. The Mine and the Mint: Sources for the Writings of Thomas De Quincey. Carbondale, Southern Illinois University Press, 1965.

3399 Jordan, J. E. Thomas De Quincey; Literary Critic: His Method and Achievement. Berkeley, University of California Press, 1952.

3400 Metcalf, J. C. De Quincey: A Portrait. Cambridge, Mass., Harvard University Press, 1940.

3401 Proctor, S. K. De Quincey's Theory of Literature. Ann Arbor, University of Michigan Press, 1943.

William Hazlitt (1778-1830)
WORKS

3402 Characters of Shakespeare's Plays, 1817
3403 The Round Table, 1817
3404 A View of the English Stage, 1818
3405 Lectures on the English Poets, 1818
3406 Lectures on the English Comic Writers, 1819
3407 Lectures Chiefly on the Dramatic Literature of the Age of Elizabeth, 1820
3408 Table-Talk, 1821-22, 1825

BIBLIOGRAPHIES

3409 Keynes, G. L. Bibliography of William Hazlitt. London, Nonesuch Press, 1931.

TEXTS

3410 Howe, P. P., ed. Works. New York, AMS Press, 1968. 21 vols.

3411 Sikes, H. M., ed. The Hazlitt Sampler: Selections from His Familiar, Literary and Critical Essays. Greenwich, Conn., Fawcett Publications, 1942.

CRITICISM

3412 Albrecht, W. P. Hazlitt and the Creative Imagination. Lawrence, University of Kansas Press, 1965.

3413 Archer, W., and W. Lowe, eds. Hazlitt on Theatre. London, Hill & Wang, 1957.

3414 Baker, H. Hazlitt. Cambridge, Mass., Harvard University Press, 1962.

Charles Lamb (1775-1834)
WORKS

3415 Tales from Shakespeare, 1807
3416 Specimens of English Dramatic Poets, 1808
3417 Elia, 1823, 1835
3418 The Last Essays of Elia, 1833

BIBLIOGRAPHIES

3419 Thomson, J. C. Bibliography of the Writings of Charles and Mary Lamb. Hull, Tutin, 1908.

TEXTS

3420 Brown, J. M., ed. The Portable Lamb. New York, Viking, 1949.

3421 Hallward, N. L., and S. C. Hill, eds. The Last Essays of Elia. New York, St. Martin's, 1968.

3422 Lucas, E. V., ed. Works. London, Methuen, 1912.

3423 _____ , ed. Letters. New Haven, Conn., Yale University Press, 1935. 3 vols.

CRITICISM

3424 Barnett, G. L. Charles Lamb: The Evolution of Elia. Bloomington, Indiana University Press, 1964.

3425 Blunden, E. C. Lamb and His Contemporaries. Cambridge, Cambridge University Press, 1937.

John Stuart Mill (1806-1873)

WORKS

3426 Utilitarianism, 1863   3427 Autobiography, 1873

BIBLIOGRAPHIES

3428 McMinn, N., J. R. Hainds, and J. M. McCrimmon, eds. Bibliography of the Published Writings of Mill, Edited from His Manuscript. Evanston, Northwestern University Press, 1945.

TEXTS

3429 Autobiography. Boston, Houghton, 1969.

3430 Collected Works. Toronto, University of Toronto Press, 1963.

3431 Piest, O., ed. Utilitarianism. 2d ed. New York, Liberal Arts Press, 1957.

3432 Stillinger, J., ed. The Early Draft of John Stuart Mill's Autobiography. Urbana, University of Illinois Press, 1961.

CRITICISM

3433 Ellery, J. B. John Stuart Mill. New York, Twayne, 1964.

3434 Robson, J. M. The Improvement of Mankind: The Social and Political Thought of John Stuart Mill. Toronto, University of Toronto Press, 1968.

3435 Sharpless, F. P. The Literary Criticisms of John Stuart Mill. The Hague, Mouton, 1967.

3436 Woods, T. Poetry and Philosophy: A Study in the Thought of John Stuart Mill. London, Hutchinson, 1961.

John Ruskin (1819-1900)

WORKS

3437 Modern Painters, 1846   3439 The Stones of Venice, 1853
3438 Pre-Raphaelitism, 1851

TEXTS

3440 Bloom, H., ed. The Literary Criticism of John Ruskin. Garden City, N. Y., Doubleday, 1965.

3441 Cook, E. T., and A. Wedderburn, eds. Complete Works. New York, Longmans, Green, 1903-1912. 39 vols.

3442 Evans, J., and J. H. Whitehouse, eds. The Diaries of John Ruskin. Oxford, Clarendon Press, 1959.

3443 Rosenberg, J. D., ed. The Genius of John Ruskin: Selections from His Writings. Boston, Houghton, 1963.

3444 Viljoen, H. G., ed. The Brantwood Diary of John Ruskin: Together with Selected Letters and Sketches of Persons Mentioned. New Haven, Conn., Yale University Press, 1971.

CRITICISM

3445 Clark, K., ed. Ruskin Today. London, Murray, 1964.

3446 Landow, G. R. The Aesthetic and Critical Theories of John Ruskin. Princeton, University of Princeton Press, 1971.

3447 Rosenberg, J. D. The Darkening Glass: A Portrait of Ruskin's Genius. New York, Columbia University Press, 1962.

3448 Townsend, F. G. Ruskin and the Landscape Feeling: A Critical Analysis of His Thought During the Crucial Years of His Life, 1843-56. Urbana, University of Illinois Press, 1951.

TWENTIETH CENTURY

GENERAL WORKS—BIBLIOGRAPHIES

3449 Eastwood, W., and J. T. Good, eds. Signposts: A Guide to Modern English Literature. Cambridge, Cambridge University Press, 1960.

3450 Temple, R. Z., comp. and ed., assisted by M. Tucker. Twentieth Century British Literature: A Reference Guide and Bibliography. New York, Ungar, 1968.

GENERAL WORKS—TEXTS AND CRITICISM

3451 Fleischmann, W. B., ed. Encyclopedia of World Literature in the Twentieth Century. I: A-F. New York, Ungar, 1969.

3452 Ford, B., et al., eds. The Modern Age. Baltimore, Penguin, 1969.

3453 Frye, N. The Modern Century. Oxford, Oxford University Press, 1967.

3454 Goldberg, G. J., and N. M., eds. The Critical Spectrum: The Major Schools of Modern Literary Criticism Explained and Illustrated for Today's Reader. Englewood Cliffs, N. J., Prentice-Hall, 1962.

3455 Grigson, G., ed. The Concise Encyclopedia of Modern World Literature. New York, Hawthorne Books, 1963.

3456 Hough, G. Image and Experience: Studies in a Literary Revolution. London, Duckworth, 1960.

3457 Richardson, K. Twentieth Century Writing: A Reader's Guide to Contemporary Literature. New York, Transatlantic, 1970.

3458 Symons, J. The Thirties: A Dream Revolved. London, Cresset Press, 1960.

3459 Temple, R. Z., and M. Tucker, comps. and eds. A Library of Literary Criticism: Modern British Literature. New York, Ungar, 1966. 3 vols.

3460 Wellek, R. A History of Modern Criticism, 1750-1950. New Haven, Conn., Yale University Press, 1955. 4 vols.

DRAMA—BIBLIOGRAPHIES

3461 Adelman, I., and R. Dworkin, eds. Modern Drama: A Check List of Critical Literature on Twentieth Century Plays. Metuchen, N. J., Scarecrow, 1967.

3462 Salem, J. M. A Guide to Critical Reviews. Part III, British and Continental Drama from Ibsen to Pinter. Metuchen, N. J., Scarecrow, 1968.

DRAMA—TEXTS

3463 Barnet, S., M. Berman, and W. Burto, eds. The Genius of the Irish Theatre. New York, New American Library, 1960.

3464 Block, H. M., and R. G. Shedd, eds. Masters of Modern Drama. New York, Random, 1962.

3465 Brown, J. R., ed. Modern British Dramatists. Englewood Cliffs, N. J., Prentice-Hall, 1968.

3466 Cerf, B., and V. H. Cartwell, eds. Twenty-Four Favorite One-Act Plays. New York, Doubleday, 1958.

3467 Corrigan, R. W., ed. The Modern Theatre. New York, Macmillan, 1964.

3468 _____ , ed. Masterpieces of English Drama: The Twentieth Century. New York, Dell, 1968.

3469 Hogan, R. G., ed. Seven Irish Plays, 1946-1964. Minneapolis, University of Minnesota Press, 1967.

3470 Popkin, H., ed. The New British Drama. New York, Grove, 1964.

The Best Plays of 1919-1967. New York, Dodd, 1920– .

3471 Mantle, B., ed. The Best Plays of 1919-30 to 1946-47. New York, Dodd, annual.

3472 Chapman, J., ed. The Burns Mantle Best Plays, 1947-48 to 1951-52. New York, Dodd, annual.

3473 Kronenberger, L. The Best Plays of 1952-53 to 1960-61. New York, Dodd, annual.

3474 Hewes, H., ed. The Best Plays of 1960-62 to 1963-64. New York, Dodd, annual.

3475 Guernsey, O., ed. The Best Plays of 1964-65 to 1966-67. New York, Dodd, annual.

3476 The Modern Theatre: An Anthology. New York, Doubleday, 1955.
6 vols.

DRAMA—CRITICISM

3477 Bentley, E. R. The Playwright as Thinker: A Study of Drama in
Modern Times. New York, Harcourt, 1967.

3478 _____ . The Theory of Modern Stage: An Introduction to
Modern Theatre and Drama. Baltimore, Penguin, 1968.

3479 Brown, J. R., ed. Modern British Dramatists: A Collection of
Critical Essays. Englewood Cliffs, N. J., Prentice-Hall, 1968.

3480 Brustein, R. The Theatre of Revolt: An Approach to the Modern
Drama. Boston, Little-Atlantic, 1964.

3481 Clark, B. H., and G. Freedley. A History of Modern Drama. New
York, Appleton, 1947.

3482 Clurman, H. The Naked Image: Observation on the Modern Theatre.
New York, Macmillan, 1966.

3483 Dickinson, H. Myth on the Modern Stage. Urbana, University of
Illinois Press, 1969.

3484 Dietrich, R. F., W. E. Carpenter, and K. Kerrane, comps. The Art
of Modern Drama. New York, Holt, 1969.

3485 Donoghue, D. The Third Voice: Modern British and American Verse
Drama. Princeton, Princeton University Press, 1959.

3486 Ellis-Fermor, U. M. The Irish Dramatic Movement. London, Methuen, 1967.

3487 Esslin, M. The Theatre of the Absurd. Garden City, N. Y.,
Doubleday, 1961.

3488 Guthke, K. S. Modern Tragicomedy. New York, Random, 1966.

3489 Hogan, R. G. After the Irish Renaissance: A Critical History of Irish
Drama since The Plough and The Stars. Minneapolis, University of
Minnesota Press, 1967.

3490 Krutch, J. W. "Modernism" in Modern Drama: A Definition and
an Estimate. Ithaca, N. Y., Cornell University Press, 1966.

3491 Lewis, A. The Contemporary Theatre: The Significant Playwrights
of our Time. New York, Crown, 1962.

3492 Lumley, F. New Trends in Twentieth Century Drama: A Survey
Since Ibsen and Shaw. 3d ed. London, Barrie & Rockliff, 1967.

3493 Melchinger, S. Concise Encyclopedia of Modern Drama. Ed. by H. Popkin, trans. by G. Wellwarth. New York, Horizon, 1965.

3494 Nicoll, A. English Drama: A Modern Viewpoint. New York, Harrap, 1968.

3495 Reynolds, E. Modern English Drama: A Survey of the Theatre since 1900. Norman, University of Oklahoma Press, 1951.

3496 Styan, J. L. The Dark Comedy: The Development of Modern Comic Tragedy. 2d ed. London, Cambridge University Press, 1968.

3497 Sutton, G. Some Contemporary Dramatists. Port Washington, N. Y., Kennikat, 1967.

3498 Taylor, J. R. The Rise and Fall of the Well-Made Play. London, Methuen, 1968.

3499 _____ . Anger and After: A Guide to the New British Dramas. London, Methuen, 1962.

3500 Wager, W. The Dramatists Speak. New York, Longmans, 1968.

3501 Weales, G. C. Religion in Modern English Drama. Philadelphia, University of Pennsylvania Press, 1961.

3502 Williams, R. Drama from Ibsen to Eliot. London, Chatto & Windus, 1952.

3503 _____ . Modern Tragedy. Stanford, University of Stanford Press, 1966.

DRAMA—INDIVIDUAL AUTHORS

Samuel Beckett (1906–)

WORKS

3504 Whoroscope, 1930
3505 Proust, 1931
3506 More Pricks than Kicks, 1934
3507 Molloy, 1951

3508 Waiting for Godot, 1952
3509 Endgame, 1958
3510 Krapp's Last Tape, 1959
3511 Happy Days, 1961

BIBLIOGRAPHIES

3512 Federman, R., and J. Fletcher. Samuel Beckett. His Works and Critics. An Essay in Bibliography. Berkeley, University of California Press, 1970.

TEXTS

3513 Calder, J., ed. A Samuel Beckett Reader. London, Calder & Boyars, 1967.

3514 Endgame. Trans. by the author. New York, Grove, 1958.

3515 Happy Days. Play in Two Acts. New York, Grove, 1970.

3516 Krapp's Last Tape and Other Dramatic Pieces. New York, Grove, 1970.

3517 Molloy. New York, Grove, 1970.

3518 More Pricks than Kicks. New York, Grove, 1970.

3519 Proust. New York, Grove, 1970.

3520 Waiting for Godot. A Tragicomedy in Two Acts. Trans. by the author. New York, Grove, 1970.

CRITICISM

3521 Cohn, R. Samuel Beckett: The Comic Gamut. New Brunswick, N. J., Rutgers University Press, 1962.

3522 _____ . Casebook on Waiting for Godot. New York, Grove, 1967.

3523 Fletcher, J. The Novels of Samuel Beckett. 2d ed. New York, Barnes & Noble, 1970.

3524 _____ . Samuel Beckett's Art. New York, Barnes & Noble, 1967.

3525 Grossvogel, D. I. Four Playwrights and a Postscript: Brecht, Ionesco, Beckett, Genet. Ithaca, N. Y., Cornell University Press, 1962.

3526 Jacobsen, J., and W. R. Mueller. The Testament of Samuel Beckett. London, Faber, 1968.

3527 Simpson, A. Beckett and Behan and a Theatre in Dublin. New York, Hillary House, 1962.

3528 Tindall, W. Y. Samuel Beckett. New York, Columbia University Press, 1964.

3529 Webb, E. Samuel Beckett: A Study of his Novels. Seattle, University of Washington Press, 1970.

William Somerset Maugham (1874-1965)
WORKS

3530	Of Human Bondage, 1915	3533	The Summing Up, 1938
3531	The Moon and Sixpence, 1919	3534	The Razor's Edge, 1944
		3535	A Winter's Notebook, 1949
3532	Cakes and Ale, 1930	3536	Short Stories, 1951

BIBLIOGRAPHIES

3537 Sanders, C., ed. and comp. Somerset Maugham: An Annotated Bibliography of the Writings about Him. Dekalb, Northern Illinois University Press, 1970.

3538 Toolestott, R. The Writings of William Somerset Maugham: A Bibliography. London, Rota, 1956.

TEXTS

3539 Complete Short Stories. New York, Doubleday, 1952. 2 vols.

3540 Jonas, K. W., ed. The World of Somerset Maugham: An Anthology. London, P. Owen, 1959.

3541 The Maugham Reader. Garden City, N. Y., Doubleday, 1950.

3542 Plays. Boston, Mass., Baker, 1968. 6 vols.

3543 Selected Novels. London, Heinemann, 1953. 3 vols.

CRITICISM

3544 Barnes, R. E. The Dramatic Comedy of William Somerset Maugham. The Hague, Mouton, 1968.

3545 Brander, L. Somerset Maugham: A Guide. Edinburgh, Oliver & Boyd, 1963.

3546 Cordell, R. A. Somerset Maugham: A Biographical and Critical Study. 2d ed. Bloomington, Indiana University Press, 1969.

3547 Nichols, B. A Case of Human Bondage. London, Secker & Warburg, 1966.

Sean O' Casey (1884-1964)

WORKS

3548 Juno and the Peacock, 1925
3549 Autobiography, 1939-63
3550 Red Roses for Me, 1942
3551 Cockadoodle Dandy, 1949
3552 Collected Plays, 1949

TEXTS

3553 Cock-A-Doodle Dandy. London, Macmillan, 1949.

3554 Collected Plays. London, St. Martin's, 1950-1951.

3555 Juno and the Peacock. The Shadow of a Gunman. New York, Macmillan, 1925.

3556 Mirror in my House: His Autobiographies. New York, Macmillan, 1939-1954. 6 vols.

3557 Red Roses for Me. London, Macmillan, 1942.

3558 Selected Plays. Introd. by John Gessner. New York, Braziller, 1956.

CRITICISM

3559 Cowasjee, S. Sean O' Casey: The Man Behind the Plays. New York, St. Martin's, 1964.

3560 Fallon, G. Sean O' Casey: The Man I Knew. London, Routledge & K. Paul, 1965.

3561 Hogan, R. G. The Experiments of Sean O' Casey. New York, St. Martin's, 1960.

3562 Koslow, J. Sean O' Casey: The Man and his Plays. New York, Citadel Press, 1966.

3563 Krause, D. Sean O' Casey: The Man and his Work. New York, Collier, 1960.

George Bernard Shaw (1856-1950)

WORKS

3564 An Unsocial Socialist, 1884
3565 Ghosts, 1891
3566 Arms and the Man, 1894
3567 Candida, 1895
3568 The Devil's Disciple, 1897
3569 Plays Pleasant and Unpleasant, 1898
3570 You Never Can Tell, 1899
3571 Major Barbara, 1905
3572 Man and Superman, 1905
3573 Caesar and Cleopatra, 1906
3574 The Doctor's Dilemma, 1906
3575 Androcles and the Lion, 1913
3576 Heartbreak House, 1913
3577 Pygmalion, 1913
3578 Back to Methuselah, 1921
3579 Saint Joan, 1923

TEXTS

3580 Burton, H. M., ed. Prose Anthology. Greenwich, Conn., Fawcett, 1968.

3581 Collected Works of Bernard Shaw. Ed. A. St. Lawrence. New York, Wise, 1930.

3582 Complete Plays. New York, Dodd, 1962. 6 vols.

3583 Downer, A. S., ed. The Theatre of Bernard Shaw. New York, Dodd, 1961. 2 vols.

3584 Laurence, D. H., ed. Selected Non-Dramatic Writings. Boston, Houghton, 1968.

3585 _____ , ed. Collected Letters, 1874-1897. New York, Dodd, 1964.

3586 Matthews, J. F., ed. Shaw's Dramatic Criticism: A Selection. New York, Hill & Wang, 1959.

3587 Selected Novels of George Bernard Shaw. New York, Caxton, 1946.

3588 Tillett, J., ed. Bernard Shaw: Three Shorter Plays. London, Heinemann, 1968.

3589 Tompkins, P., ed. To a Young Actress: The Letters of Bernard Shaw to Molly Tompkins. New York, Potter, 1960.

3590 Ward, A. C., ed. Plays and Players: Selected Essays. Oxford, World's Classics, 1952.

CRITICISM

3591 Bentley, E. R. Bernard Shaw: A Reconsideration. New York, New Directions, 1957.

3592 Broad, C. L., and V. M. Dictionary to the Plays and Novels of Bernard Shaw. London, Black, 1929. Repr. New York, Haskell House, 1969.

3593 Carpenter, C. Bernard Shaw and the Art of Destroying Ideals: The Early Plays. Madison, University of Wisconsin Press, 1969.

3594 Dietrich, R. F. Portrait of the Artist as a Young Superman: A Study of Shaw's Novels. Gainesville, University of Florida Press, 1969.

3595 Fromm, H. Bernard Shaw and the Theatre in the Nineties: A Study of Shaw's Dramatic Criticism. Lawrence, University of Kansas Press, 1967.

3596 Kaufmann, R. J., ed. George Bernard Shaw: A Collection of Critical Essays. Englewood Cliffs, N. J., Prentice-Hall, 1965.

3597 Kronenberger, L., ed. George Bernard Shaw: A Critical Survey. Cleveland, World Publishing Company, 1953.

3598 Meisel, M. Shaw and the Nineteenth Century Theatre. Princeton, Princeton University Press, 1963.

3599 Ohmann, R. M. Shaw: The Style and the Man. Middletown, Conn., Wesleyan University Press, 1962.

3600 Pearson, H. Bernard Shaw: His Life and Personality. New York, Atheneum, 1963.

3601 Purdom, C. B., ed. A Guide to the Plays of Bernard Shaw. London, Methuen, 1963.

3602 Rosset, B. C. Shaw of Dublin. The Formative Years. University Park, Pennsylvania State University Press, 1964.

3603 Shenfield, M. George Bernard Shaw: A Pictorial Biography. New York, Viking, 1962.

3604 Wagenknecht, E. C. A Guide to Bernard Shaw. New York, Appleton, 1929. Repr. New York, Russell & Russell, 1971.

3605 Williamson, A. Bernard Shaw: Man and Artist. New York, Crowell-Collier, 1963.

3606 Woodbridge, H. E. George Bernard Shaw, Creative Artist. Carbondale, Southern Illinois University Press, 1963.

John Millington Synge (1871-1909)

WORKS

3607 Riders to the Sea, 1905

3608 The Playboy of the Western World, 1907

3609 The Tinker's Wedding, 1907

3610 Deidre of the Sorrows, 1910

TEXTS

3611 The Complete Plays. New York, Random, 1960.

3612 The Complete Works. New York, Random, 1968.

3613 Henn, T. R., ed. The Plays and Poems of John Millington Synge. London, Methuen, 1963.

3614 Skelton, R., ed. John Millington Synge: Collected Works. 5 vols. London, Oxford University Press, 1962.

CRITICISM

3615 Corkery, D. Synge and the Anglo-Irish Literature. New York, Russell & Russell, 1965.

3616 Johnston, D. John Millington Synge. New York, Columbia University Press, 1965.

3617 Price, A. F. The Autobiography of John Millington Synge. Philadelphia, Dufour, 1967.

3618 _____ . Synge and Anglo-Irish Drama. New York, Barnes & Noble, 1961.

3619 Saddlemyer, A. John Millington Synge and Modern Comedy. Dublin, Dolmen Press, 1968.

3620 Solomont, S. The Comic Effect of Playboy of the Western World. Bangor, Me., Signalman Press, 1962.

POETRY—TEXTS

3621 Allott, K., ed. The Penguin Book of Contemporary Verse. London, Penguin, 1962.

3622 Cecil, L. D., and A. Tate, eds. Modern Verse in English, 1900-1950. New York, Macmillan, 1958.

3623 Daiches, D., and W. Charvart, eds. Poems in English, 1930-1940. New York, Ronald, 1950.

3624 Durrell, L., ed. New Poems, 1963. A British P.E.N. Anthology. New York, Harcourt, 1964.

3625 Gardner, B., ed. The Terrible Rain: The War Poets, 1939-1945: An Anthology. London, Methuen, 1966.

3626 _____ , ed. Up the Line to Death: The War Poets, 1914-1919: An Anthology. London, Methuen, 1964.

3627 Griffiths, B., ed. Welsh Voices: An Anthology of New Poetry from Wales. London, Dent, 1967.

3628 Jennings, E., ed. An Anthology of Modern Verse, 1940-1960. London, Methuen, 1961.

3629 Lindsay, J. M., ed. Modern Scottish Poetry: An Anthology of the Scottish Renaissance. London, Faber & Faber, 1966.

3630 Macbeth, G., ed. Poetry 1900 to 1965: An Anthology. London, Longmans, 1967.

3631 Rosenthal, M. L., ed. The New Modern Poetry Since World War II. New York, Oxford University Press, 1969.

3632 Untermeyer, L., ed. Modern British Poetry. 6th rev. ed. New York, Harcourt, 1962.

3633 Yeats, W. B., ed. The Oxford Book of Modern Verse: 1892-1935. Oxford, Oxford University Press, 1936.

POETRY—CRITICISM

3634 Coffman, S. K., Jr. Imagism: A Chapter for the History of Modern Poetry. Norman, University of Oklahoma Press, 1951.

3635 Cox, C. B., and A. E. Dyson. Modern Poetry: Studies in Practical Criticism. London, E. Arnold, 1963.

3636 Deutsch, B. Poetry in Outline. New York, Doubleday, 1963.

3637 Drew, E. Poetry: A Modern Guide to its Understanding and Enjoyment. New York, Norton, 1959.

3638 Duncan, J. E. The Revival of the Metaphysical Poetry: The History of a Style, 1800 to the Present. Minneapolis, University of Minnesota Press, 1959.

3639 Gross, H. Sound and Form in Modern Poetry. Ann Arbor, University of Michigan Press, 1964.

3640 Hollander, J., ed. Modern Poetry: Essays in Criticism. London, Oxford University Press, 1968.

3641 Hughes, G. Imagism and the Imagists: A Study in Modern Poetry. Stanford, Stanford University Press, 1931.

3642 Johnson, J. H. English Poetry of the First World War. Princeton, Princeton University Press, 1964.

3643 Miller, J. H. Poets of Reality: Six Twentieth Century Writers. Cambridge, Mass., Harvard University Press, 1965.

3644 O'Connor, W. V. Sense and Sensibility in Modern Poetry. New York, Barnes & Noble, 1963.

3645 Pinto, V. de Sola. Critics in English Poetry, 1880-1940. New York, Harper, 1957.

3646 Pratt, J. C. The Meaning of Modern Poetry. Garden City, N. Y., Doubleday, 1962.

3647 Rosenthal, M. L. The Modern Poets: A Critical Introduction. Oxford, Galaxy Books, 1960.

3648 _____ . The New Poets: American and British Poetry Since World War II. Oxford, Galaxy Books, 1967.

3649 Wheelwright, P. Metaphor and Reality. Bloomington, Indiana University Press, 1962.

POETRY—INDIVIDUAL AUTHORS

Wystan Hugh Auden (1907–)

WORKS

3650 Poems, 1930
3651 The Orators, 1932
3652 The Dance of Death, 1933
3653 The Dog Beneath the Skin, 1935
3654 Look, Stranger, 1936
3655 The Ascent, F.6, 1936
3656 New Year Letter, 1941
3657 For the Time Being, 1944
3658 The Age of Anxiety, 1947
3659 The Shield of Achilles, 1955
3660 Homage to Clio, 1960
3661 About the House, 1966

BIBLIOGRAPHIES

3662 Broomfield, B. C. W. H. Auden: A Bibliography: The Early Years through 1955. Charlottesville, Virginia University Press, 1964.

3663 Callan, E. An Annotated Check List of the Works of W. H. Auden. Denver, Swallow, 1958.

TEXTS

3664 Collected Poetry. New York, Random, 1945.

3665 Selected Poetry. New York, Modern Library, 1959.

CRITICISM

3666 Beach, J. W. The Making of the Auden Canon. Minneapolis, University of Minnesota Press, 1957.

3667 Blair, J. G. The Poetic Art of W. H. Auden. Princeton, Princeton University Press, 1965.

3668 Fuller, J. A Reader's Guide to W. H. Auden. New York, Farrar, 1970.

3669 Hoggart, R. Auden: An Introductory Essay. New York, Hillary House, 1956.

3670 Nelson, G. Changes of Heart: A Study of the Poetry of W. H. Auden. Berkeley, University of California Press, 1969.

3671 Spears, M. K. The Poetry of W. H. Auden: The Disenchanted Island. New York, Oxford University Press, 1963.

3672 _____ . Auden: A Collection of Critical Essays. Englewood Cliffs, N. J., Prentice-Hall, 1964.

T. S. Eliot (1888-1965)

WORKS

3673 The Sacred Wood, 1920
3674 The Waste Land, 1922
3675 Ash Wednesday, 1930
3676 Selected Essays, 1932
3677 Sweeney Agonistes, 1932
3678 The Rock, 1934

3679 Murder in the Cathedral, 1935
3680 Collected Poems, 1936
3681 The Cocktail Party, 1940
3682 Four Quarters, 1943
3683 On Poetry and Poets, 1957

BIBLIOGRAPHIES

3684 Gallup, D. T. S. Eliot: A Bibliography. Rev. ed. New York, Harcourt, 1969.

3685 Gallup, D. A Bibliographical Check List of the Writings of T. S. Eliot Including his Contributions to Periodicals and Translations of his Work into Foreign Languages. New Haven, Conn., Yale University Press, 1947.

TEXTS

3686 Collected Poems, 1969-1962. New York, Harcourt, 1965.

3687 Complete Poems and Plays, 1909-1950. New York, Harcourt, 1952.

3688 On Poetry and Poets. New York, Farrar, 1957.

3689 The Sacred Wood: Essays on Poetry and Criticism. 6th ed. New York, Barnes & Noble, 1948.

3690 Selected Essays, 1917-1932. New York, Harcourt, 1932.

3691 Selected Poems. New York, Harcourt, 1967.

3692 The Use of Poetry and the Use of Criticism. New York, Barnes & Noble, 1955.

CRITICISM

3693 Bergsten, S. Time and Eternity: A Study in the Structure and Symbolism of T. S. Eliot's Four Quarters. Stockholm, Bonniers, 1960.

3694 Brombert, V. H. The Criticism of T. S. Eliot, Problems of an "Impersonal Theory" of Poetry. New Haven, Conn., Yale University Press, 1949.

3695 Browne, E. M. The Making of T. S. Eliot's Plays. London, Cambridge University Press, 1969.

3696 Drew, E. A. T. S. Eliot: The Design of His Poetry. New York, Scribner's, 1961.

3697 Fabricius, J. The Unconscious and Mr. Eliot: A Study in Expressionism. Copenhagen, Nyt Nordisk, 1967.

3698 Freed, L. T. S. Eliot: Aesthetics and History. La Salle, Open Court, 1962.

3699 Frye, N. T. S. Eliot. New York, Barnes & Noble, 1966.

3700 Gardner, H. T. S. Eliot and the English Poetic Tradition. Nottingham, University of Nottingham Press, 1966.

3701 _____ . The Art of T. S. Eliot. New York, Cressett, 1968.

3702 Ishak, F. M. The Mystical Philosophy of T. S. Eliot. New Haven, Conn., College and University Press, 1971.

3703 Jones, G. Approach to the Purpose: A Study of the Poetry of T. S. Eliot. New York, Barnes & Noble, 1964.

3704 Kenner, H. T. S. Eliot: A Collection of Critical Essays. Englewood Cliffs, N. J., Prentice-Hall, 1966.

3705 Lucy, S. T. S. Eliot and the Idea of Tradition. New York, Barnes & Noble, 1960.

3706 Mason, W. H. T. S. Eliot's Murder in the Cathedral. New York, Barnes & Noble, 1963.

3707 Matthiessen, F. O. The Achievement of T. S. Eliot: An Essay on the Nature of Poetry. Oxford, Oxford University Press, 1958.

3708 Smith, C. H. T. S. Eliot's Dramatic Theory and Practice from Sweeney Agonistes to the Elder Statesman. Princeton, Princeton University Press, 1963.

3709 Smith, G. Eliot's Poetry and Plays: A Study in Sources and Meaning. Chicago, University of Chicago Press, 1956.

3710 Southam, B. C. A Guide to the Selected Poems of T. S. Eliot. New York, Harcourt, 1969.

3711 Tate, A., ed. T. S. Eliot, the Man and his Work: A Critical Evaluation by 26 Distinguished Writers. New York, Delacorte Press, 1966.

3712 Thompson, E. T. S. Eliot: The Metaphysical Perspective. Carbondale, Southern Illinois University Press, 1963.

3713 Unger, L. T. S. Eliot: Moments and Patterns. Minneapolis, University of Minnesota Press, 1966.

3714 Williams, H. T. S. Eliot: The Waste Land. London, E. Arnold, 1968.

3715 Williamson, G. A Reader's Guide to T. S. Eliot: A Poem-by-Poem Analysis. New York, Farrar, 1955.

3716 Wright, G. The Poet and the Poem: The Personae of Eliot, Yeats, and Pound. Berkeley, University of California Press, 1960.

Dylan Thomas (1914-1953)

WORKS

3717 18 Poems, 1934
3718 25 Poems, 1936
3719 The Map of Love, 1939
3720 Portrait of the Artist as a Young Dog, 1940
3721 Deaths and Entrances, 1946
3722 Collected Poems, 1952
3723 Under Milk Wood, 1954

BIBLIOGRAPHIES

3724 Maud, R. N. Dylan Thomas in Print: A Bibliographical History. Pittsburgh, University of Pittsburgh Press, 1970.

3725 Rolph, J. A. Dylan Thomas: A Bibliography. London, Dent, 1956.

TEXTS

3726 Collected Poems, 1934-1953. New York, New Directions, 1953.

3727 FitzGibbon, C., ed. Selected Letters. New York, New Directions, 1967.

3728 Jones, D., ed. The Poems of Dylan Thomas. New York, New Directions, 1971.

3729 Maud, R. N., and A. T. Davies, eds. The Colour of Saying: An Anthology of Verse Spoken by Dylan Thomas. London, Dent, 1963.

3730 Selected Writings. Ed. J. L. Sweeney. New York, New Directions, 1947.

3731 Watkins, V., ed. Letters to Vernon Watkins. New York, New Directions, 1957.

CRITICISM

3732 Ackerman, J. Dylan Thomas: His Life and Work. London, Oxford University Press, 1964.

3733 Cox, C. B., ed. Dylan Thomas: A Collection of Critical Essays. Englewood Cliffs, N. J., Prentice-Hall, 1966.

3734 Davies, A. T. Dylan: Druid of the Broken Body. New York, Barnes & Noble, 1966.

3735 Emery, C. The World of Dylan Thomas. Coral Gables, Fla., University of Miami Press, 1962.

3736 FitzGibbon, C. The Life of Dylan Thomas. Boston, Little-Atlantic, 1965.

3737 Jones, T. H. Dylan Thomas. New York, Barnes & Noble, 1964.

3738 Kleinman, H. H. The Religious Sonnet of Dylan Thomas: A Study in Imagery and Meaning. Berkeley, University of California Press, 1963.

3739 Moynihan, W. T. The Craft and Art of Dylan Thomas. Ithaca, N. Y., Cornell University Press, 1966.

3740 Murdy, L. B. Sound and Sense in Dylan Thomas Poetry. The Hague, Mouton, 1966.

3741 Olson, E. The Poetry of Dylan Thomas. Chicago, University of Chicago Press, 1954.

3742 Read, B. The Days of Dylan Thomas. New York, McGraw-Hill, 1964.

3743 Reddington, A. M. Dylan Thomas: A Journey from Darkness to Light. New York, Paulist, 1968.

3744 Stanford, D. Dylan Thomas: A Literary Study. Rev. ed. New York, Citadel Press, 1964.

3745 Tedlock, E. W., ed. Dylan Thomas: The Legend and the Poet. A Collection of Biographical and Critical Essays. London, Heinemann, 1961.

3746 Tindall, W. Y. A Reader's Guide to Dylan Thomas. New York, Farrar, 1962.

3747 Williams, R. C. A Concordance to the Collected Poems of Dylan Thomas. Lincoln, University of Nebraska Press, 1968.

William Butler Yeats (1865-1939)
WORKS

3748 The Celtic Twilight, 1893
3749 The Land of Heart's Desire, 1894
3750 The Adoration of the Magi, 1897
3751 The Wind Among the Reeds, 1899
3752 The Shadowy Waters, 1900
3753 The Hour Glass, 1903
3754 The King's Threshold, 1904
3755 Deidre, 1907
3756 Poems Written in Discouragement, 1913
3757 Responsibilities, 1914
3758 The Wild Swans at Coole, 1917
3759 Michael Roberts and the Dancer, 1921
3760 The Cat and the Moon, 1924
3761 Vision, 1925
3762 Autobiographies, 1926
3763 The Tower, 1928
3764 The Cavalry, 1930
3765 The Resurrection, 1931
3766 The Winding Stair, 1933
3767 A Fool Moon in March, 1935
3768 Last Poems and Plays, 1941

BIBLIOGRAPHIES

3769 Wade, A. A Bibliography of the Writings of W. B. Yeats. Rev. 3d ed. by R. K. Alspach. London, Hart-Davis, 1969.

TEXTS

3770 Alspach, R. K., and C. C., eds. The Variorum Edition of the Plays of W. B. Yeats. New York, Macmillan, 1966.

3771 Stallworthy, J., ed. Yeats: Last Poems. London, Macmillan, 1968.

CRITICISM

3772 Bloom, H. Yeats. Oxford, Oxford University Press, 1970.

3773 Bornstein, G. Yeats and Shelley. Chicago, University of Chicago Press, 1970.

3774 Bradford, C. B. Yeats at Work. Carbondale, Southern Illinois University Press, 1965.

3775 Donoghue, D., and J. R. Mulryne, eds. An Honoured Guest: New Essays on W. B. Yeats. London, E. Arnold, 1965.

3776 Ellmann, R. Yeats: The Man and the Masks. New York, Dutton, 1948.

3777 _____ . The Identity of Yeats. Oxford, Galaxy, 1954.

3778 Gordon, D. J., et al., eds. W. B. Yeats: Images of a Poet. New York, Barnes & Noble, 1961.

3779 Hall, J., and M. Steinman, eds. The Permanence of Yeats: Selected Criticism. New York, Collier, 1950.

3780 Henn, T. R. The Lonely Tower: Studies in the Poetry of Yeats. London, Methuen, 1965.

3781 _____ . W. B. Yeats and the Poetry of War. London, Oxford University Press, 1967.

3782 Jeffares, A. N., ed. W. B. Yeats: Selected Criticism. London, Macmillan, 1964.

3783 _____ . W. B. Yeats: Man and Poet. New York, Barnes & Noble, 1966.

3784 _____ . The Poems of W. B. Yeats. London, E. Arnold, 1961.

3785 _____ , and G. W. Cross, eds. In Excited Reverie: A Centenary Tribute to W. B. Yeats, 1865-1939. London, Macmillan, 1965.

3786 Kermode, F. The Romantic Image. New York, Random, 1964.

3787 Marcus, R. L. Yeats and the Beginning of Irish Renaissance. Ithaca, N. Y., Cornell University Press, 1970.

3788 Maxwell, D. E. S., and S. B. Bushrui, eds. W. B. Yeats, 1865-1965; Centenary Essays on the Art of W. B. Yeats. Ibadan, International Publications Service, 1965.

3789 Melchiori, G. The Whole Mystery of Art: Pattern Into Poetry in the Work of W. B. Yeats. London, Routledge & K. Paul, 1960.

3790 Menon, V. K. Narayana. The Development of W. B. Yeats. Philadelphia, Dufour, 1961.

3791 Nathan, L. E. The Tragic Drama of W. B. Yeats: Figures in a Dance. New York, Columbia University Press, 1965.

3792 Parrish, S. M., and J. A. Painter, A Concordance to the Poems of W. B. Yeats. Ithaca, N. Y., Cornell University Press, 1963.

3793 Reid, B. L. William Butler Yeats: The Lyric of Tragedy. Norman, University of Oklahoma Press, 1961.

3794 Ronsley, J. Yeats' Autobiography: Life as Symbolic Pattern. Cambridge, Mass., Harvard University Press, 1968.

3795 Ryan, Sister Rosalie C. S. J. Symbolic Elements in the Plays of William Butler Yeats, 1892-1921. Washington, Catholic University Press, 1952.

3796 Saul, G. B. Prolegomena to the Study of Yeats' Poems. New York, Octagon, 1971.

3797 _____ . Prolegomena to the Study of Yeats' Plays. New York, Octagon, 1971.

3798 Seiden, M. I. William Butler Yeats: The Poet as Myth Maker, 1865-1939. East Lansing, Michigan State University Press, 1962.

3799 Skelton, R., and A. Saddlemyer, eds. The World of W. B. Yeats: Essays in Perspective. Seattle, University of Washington Press, 1967.

3800 Stock, A. G. W. B. Yeats: His Poetry and Thought. Cambridge, Cambridge University Press, 1961.

3801 Unterecker, J., ed. Yeats: A Collection of Critical Essays. Englewood Cliffs, N. J., Prentice-Hall, 1963.

3802 _____ . A Reader's Guide to William Butler Yeats. New York, Farrar, 1959.

3803 Ure, P. Yeats the Playwright: A Commentary on Character and Design in the Major Plays. New York, Barnes & Noble, 1963.

3804 _____ . Towards a Mythology: Studies in the Poetry of Yeats. New York, Russell & Russell, 1967.

3805 Vendler, H. H. Yeats's "Vision" and the Later Plays. Cambridge, Mass., Harvard University Press, 1962.

3806 Whitaker, T. R. The Poetry of William Butler Yeats. Denver, Swallow, 1960.

3807 Wilson, F. A. C. Yeats's Iconography. New York, Macmillan, 1960.

3808 Wright, G. The Poet in the Poem: The Personae of Eliot, Yeats, and Pound. Berkeley, University of California Press, 1960.

FICTION—BIBLIOGRAPHIES

3809 Awad, R., comp. A Bibliography of the English Novel After the Second World War. Vol. II. Cairo, no publisher, 1964.

3810 Bufkin, E. C. The Twentieth Century Novel in England: A Check-list. Athens, University of Georgia Press, 1967.

3811 Temple, R. Z., comp. and ed. Twentieth Century British Literature: A Reference Guide and Bibliography. New York, Ungar, 1968.

3812 Walker, W. S. Twentieth Century Short Story Explications. 2d ed. Hamden, Conn., Shoe String Press, 1968.

FICTION—TEXTS

3813 Davis, R. G., ed. Ten Modern Masters: An Anthology of the Short Story. 2d ed. New York, Harcourt, 1952.

3814 Havighurst, W., ed. Masters of the Modern Short Story. New York, Harcourt, 1945.

3815 Newman, F. B., M. Felheim, and W. R. Steinhoff, eds. Modern Short Stories. New York, Oxford University Press, 1951.

FICTION—CRITICISM

3816 Allen, W. Tradition and Dream: A Critical Survey of British and American Fiction from 1920's to the Present Day. Harmondsworth, Penguin, 1965.

3817 Axthelm, P. M. The Modern Confessional Novel. New Haven, Conn., Yale University Press, 1967.

3818 Church, M. Time and Reality: Studies in Contemporary Fiction. Chapel Hill, University of North Carolina Press, 1963.

3819 Edel, L. The Modern Psychological Novel. New York, Grosset University Library, 1964.

3820 Friedman, A. The Turn of the Novel. New York, Oxford University Press, 1966.

3821 Gindin, J. Postwar British Fiction: New Accents and Attitudes. Berkeley, University of California Press, 1962.

3822 Hall, J. The Tragic Comedians: Seven Modern British Novelists. Bloomington, Indiana University Press, 1963.

3823 Hardy, J. E. Man in the Modern Novel. Seattle, University of Washington Press, 1964.

3824 Humphreys, R. Stream of Consciousness in the Modern Novel. Berkeley, University of California Press, 1954.

3825 Jones, P. M., ed. English Critical Essays: Twentieth Century. Oxford, Oxford University Press, 1968.

3826 Karl, F. R. The Contemporary English Novel. New York, Farrar, 1962.

3827 _____ . A Reader's Guide to Contemporary English Novel. New York, Farrar, 1963.

3828 Kostelanez, R. On Contemporary Literature: An Anthology of Critical Essays on the Major Movements and Writers of Contemporary Literature. Cliffside Park, N. J., Avon Books, 1964.

3829 Schorer, M., ed. Modern British Fiction. New York, Oxford University Press, 1961.

3830 Stallman, R. W. The Art of Modern Fiction. New York, Rinehart, 1949.

3831 Stevenson, L. The History of the English Novel. XI: Yesterday and After. New York, Barnes & Noble, 1967.

3832 Tindall, W. Y. Forces in Modern British Literature, 1885-1956. New York, Vintage, 1956.

3833 Ward, A. C. Twentieth Century English Literature, 1901-1960. New York, Barnes & Noble, 1964.

3834 Webster, H. C. After the Trauma: Representative British Novelists since 1920. Lexington, University of Kentucky Press, 1970.

3835 West, R. B. Modern Library Criticism. New York, Rinehart, 1952.

FICTION—INDIVIDUAL AUTHORS

Joseph Conrad (1857-1924)

WORKS

3836 The Nigger of the "Narcissus", 1897
3837 Lord Jim, 1900
3838 Heart of Darkness, 1902
3839 Youth, 1902
3840 Typhoon, 1903
3841 Nostromo, 1904
3842 The Mirror of the Sea, 1906
3843 Chance, Victory, 1915
3844 The Rover, 1923

BIBLIOGRAPHIES

3845 Ehrsam, T. G., comp. A Bibliography of Joseph Conrad. Metuchen, N. J., Scarecrow, 1969.

3846 Wise, T. J. A Bibliography of the Writings of Joseph Conrad. (1895-1921). London, Dawsons, 1964.

TEXTS

3847 Conrad's Short Stories Complete. Garden City, N. Y., Doubleday, 1923.

3848 Garnett, E., ed. Collected Letters. Indianapolis, Bobbs-Merrill, 1928.

3849 Hoppe, A. J., ed. The Conrad Companion. London, Phoenix, 1947.

3850 The Mirror of the Sea. Garden City, N. Y., Doubleday, 1932.

3851 Moser, T. C., ed. Lord Jim. New York, Norton, 1968.

3852 The Niger of the "Narcissus." Garden City, N. Y., Doubleday, 1924.

3853 Nostromo. Garden City, N. Y., Doubleday, 1914.

3854 An Outcast of the Islands. Garden City, N. Y., Doubleday, 1914.

3855 The Rescue. Garden City, N. Y., Doubleday, 1920.

3856 Romance. Garden City, N. Y., Doubleday, 1914.

3857 The Rover. Garden City, N. Y., Doubleday, 1923.

3858 Tales of Land and Sea. Garden City, N. Y., Doubleday, 1953.

3859 Typhoon. New York, Putnam, 1902.

3860 Victory. New York, Modern Library, 1921.

3861 Wright, W. F., ed. Joseph Conrad on Fiction. Lincoln, University of Nebraska Press, 1964.

3862 Zabel, D., ed. The Portable Conrad. New York, Viking, 1947.

3863 Zabel, D., ed. Tales of the East and West. Garden City, N. Y., Doubleday, 1958.

CRITICISM

3864 Boyle, T. E. Symbol and Meaning in the Fiction of Joseph Conrad. The Hague, Mouton, 1965.

3865 Conrad, B. My Father: Joseph Conrad. New York, Coward-McCann, 1970.

3866 Conrad, J. Joseph Conrad and his Circle. 2d ed. New York, Kennikat, 1964.

3867 Cushwa, F. W. An Introduction to Conrad. Garden City, N. Y., Doubleday, 1933.

3868 Dean, L. F., ed. Heart of Darkness: Backgrounds and Criticisms. Englewood Cliffs, N. J., Prentice-Hall, 1960.

3869 Fleishman, A. Conrad's Politics: Community and Anarchy in the Fiction of Joseph Conrad. Baltimore, Johns Hopkins, 1968.

3870 Ford, F. M. Joseph Conrad. New York, Octagon, 1965.

3871 Gillon, A. The Eternal Solitary: A Study of Joseph Conrad. New York, Twayne, 1960.

3872 Guerard, A. J. Conrad the Novelist. Cambridge, Mass., Harvard University Press, 1958.

3873 Gurko, L. Joseph Conrad: Giant in Exile. New York, Macmillan, 1962.

3874 Hay, E. The Political Novels of Joseph Conrad: A Critical Study. Chicago, University of Chicago Press, 1963.

3875 Hodges, R. R. The Dual Heritage of Joseph Conrad. The Hague, Mouton, 1967.

3876 Hoffman, S. de V. Comedy and Form in the Fiction of Joseph Conrad. The Hague, Mouton, 1969.

3877 Jean-Aubery, G. Sea-Dreamer: A Definitive Biography. Trans. by H. Sebba. Hamden, Conn., Shoe String Press, 1957.

3878 Karl, F. R. A Reader's Guide to Joseph Conrad: Extended Analysis of the Novels and Shorter Fiction. New York, Farrar, 1960.

3879 Kirschner, P. Conrad: The Psychologist as Artist. Edinburgh, Oliver & Boyd, 1968.

3880 Kuehn, R. E., ed. Twentieth Century Interpretations of Lord Jim: A Collection of Critical Essays. Englewood Cliffs, N. J., Prentice-Hall, 1969.

3881 Meyer, B. C. Joseph Conrad: A Psychoanalytic Biography. Princeton, Princeton University Press, 1967.

3882 Mudrick, M., ed. Conrad: A Collection of Critical Essays. Englewood Cliffs, N. J., Prentice-Hall, 1966.

3883 Palmer, J. A. Joseph Conrad's Fiction: A Study in Literary Growth. Ithaca, N. Y., Cornell University Press, 1968.

3884 Said, E. W. Joseph Conrad and the Fiction of Autobiography. Cambridge, Mass., Harvard University Press, 1966.

3885 Stallman, R. W., ed. The Art of Joseph Conrad: A Critical Symposium. East Lansing, Michigan State University Press, 1960.

3886 Stewart, J. I. M. Joseph Conrad. New York, Longmans, 1968.

3887 Wright, W. F. Romance and Tragedy in Joseph Conrad. Lincoln, University of Nebraska Press, 1949.

Edward Morgan Forster (1879-1970)

WORKS

3888 Where Angels Fear to Tread, 1905

3889 The Longest Journey, 1907

3890 A Room with a View, 1908

3891 Howard's End, 1910

3892 The Celestial Omnibus, 1911

3893 A Passage to India, 1924

3894 Aspects of the Novel, 1927

3895 Marianne Thornton, 1956

BIBLIOGRAPHIES

3896 Kirkpatrick, B. J. A Bibliography of E. M. Forster. London, Hart-Davis, 1968.

TEXTS

3897 The Celestial Omnibus and Other Stories. New York, Knopf, 1923.

3898 Collected Short Stories. London, Sidgwick & Jackson, 1947.

3899 Collected Tales. New York, Knopf, 1947.

3900 Colmer, J., ed. A Passage to India. London, E. Arnold, 1967.

3901 The Longest Journey. Norfolk, Conn., New Directions, 1943.

3902 A Room with a View. Norfolk, Conn., New Directions, 1943.

3903 Where Angels Fear to Tread. New York, Knopf, 1920.

CRITICISM

3904 Beer, J. B. The Achievement of E. M. Forster. London, Chatto & Windus, 1962.

3905 Borrello, A. An E. M. Forster Dictionary. Metuchen, N. J., Scarecrow, 1971.

3906 Bradbury, M., ed. E. M. Forster: A Collection of Critical Essays. Englewood Cliffs, N. J., Prentice-Hall, 1966.

3907 Brander, L. E. M. Forster: A Critical Study. London, Hart-Davis, 1968.

3908 Crews, F. C. E. M. Forster: The Perils of Humanism. Princeton, Princeton University Press, 1962.

3909 Godfrey, D. E. M. Forster's Other Kingdom. Edinburgh, Oliver & Boyd, 1968.

3910 Johnstone, J. K. The Bloomsbury Group. New York, Farrar, 1963.

3911 MacCauley, Dame Rose. The Writings of E. M. Forster. New York, Barnes & Noble, 1971.

3912 McConkey, J. The Novels of E. M. Forster. Ithaca, N. Y., Cornell University Press, 1957.

3913 Moody, P. A Critical Commentary on E. M. Forster's A Passage to India. London, Macmillan, 1968.

3914 Moore, H. T. E. M. Forster. New York, Columbia University Press, 1965.

3915 Shahane, V. A., ed. Perspectives on E. M. Forster's A Passage to India: A Collection of Critical Essays. New York, Barnes & Noble, 1968.

3916 Shusterman, D. The Quest for Certitude in E. M. Forster's Fiction. Bloomington, Indiana University Press, 1965.

3917 Stone, W. The Cave and the Mountain: A Study of E. M. Forster. Stanford, Stanford University Press, 1966.

3918 Thomson, G. H. The Fiction of E. M. Forster. Detroit, Wayne State University Press, 1967.

3919 Trilling, L. E. M. Forster. A Critical Guidebook. New York, New Directions, 1964.

3920 Wilde, A. Art and Order: A Study of E. M. Forster. New York, New York University Press, 1964.

Graham Greene (1904–)

WORKS

3921 The Man Within, 1929
3922 Rumour at Nightfall, 1931
3923 Brighton Rock, 1938
3924 The Heart of the Matter, 1948
3925 The End of the Affair, 1951
3926 Living Room, 1953
3927 Twenty-One Stories, 1954

3928 The Potting Shed, 1957
3929 Our Man in Havana, 1958
3930 The Complaisant Lover, 1959
3931 In Search of a Character, 1961
3932 The Comedians, 1966
3933 May We Borrow your Husband? And Other Comedies of the Sexual Life, 1967

BIBLIOGRAPHIES

3934 Vann, J. D. Graham Greene: A Checklist of Criticism. Kent, Ohio, Kent State University Press, 1970.

TEXTS

3935 Collected Essays. London, Sydney, 1969.

3936 The Comedians. New York, Viking, 1966.

3937 The Complaisant Lover. New York, Viking, 1959.

3938 The End of the Affair. New York, Viking, 1951.

3939 The Heart of the Matter. New York, Viking, 1948.

3940 The Living Room. New York, Viking, 1953.

3941 The Man Within. New York, Viking, 1947.

3942 Our Man in Havana. New York, Viking, 1958.

3943 In Search of a Character. New York, Viking, 1961.

3944 The Potting Shed. New York, Viking, 1947.

3945 Twenty-One Stories. New York, Viking, 1962.

CRITICISM

3946 Atkins, J. Graham Greene. New York, Humanities Press, 1966.

3947 DeVitis, A. A. Graham Greene. New York, Twayne, 1964.

3948 Evans, R. O., ed. Graham Greene: Some Critical Considerations. Lexington, University of Kentucky Press, 1963.

3949 Lodge, D. Graham Greene. New York, Columbia University Press, 1966.

3950 Stratford, P. Faith and Fiction: Creative Process in Greene and Mauriac. Notre Dame, Ind., University of Notre Dame Press, 1964.

Aldous Huxley (1894-1963)

WORKS

3951	Poems, 1916-31	3958	Eyeless in Gaza, 1936
3952	Short Stories, 1920-30	3959	Time Must Have a Stop, 1945
3953	Essays, 1923-56	3960	Ape and Essence, 1949
3954	Plays, 1924-55	3961	The Devils of Loudun, 1952
3955	Point Counter Point, 1928	3962	The Doors of Perception,
3956	Antic Hay, 1932		1954
3957	Brave New World, 1932,	3963	Island, 1962
	1958		

BIBLIOGRAPHIES

3964 Eschebach, C. J., and J. L. Shober, eds. Aldous Huxley: A Bibliography, 1916-1959. Berkeley, University of California Press, 1961.

TEXTS

3965 Antic Hay. New York, Doran, 1923.

3966 Ape and Essence. New York, Harper, 1948.

3967 Collected Essays. New York, Harper, 1959.

3968 Collected Short Stories. London, Chatto & Windus, 1957.

3969 The Devils of Loudun. New York, Harper, 1952.

3970 The Doors of Perception and Heaven and Hell. New York, Harper, 1956.

3971 Eyeglass in Gaza. New York, Harper, 1936.

3972 Island. New York, Harper, 1962.

3973 Point Counter Point. New York, Harper, 1947.

3974 Rolo, C. J., ed. Brave New World. New York, Harper, 1960.

3975 Smith, G., ed. Letters of Aldous Huxley. New York, Harper, 1970.

3976 Stories, Essays and Poems by Aldous Huxley. London, Dent, 1949.

CRITICISM

3977 Atkins, J. Aldous Huxley: A Literary Study. New York, Orion Press, 1968.

3978 Ghose, S. Aldous Huxley: A Cynical Salvationist. New York, Asia Publishing House, 1962.

3979 Henderson, A. Aldous Huxley. New York, Russell & Russell, 1964.

3980 Huxley, J., ed. Aldous Huxley: A Memorial Volume. New York, Harper, 1966.

3981 Huxley, L. A. This Timeless Moment: A Personal View of Aldous Huxley. London, Hogarth, 1969.

3982 Lowry, W. M. Aldous Huxley: Humanist and Mystic. The Revolt against the Reason in the Twentieth Century. Urbana, University of Illinois Press, 1941.

3983 Meckier, J. Aldous Huxley: Satire and Structure. London, Chatto & Windus, 1969.

3984 Rowering, P. Aldous Huxley: A Study of the Major Novels. London, Athlone, 1968.

James Joyce (1882-1941)

WORKS

3985 Dubliners, 1914
3986 A Portrait of the Artist as a Young Man, 1916

3987 Ulysses, 1922
3988 Finnegans Wake, 1939

BIBLIOGRAPHIES

3989 Deming, R. H. A Bibliography of James Joyce Studies. Lawrence, University of Kansas Press, 1964.

3990 Parker, A. James Joyce: A Bibliography. Boston, Faxon, 1948.

3991 Slocum, J. J., and H. Cahoon. A Bibliography of James Joyce, 1882-1941. London, Hart-Davis, 1953.

TEXTS

3992 Anderson, C. G., and R. Ellmann, eds. A Portrait of the Artist as a Young Man. London, Cape, 1968.

3993 Collected Poems by James Joyce. New York, Viking, 1937.

3994 Dubliners. New York, Modern Library, 1926.

3995 Finnegans Wake. New York, Viking, 1936.

3996 Gilbert, S., ed. Letters. New York, Viking, 1957.

3997 Levin, H., ed. The Portable James Joyce. New York, Viking, 1947.

3998 Mason, E., and R. Ellmann, eds. Critical Writings. New York, Viking, 1959.

3999 Spencer, T., ed. Stephen Hero. Norfolk, Conn., New Directions, 1963.

4000 Ulysses. New York, Modern Library, 1942.

CRITICISM

4001 Adams, R. M. Surface and Symbol: The Consistency of James Joyce's Ulysses. New York, Oxford University Press, 1962.

4002 Beck, W. Joyce's Dubliners: Substance, Vision and Art. Durham, N. C., Duke University Press, 1969.

4003 Budgen, F. James Joyce and the Making of Ulysses. Bloomington, Indiana University Press, 1960.

4004 Curran, C. James Joyce Remembered. New York, Oxford University Press, 1968.

4005 Dalton, J. P., and C. Hart, eds. Twelve and a Tilly: Essays on the Occasion of the 25th Anniversary of Finnegans Wake. Evanston, Ill., Northwestern University Press, 1965.

4006 Deming, R. H., comp. and ed. James Joyce: The Critical Heritage. New York, Barnes & Noble, 1970.

4007 Ellmann, R. James Joyce. New York, Oxford University Press, 1959.

4008 _____ . Joyce in Love. Ithaca, N. Y., Cornell University Press, 1959.

4009 Givens, S., ed. James Joyce: Two Decades of Criticism. New York, Vanguard, 1963.

4010 Goldberg, S. L. The Classical Temper: A Study of James Joyce's Ulysses. London, Chatto & Windus, 1961.

4011 Hart, C. A Concordance to Finnegans Wake. Minneapolis, University of Minnesota Press, 1963.

4012 _____ . James Joyce's Ulysses. University Park, Pennsylvania State University Press, 1969.

4013 Joyce, S., ed. My Brother's Keeper: James Joyce's Early Years. New York, McGraw-Hill, 1958.

4014 Kain, R. M. Fabulous Voyager, James Joyce's Ulysses. New York, Viking, 1959.

4015 Kenner, H. Dublin's Joyce. London, Beacon, 1962.

4016 Levin, H. James Joyce: A Critical Introduction. London, Faber, 1968.

4017 Litz, A. W. James Joyce. New York, Twayne, 1966.

4018 Litz, A. W. The Art of James Joyce: Method and Design in Ulysses and Finnegans Wake. London, Oxford University Press, 1961.

4019 Magalaner, M., ed. A James Joyce Miscellany. Third Series. Carbondale, Southern Illinois University Press, 1961.

4020 O'Brien, D. The Conscience of James Joyce. Princeton, Princeton University Press, 1968.

4021 Smith, P. J. A Key to the Ulysses of James Joyce. New York, Haskell House, 1969.

4022 Staley, T. F., ed. James Joyce Today: Essays on the Major Works. Bloomington, Indiana University Press, 1966.

4023 _____ , and B. Benstock, eds. Approaches to Ulysses: Ten Essays. Pittsburgh, University of Pittsburgh Press, 1970.

4024 Tindall, W. Y. A Reader's Guide to Finnegans Wake. New York, Farrar, 1969.

David Herbert Lawrence (1885-1930)

WORKS

4025 The White Peacock, 1911

4026 Poems, 1913-33

4027 Sons and Lovers, 1913

4028 Plays, 1914-34

4029 The Rainbow, 1915

4030 Women in Love, 1920

4031 The Lost Girl, 1920

4032 Essays, 1921-29

4033 Lady Chatterly's Lover, 1928

4034 The Virgin and the Gipsy, 1930

BIBLIOGRAPHIES

4035 McDonald, E. D. A Bibliography of the Writings of D. H. Lawrence. Philadelphia, Centaur Book Shop, 1925. Repr. New York, Kraus, 1969.

4036 Roberts, F. W. A Bibliography of D. H. Lawrence. London, Hart-Davis, 1963.

TEXTS

4037 Beal, A., ed. Selected Literary Criticism. London, Heinemann, 1967.

4038 Collected Poems. New York, J. Cape, 1929.

4039 Complete Plays. New York, Viking, 1966.

4040 Lady Chatterly's Lover. New York, Grove, 1959.

4041 The Lost Girl. New York, Seltzer, 1921.

4042 Moore, H. T., ed. The Collected Letters of D. H. Lawrence. 2 vols. New York, Viking, 1962.

4043 _____ , ed. D. H. Lawrence's Letters to Bertrand Russell. New York, Gotham Books Mart, 1948.

4044 Pinto, V. de Sola, and W. Roberta, eds. Complete Poems. New York, Viking, 1964.

4045 The Rainbow. New York, Modern Library, 1927.

4046 Sons and Lovers. New York, Viking, 1968.

4047 Tindall, W. Y., ed. The Plumed Serpent. New York, Knopf, 1926.

4048 _____ , ed. The Later D. H. Lawrence. New York, Knopf, 1952.

4049 Trilling, D., ed. The Portable D. H. Lawrence. New York, Viking, 1947.

4050 The Virgin and the Gypsy. London, Martin Secker, 1930.

4051 The White Peacock. Carbondale, Southern Illinois University Press, 1966.

4052 Women in Love. New York, Modern Library, 1920.

CRITICISM

4053 Chambers, J. D. D. H. Lawrence: A Personal Record. New York, Barnes & Noble, 1965.

4054 Clarke, C. River of Dissolution: D. H. Lawrence and English Romanticism. London, Routledge & K. Paul, 1969.

4055 Draper, R. P., ed. D. H. Lawrence: The Critical Heritage. New York, Barnes & Noble, 1970.

4056 Ford, G. H. Double Measure: A Study of the Novels and Stories of D. H. Lawrence. New York, Holt, 1965.

4057 Goodheart, E. The Utopian Vision of D. H. Lawrence. Chicago, University of Chicago Press, 1963.

4058 Gordon, D. J. D. H. Lawrence as a Literary Critic. New Haven, Conn., Yale University Press, 1966.

4059 Leavis, F. R. D. H. Lawrence, Novelist. New York, Knopf, 1956.

4060 Levy, M., ed. Paintings of D. H. Lawrence. New York, Viking, 1964.

4061 Moore, H. T. A D. H. Lawrence Miscellany. Carbondale, Southern Illinois University Press, 1959.

4062 _____ . The Life and Works of D. H. Lawrence. New York, Twayne, 1963.

4063 Moynahan, J. The Dead of Life: The Novels and Tales of D. H. Lawrence. Princeton, Princeton University Press, 1963.

4064 Nehls, E., ed. D. H. Lawrence: A Composite Biography. Madison, University of Wisconsin Press, 1959.

4065 Spilka, M., ed. D. H. Lawrence: A Collection of Critical Essays. Englewood Cliffs, N. J., Prentice-Hall, 1963.

4066 _____ . The Love Ethic of D. H. Lawrence. Bloomington, Indiana University Press, 1955.

4067 Tedlock, E. W., Jr. D. H. Lawrence, Artist and Rebel: A Study of Lawrence's Fiction. Albuquerque, University of New Mexico Press, 1963.

4068 _____ . Lawrence and Sons and Lovers: Sources and Criticism. New York, New York University Press, 1965.

4069 Vivas, E. D. H. Lawrence: The Failure and Triumph of Art. Evanston, Ill., Northwestern University Press, 1960.

4070 Widmer, K. The Art of Perversity: D. H. Lawrence's Shorter Fictions. Seattle, University of Washington Press, 1962.

Katherine Mansfield (1888-1923)

WORKS

4071 Bliss and Other Stories, 1920
4072 The Garden Party and Other Stories, 1922
4073 Poems, 1923
4074 The Dove's Nest and Other Stories, 1923
4075 Something Childish and Other Stories, 1924

BIBLIOGRAPHIES

4076 Mantz, R. E. The Critical Bibliography of Katherine Mansfield. New York, B. Franklin, 1969.

TEXTS

4077 Bowen, E., ed. Stories. New York, Random, 1956.

4078 Murry, M. J., ed. Journal. New York, Knopf, 1928.

4079 Short Stories. New York, Knopf, 1937.

CRITICISM

4080 Berkman, S. Katherine Mansfield: A Critical Study. New Haven, Conn., Yale University Press, 1951.

4081 Daly, S. Katherine Mansfield. New York, Twayne, 1965.

4082 Gordon, I. A. Katherine Mansfield. London, British Book Centre, 1968.

4083 Hormasji, N. Katherine Mansfield: An Appraisal. London, Collins, 1967.

George Orwell (1903-1950)

WORKS

4084 Homage to Catalonia, 1938
4085 Animal Farm, 1945
4086 Critical Essays, 1946
4087 Nineteen Eighty-Four, 1949
4088 Shooting an Elephant, 1950

TEXTS

4089 Animal Farm. New York, Harcourt, 1946.

4090 Collected Essays. 2d ed. London, Secker & Warburg, 1961.

4091 Homage to Catalonia. New York, Harcourt, 1952.

4092 Nineteen Eighty-Four. New York, Harcourt, 1949.

4093 Rovere, R. R., ed. The Orwell Reader. New York, Harcourt, 1961.

CRITICISM

4094 Alldritt, K. The Making of George Orwell: An Essay in Literary History. London, E. Arnold, 1969.

4095 Hopkinson, T. George Orwell. London, Longmans, Green, 1962.

4096 Rees, R. George Orwell, Fugitive from the Camp of Victory. Carbondale, Southern Illinois University Press, 1962.

4097 Voorhees, R. J. The Paradox of George Orwell. Lafayette, Ind., Purdue Research Foundation, 1961.

4098 Woodcock, G. The Crystal Spirit: A Study of George Orwell. Boston, Little, Brown, 1966.

Virginia Woolf (1882-1941)

WORKS

4099 The Voyage Out, 1915	4103 To the Lighthouse, 1927
4100 Night and Day, 1919	4104 Orlando, 1928
4101 Jacob's Room, 1922	4105 The Waves, 1931
4102 Mrs. Dalloway, 1925	4106 The Years, 1937

BIBLIOGRAPHIES

4107 Kirkpatrick, B. J. A Bibliography of Virginia Woolf. London, Hart-Davis, 1967.

TEXTS

4108 Collected Essays. New York, Harper, 1967.

4109 Jacob's Room. London, Hogarth, 1945.

4110 To the Lighthouse. London, Hogarth, 1943.

4111 Mrs. Dallaway. New York, Modern Library, 1928.

4112 Night and Day. London, Hogarth, 1919.

4113 Orlando. New York, Harcourt, 1928.

4114 The Voyage Out. London, Hogarth, 1965.

4115 The Waves. London, Hogarth, 1943.

4116 The Years. New York, Harcourt, 1937.

CRITICISM

4117 Bennett, J. Virginia Woolf: Her Art as a Novelist. 2d ed. Cambridge, Cambridge University Press, 1964.

4118 Blackstone, B. Virginia Woolf: A Commentary. London, British Book Centre, 1949.

4119 Brewster, D. Virginia Woolf. New York, New York University Press, 1962.

4120 Daiches, D. Virginia Woolf. Rev. ed. New York, New Directions, 1963.

4121 Guiguest, J. Virginia Woolf and her Works. Trans. by Jean Stewart. New York, Harcourt, 1966.

4122 Hafley, J. R. The Glass Roof: Virginia Woolf as a Novelist. New York, Russell & Russell, 1963.

4123 Marder, H. Feminism and Art: A Study of Virginia Woolf. Chicago, University of Chicago Press, 1968.

4124 Moody, A. D. Virginia Woolf. Edinburgh, Oliver & Boyd, 1963.

4125 Richter, H. Virginia Woolf: The Inward Voyage. Princeton, Princeton University Press, 1970.

4126 Thakur, N. C. The Symbolism of Virginia Woolf. Oxford, Oxford University Press, 1965.

4127 Woodring, C. Virginia Woolf. New York, Columbia University Press, 1966.

4128 Woolf, L. Downhill All the Way: An Autobiography of the Years 1919-1939. London, Hogarth, 1967.

AUTHOR AND SUBJECT INDEX

In order to conserve space, authors and editors are listed by their last names and initials only. References are to item number, not to page number. Please note that all numbers for subject entries are in bold face, and that they follow author entries. Thus, Daniel, S., has the following references: 1240-1248, 1250-1253 (author entries) and **1249, 1254-1255, 1269, 1449** (subject entries). Anonymous works are listed by title—thus, Vision Concerning Piers Plowman, 621-624 (texts) and **548, 625-635, 652** (criticism about this text).

Brooke, R., 1206
Brooke, T., 848
Brooks, H. F., 581
Brooks, K., 1858
Brooks, K. R., 410
Broomfield, B. C., 3662
Broomfield, M. W., 490
Broughton, B. B., 667, 668
Broughton, L. N., 2819, 2829
Brower, R. A., 2063
Brown, A., 148
Brown, C., 531, 532, 684
Brown, D., 3194
Brown, E. K., 2810, 3352, 3362
Brown, I., 3029, 3112
Brown, J. M., 3420
Brown, J. R., 932, 3465, 3479
Brown, K. C., 2352
Brown, R. S., Jr., 2293
Brown, S.J.M., 220
Brown, W. C., 1935
Browne, E. M., 3695
Browne, G. F., 441
Browne, T., 1570-1572, 1574-1577; 1573, 1578-1580
Browning, R., 2812-2818, 2820-2827; 269, 2523, 2719, 2819, 2828-2846, 2966, 3368
Bruner, D. K., 2997
Brustein, R., 3480
Bryan, W. F., 582
Bryson, J., 3353
Buck, P. M., Jr., 85, 2445
Buckler, W. E., 3354
Buckley, J. H., 2783, 2789, 2802, 2963
Bucknill, J. C., 933
Budgen, F., 4003
Budick, S., 1731
Bufkin, E. C., 3810
Bullen, A. H., 1187
Bullen, T. S., 2200

Bullett, G., 1271, 1342, 1350
Bullitt, J. M., 2266, 2386
Bullough, G., 934, 935, 1364
Bunyan, J., 2123-2126, 2128-2134; 1889, 2127, 2135-2140
Burgess, C. F., 1794, 1795
Burke, E., 2324-2327, 2330-2335; 1659, 2328-2329, 2336-2341, 2451
Burke, F., 1160
Burns, R., 1993, 1996-2005; 1665, 1994-1995, 2006-2014
Burrows, L., 2830
Burto, W., 3463
Burton, E., 724
Burton, H. M., 3113, 3580
Burton, R., 1581-1582, 1583-1586; 1587-1589
Bush, D., 78, 184, 185, 725-727, 1095, 1213, 1856, 1857, 1878, 1879, 2552, 2668
Bushrui, S. B., 3788
Butler, S., 3071-3076, 3078-3081; 3077
Butt, J., 2054, 3114
Butter, P., 2985
Buxton, C. R., 1880
Buxton, J., 1280, 1451
Byrne, M. C., 1168
Byron, G. G., 2563-2570, 2572-2581; 2540, 2554, 2571, 2582-2609

Caedmon, 391-394, 395-401; 402
Cahoon, H., 3991
Calder, J., 3513
Caldwell, E. N., 3291
Callan, E., 3663
Cameron, K. N., 2702-2704, 2711, 2729
Campbell, A., 442
Campbell, J. J., 335
Campbell, L. B., 936, 1228

Dennis, N., 2270
Dent, R. W., 1207
DeQuincey, T., 3394, 3395-3396;
3397-3401
Dessen, A. C., 1139
Deutsch, B., 3636
DeVane, M. P., 2956
DeVane, W. C., 2821
DeVane, W. L., 2956
DeVitis, A. A., 3947
Devlin, C., 2850
Devlin, D. D., 3272
Dewhurst, K., 2416
Dick, H. G., 1559
Dickens, C., 3092-3102, 3107-3109;
2110, 3004, 3013, 3103-3106,
3110-3151
Dickins, B., 477
Dickinson, H., 3483
Dietrich, R. F., 3484, 3594
Dilligan, R. J., 2859
Dilworth, E. N., 2239
Dinkins, P., 650
Disher, M. W., 2468
Dixon, C., 1504
Dixon, P., 2064
Dixon, W. M., 2964
Dobbie, E.V.K., 337, 354, 373, 375,
386, 401, 411, 415, 444
Dobrée, B., 71, 78, 1658, 1680,
1700, 1703, 2065, 2586, 2906,
3395
Dobson, A., 1809, 1810, 2203
Dodd, M. E., 3325
Dodds, J. W., 2449, 3305
Dodge, R.E.N., 1317
Dodsley, R., 508
Donaldson, E. T., 355, 570, 621
Donne, J., 1366, 1402-1408, 1410-
1421, 1839; 1216, 1217, 1373-
1375, 1384, 1387, 1409, 1422-
1439
Donno, E. S., 1222

Donoghue, D., 3485, 3775
Donovan, F. R., 3120
Donovan, R. A., 2110
Donow, H. S., 1254
Doran, M., 791
Doughty, O., 2916, 2918
Douglas, D. C., 456
Dowden, E., 958
Downer, A. S., 126, 3583
Downes, D., 2860
Downs, B. W., 2204
Draper, J. W., 959, 1937
Draper, R. P., 4055
Drayton, M., 1440-1448, 1451-
1452; 1249, 1254, 1269, 1449-
1450, 1453-1454
Dream of the Rood, 394
Drew, E., 189, 3637
Drew, E. A., 3696
Drew, P., 2835
Driver, T. S., 960
Dronke, P., 546
Dryden, J., 1532, 1683, 1707-1717,
1717, 1719-1729, 1839, 1930;
1665, 1718, 1730-1751
Duckett, E. S., 450, 461
Duffin, H. C., 3365
Duncan, J. E., 3638
Dunn, C. W., 571
Dunn, E. C., 3325
Dunn, T. A., 1174
Dunn, W. P., 1579
Dunning, T. P., 382
Dunseath, T. K., 1324
Dupeé, F. W., 3107
Durham, W. H., 2299
Durr, R. A., 1509
Durrant, G., 2756
Durrell, L., 3624
Dworkin, R., 3461
Dyer, I. W., 3386
Dyson, A. E., 3121, 3635

Van de Voort, D., 655
Van Doren, C., 2264
Van Doren, M., 212, 1048, 1749,
    2021, 2751
Van Dorsten, J. A., 1289
Van Duzer, H. S., 3300
Van Gelder, H. A. Enno, 754
Van Ghent, D., 262
Vann, J. D., 3934
Van Patten, N., 16
Vasta, E., 504, 634, 635
Vaughan, H., 1498-1501, 1504-
    1508; **1374, 1375, 1502-1503,
    1509-1512**
Velz, J. W., 1049
Vendler, H. H., 3805
Venezky, A. S., 113
Verschoyle, D., 263
Vickers, B., 213, 1569, 2283
Victorian Literature, **314, 315, 2444,
    2468, 2472, 2779-2782, 2788-
    2797, 2798, 2809-2811, 2937,
    2990, 2993, 2997-2999, 3003,
    3012-3014, 3349**
Viljoen, H. G., 3444
Vinaver, E., 707, 716
Visiak, E. H., 1871
Visick, M., 3068
Vision Concerning Piers Plowman,
    621-624; **548, 625-635, 652**
Vivas, E., 4069
Vogler, T. A., 3069
Voigt, M., 2284
Voitle, R., 2403
Voorhees, R. J., 4097
Vos, N., 152
Vries, J.P.M.L., 214

Wade, A., 3769
Wadlock, A.J.A., 1919
Wagenknecht, E. C., 609, 3604
Wager, W., 3500

Wagner, B. M., 1050
Wahba, M., 2385
Wain, J., 3188
Waingrow, M., 1931, 2105
Waite, A. E., 666
Walcott, F. G., 3377
Walcutt, C. C., 215
Walker, J. A., 323
Walker, R. S., 1129
Walker, W. S., 3812
Wallace, J. M., 1497
Wallace, M. W., 1290
Waller, A. R., 81, 2356
Wallerstein, R. C., 1371, 1391,
    1398, 1526
Walpole, H., 2286-2288, 2291-
    2293; **1775, 2289-2290, 2294-
    2296, 2713**
Walsh, J., 2987
Walsh, W. S., 264
Wanderer, 382, 388
Ward, A. C., 80, 3590, 3833
Ward, A. W., 81
Ward, C. E., 706, 1729, 1750
Ward, M., 2846
Warhaft, S., 1562
Warner, O., 1803
Warnke, F., 205
Warren, A., 63, 1399
Warren, A. H., 2525
Warren, R. P., 160
Warton, T., 216
Warwick, R., 1621
Wasserman, E. R., 1946, 2727
Watkins, V., 3731
Watkins, W.B.C., 1339, 2244, 2404,
    2405
Watson, C. B., 1051
Watson, E. B., 2475
Watson, G., 17, 18, 59, 2628
Watt, I., 265, 1673, 2166, 3042
Weales, G. C., 1763, 3501